GREED

~~GOD~~ BLESS

AMERICA?

Peace!

Joseph Redmann

~~GOD~~ GREED BLESS AMERICA?

God Never Will Bless America

JOSEPH ALAN REDMAN

TATE PUBLISHING
AND ENTERPRISES, LLC

Published by Tate Publishing & Enterprises, LLC
127 E. Trade Center Terrace | Mustang, Oklahoma 73064 USA
1.888.361.9473 | www.tatepublishing.com

Tate Publishing is committed to excellence in the publishing industry. The company reflects the philosophy established by the founders, based on Psalm 68:11,
"The Lord gave the word and great was the company of those who published it."

Book design copyright © 2012 by Tate Publishing, LLC. All rights reserved.
Cover design by Kristen Verser
Interior design by Chelsea Womble

Published in the United States of America

ISBN: 978-1-61862-185-6
1. Religion / Christian Life / Social Issues
2. Religion / Religion, Politics & State
12.02.06

TABLE OF CONTENTS

INTRODUCTION

I tremble for my country when I reflect that God is just.

Thomas Jefferson

I have no country to fight for: my country is the earth, and
I am a citizen of the world.

Eugene V. Debs

In the days following the September 11, 2001 terrorist attacks on
the United States, many Americans demonstrated their patriotism by flying American flags at homes, places of business, places
of worship, and by placing flag magnets and bumper stickers on
cars and trucks. The president, vice-president, cabinet members,
and members of Congress, sported new American-flag lapel
pins. Most main-stream television news broadcasters also wore
new American-flag pins. Sounds of "God Bless America" came
from radio, television, and many worship services throughout the
nation. The first message delivered by the media was, "We're at
war!" and the call went out, encouraging young men and women
to enlist in the military.[1] There were additional messages, each
targeting a different emotional level of the American public. I
find it interesting that very few of the messages dealt with the
Biblical concepts of loving and praying for the enemy. The
nationalistic message from politicians was, "We will do whatever
it takes to spread freedom and democracy to the world." The
capitalistic message from both the government and corporations

was, "We will survive, recover, and exceed where we were financially before the attacks, all while increasing military spending to keep us safe from attack. We will defend the land God gave us!" The imaginary spiritual message from certain radical religious commentators was, "The Axis of Evil is our enemy, and God is on the side of America!"

The first emphasis was doing everything possible to kill the enemy in Iraq and Afghanistan. The deceptive message was that our country, our way of life, and our oil-supply sources must be protected at any cost, sadly resulting in President Bush's "war on terror" and defining of his axis of evil. In the moment of heightened emotions, fear, and uncertainty, the emphasis was (and is still) on money/greed and ego-power (using the power of an office, title, or position to enhance one's self-esteem and self-perception of greatness at the expense of those in lesser or subordinate positions, regardless of the financial or personal sacrifice demanded by those in ego-power positions), as well as on an economy driven by a massive military machine, and complete lack of God-like love and gentleness when dealing with the "enemy". This is the complete opposite of the perfect model outlined for Christians in the New Testament.

One frequently misquoted Bible passage dealing with greed states:

> For the love of money is a root of all kinds of evil. Some people, eager for money, have wandered from the faith and pierced themselves with many griefs. But you, man of God, flee from all this, and pursue righteousness, godliness, faith, love, endurance and gentleness.
>
> 1 Timothy 6:10

Note that the love of money as "the root of all evil," (an incorrect quote), actually reads in the Greek text, the love of money is "a root of all *kinds* of evil." How many Americans claiming to be Christians (including presidents) flee from being eager for money and are instead going after righteousness, godliness, faith, love, endurance, and gentleness? These Christian characteristics seem to be far from the minds and behaviors of a great number of Americans. If Christians are defined by being righteous, godly, faithful, loving, enduring, and gentle, and if the argument is that we are a Christian nation, how can the same words be used to define this country as it declares, then fights, illegal wars and isolates other countries by labeling them, "The Axis of Evil?"

America prides itself on being free and capitalistic in nature. If the foundation of out-of-control capitalism is love of money or greed then the simple statement of love of money being a root of all kinds of evil describes America. The urge to gain as much money, as many possessions, and as much ego-power as possible, all at the expense of others, is far different from the command given in the New Testament book of 1 Timothy. The 1930 edition of *The New Revised Webster Dictionary Self-Pronouncing* defines capitalism as, "the possession of capital, especially its concentration in the hands of the few; the power of combined capital." The same dictionary defines nationalism as, "devotedness or loyalty to the nation as a whole." In general, America today fits this definition perfectly, more specifically, by capital ($) in the hands of the few and devotion to country.

Is out-of-control capitalism driven by intense greed combined with single-minded nationalism an indicator of a country blessed by God? If one can own multiple houses, cars, boats, and fill walk-in closets with thousands of dollars worth of clothes, while most in the world live in small structures, use walking as their primary means of transportation, (or perhaps own a bicycle, motorcycle if they are richer), and have one or two changes of clothing, is this what people mean when they sing "God Bless America?" Why do we have "In God We Trust" on our money? Is it a visual slogan we hope will convince others that while we need money to buy food and clothing, God is important too? Is trust in God simply a slogan printed or stamped on money? As Dr. W. Edwards Deming said in a workshop I attended in 1986, "Slogans don't work!" So what does work?

The four purposes of this book are first, through the use of scripture and examples from life experience, to discuss the pursuit of complete honesty, sincere godliness, constant faith, unconditional love, spiritual endurance, and compassionate gentleness as opposed to seeing how much money or how many titles one can collect during a lifetime. The second purpose is to explain why asking God to bless America, or any nation, is a concept not supported by the Christian New Testament. The third purpose is to discuss a variety of examples defining the American philosophy of individualism, ego-power, greed, and spiritually valueless activities. Fourth, I hope the questions and tasks at the end of each chapter will inspire the reader to examine their own life and inspire love and faith based actions to draw them closer to God.

Writing simply from the viewpoint of a Christian using the Bible as my guide, I cannot write from the viewpoint of a Muslim, Buddhist, or Jew, because I am a Christian. There are other resources available for comparing and contrasting various religious beliefs, but that is not the purpose of this book. I quote from the Bible to show why trusting in America doesn't matter, but trusting in God does. There may be those who question my patriotism. As we will see later in the book when discussing patriotism and nationalism, I readily agree I am not patriotic as many Americans define patriotism. However, I served voluntarily in the army twice, once as an enlisted man on active duty and in the reserves for eight years, including nineteen months in Vietnam, and once for five years as a commissioned officer in Oklahoma, West Germany, and Kansas during the Cold War. This book, however, is not about personal war stories. Instead, this book puts in plain words what must matter most to

Christians not what matters to most Americans (money, posses-sions, and ego-power.)

The fact that we are Christian-Americans should make no real difference to us. America is simply the place where we hap-pened to have been born and where we temporarily live. Because of the path down which greed, out-of-control capitalism, and misguided nationalism is dragging America, Christians should have no pride in being an American, because there are no com-mands in the New Testament to be proud, patriotic citizens devoted to a man-made government driven by greed, ego-power, and lust for war. According to the New Testament, other than paying taxes, obeying the law unless it conflicts with the New Testament, and praying for the country's leaders so we will live in peace, our job as Christians is to do something entirely different - to have complete trust only in God and to base our daily actions on loving and compassionate ways, enthusiastically demonstrat-ing our faith in God. Christians can do that, here in America, or anywhere on earth, for that matter.

Many Christians have an American passport, but we must never forget that our permanent citizenship is in the kingdom of God. Our permanent home will be in heaven, not in America. There are many who are Americans first and Christians sec-ond, or third, and some who claim the title of Christian who are not interested in God at all. There are those who say, "I cannot think of a better place to live than in America." Maybe this view comes from being comfortable with all the unnecessary excesses available to Americans every day and not from accepting the fact this country is only here for a little while. Maybe this view comes from never traveling to another country to see what the rest of the world looks like. Maybe this view comes from focus-ing too much on the material and not enough on the spiritual. This view reminds me of the view taken by early Christians in the church at Corinth. In his commentary on 1 Corinthians, Simon K. Kistemaker describes the early Christians in Corinth this way: "Instead of living as Christians in a pagan society some Corinthians were living as worldly people in a Christian community." [2] Can we insert the word "Americans" instead of "Corinthians" and make the same statement about modern-day America? Perhaps. Christians should find the following comment quite an eye-opener, "The editorial quoted Supreme Court Justice Antonin Scalia saying, 'A Christian should not support a government that suppresses the faith or one that sanctions the taking of an innocent human life.'" [3] I will comment on this later in the book.

Part of what led me to write this book are my simple observations from travels around the world and across the United States. I am blessed by having been to over thirty-eight countries and all fifty US states. One recent trip took place in 2004 when my wife and I traveled with over fifty humanitarian clowns from fourteen countries to China and Tibet. During our adventure we visited hospitals, schools, nursing homes, orphanages, and remote villages rarely, if ever, visited by regular tourists from the west. One small village school located near Lhasa, Tibet, had about one hundred children ranging from kindergarten to junior high. As we walked into the area designated as their playground, all the children sat quietly on what appeared to be enormous slabs of scrap concrete from the demolition of a building. There was no typical playground equipment. The children obviously had been coached to remain seated and quiet until we arrived. Within a few minutes, all the children were laughing, running, singing, dancing, and playing throughout the playground. Although the children wore school uniforms, most appeared to have never been laundered. Many of the children had runny noses and dental care appeared to be nonexistent as evidenced by the poor condition of their teeth and lack of oral hygiene. The hands of many children were covered with a dark layer of dirt and green mold growing on the skin of their fingers. They apparently had no soap. They obviously had no tooth paste. They had no playground equipment. They had no school books or supplies. While sitting quietly in their classroom, the children learned by their teacher reading out of textbooks for the topic at hand. The classrooms had windows, doors, two chalkboards, and no supplies one typically sees filling shelves in American schools.

These children have nothing compared to their western peers, but they are immediately able and willing to laugh and play and be silly without cell phones, electronic games, television, toys, and other junk our children believe they must have to be happy! Why? These children seem to not have the damaging level of greed we have in the west, especially in America. Their lifestyle is what they know and are accustomed to for the moment, but more importantly, separate from greed and direct, daily influence of abusive government power. Their isolated and remote location in rural Tibet does have some politically distancing advantages. They are strongly devoted to their families and their religious beliefs. But, have no fear! Within a few years they too will have the blessed appearance of fast-food restaurants and the option to buy junk at big-box discount stores! [4] There are those who will say, "See! If those children lived in America, they wouldn't have to go to school in those horrible conditions. America really is blessed by God!" Really?

Think about the current physical condition of schools in America, the low pay offered to teachers, the increasing drop-out rate of high school students, and the low ranking of American students when compared to students from other "first-world" countries. Is this an indication of a blessing from God? The following data come from a Stanford University study. Should we say, "God Bless Finland?"

*Relative Poverty Rates in Twenty-One Rich Nations
at the Turn of the Century for Children ~ Percent of
Children with Disposable Income Less than 50 percent
of Adjusted National Disposable Median Income*

Country	Data Year	Poverty Rate (% of Population)
Mexico	2002	24.8
United States	2000	21.9
Ireland	2000	17.2
Italy	2000	16.6
Spain	2000	16.1
United Kingdom	2001	15.3
Australia	2000	14.9
Canada	2000	14.9
Estonia	1999	13.6
Greece	2000	12.8
Poland	2000	12.7
Netherlands	1999	9.8
Germany	2000	9.0
Taiwan	1999	8.0
France	2000	7.9
Austria	2000	7.8
Slovenia	2000	6.9
Belgium	1999	6.7
Sweden	2000	4.2
Norway	2000	3.4
Finland	2000	2.8
Overall Average		11.0

Percent of Population[5]

One's observation of the poor as defined by western standards (little money and/or few possessions) indicates those who have few material possessions, and who live from day to day, and have no concern for titles, ego-power, or war, but focus instead on family and their religious activities, are some of the most happy people on the planet. Christians must not discount the struggle these people face in their search for food and water each day. Suffering people may not have a sense of light-hearted joy in their daily activities of trying to live, but the demonstration of their faith is strong and even in their grim circumstances (when compared to people living in the so-called first-world countries), they laugh and play more easily than many Americans. It seems those with the most money and possessions are those with the most personal problems, health problems, and unhappy outlooks on life. Is this a valid definition of the American dream? Is this an indicator of God's blessings on the country? This example is one of many the reader will be exposed to in the book.

In this book I show how belief in God and living in a way he would have us live, a life driven by love of God and a love of humanity, is more important eternally than concentrating on making more money, buying more things, and trying to boost one's own ego by keeping up with the neighbors. I explain that living for God must supersede any form of patriotism for country, nationalistic acts such as pledging to a flag, or fighting illegal and unjust wars, or any war for that matter. I make clear that God's plan for the distribution of wealth, food, clothing, shelter, and loving compassion is far beyond the feeble plan any man-made government can provide. Humanity, greed, governments, political boundaries, countries, wars, and ego-power, all are temporary. On the other hand, God and our souls are eternal.

Throughout the book are tables and charts showing a variety of data, facts, and statistics to support the arguments I make. The dates of some of this information are not as important as the data themselves. What is important are the causes and history behind the data. I encourage readers to do their own research into more current data to validate the information presented.

In addition, throughout the book, I ask the reader to think. At the end of each chapter are several *Thought Questions* and *Challenge Tasks* for the reader to consider. My hope is readers will dedicate time to think earnestly about what individual actions can be taken to be a living conduit for God's love and then to take those actions. I also hope readers will add their own actions to the lists provided at the end of the chapter, expanding our active demonstration of God's love.

It is very important for the reader to understand that while all governments and nations are in place as part of God's design, they are not entities to be adored or worshiped. God establishes the creation of governments, where they will function, and how long they will exist. How he does this is beyond our ability to comprehend. What is important for Christians is not the fate of their earthly country, but to recognize that America, or any other country on the earth, exists so that people will search for and find God. This scripture counters all nationalistic and patriotic arguments.

> From one man he made every nation of men, that they should inhabit the whole earth; and he determined the times set for them and the exact places where they should live. God did this so that men would seek him and perhaps reach out for him and find him, though he is not far from each one of us.
>
> Acts 17: 26-27

All nations and their governments are susceptible to the power of the devil as evidenced by the tumultuous history of the world from the beginning with the expulsion of Adam and Eve from the garden of Eden. I believe it is time to question our values as Christians and to answer the question as to where our true allegiance lies.

My views will seem controversial to some. Many topics are discussed in the book with the intention of encouraging the reader to think about all aspects of their own lives. Some will see me as some kind of radical, narrow-minded, Bible-banging Christian. I believe if one studies the life of Christ and his short time on earth, it will be obvious he was also a radical thinker and doer, going against all that was accepted as religious and spiritual practice of the day. The modern church needs radical thinkers and doers. As Gregory A. Boyd clearly illustrates in his book, *The Myth of a Christian Religion*, we are at a point in time where "Christians" are difficult to identify, because their actions are no different than the rest of the world. The world, and many Christians, focuses on greed, power, and the desire to gain more possessions, all at the expense of their relationship with God. It is time to change that focus. Some may take my comments as harsh and critical. Some of my comments are harsh and critical so that the reader can more readily understand the seriousness of the issues facing Christians today. They are harsh and critical of those actions and behaviors that go against the Word of God. My prayer is readers will understand my harshness is based on the hatred I feel for evil in the world and my love of God and what he expects us to do as we work out our own salvation. This book is an examination of what New Testament Scripture says about the role of Christians in relationship to the American government, and why blind devotion to any country obsessed by aggressive greed, out-of-control capitalism, and idolatrous patriotism is unhealthy for the Christian soul.

GOD BLESS AMERICA?

While on the shop and street I gazed
My body of a sudden blaze;
And twenty minutes more or less
It seemed, so great my happiness,
That I was blessed and could bless.

W.B. Yeats

'God bless us every one!' said Tiny Tim, the last of all.

Charles Dickens

New York spot gold closed today at $804.50 up over $14 per ounce. Thank you Ben Bernanke for circulating all that fresh new US currency and pushing the value of gold even higher! God bless America.[6]

This is a complex chapter covering many different but related topics. Each section in this chapter is sub-titled with a broad term describing the topic covered to help further clarify the title of the book, ~~God~~ Greed Bless America?.

How is the Word *Blessing* Defined?

It seems the passion of many Americans is the focus on self instead of selflessness; on getting instead of giving; on hating instead of loving; on *me* instead of *you*. In spite of so many stories about the apparent decline of Christian values and Christian actions by many living in America, many citizens still claim that God blesses America. "God Bless America" – what does this mean? To begin, one must define *bless*. On the whole, there are two types of blessings mentioned in the Bible – Spiritual and material. Before examining what the Bible says about blessings, let us look at one dictionary for a straightforward definition. The edition of the dictionary used for this definition is the 1930 edition of *The New Revised Webster Dictionary Self-Pronouncing*. I prefer this edition to newer editions simply because of its straightforwardness. It has not been sanitized by political correctness and offers easy-to-understand, more to-the-point definitions. These definitions are also closer to the original meanings of the words found in the Bible. And this dictionary has not removed the word "God" from its definitions, contrary to more modern editions.

> Bless: to consecrate; invoke a blessing upon; bestow happiness upon.
>
> Consecrate: to set apart as sacred; dedicated to the service of God.
>
> Sacred: pertaining to religion or religious uses.

By consecrating, or dedicating oneself to serving God, this leads to blessings – our being set apart as sacred - resulting in happiness. It looks like a very simple formula with no mention of money or power. But is this definition valid from a modern Christian point of view? There are fifteen variations of the Greek word for blessing in the New Testament. The variations, such as bless, blessing, and blessed, are used 115 times. The most commonly used word (used forty-eight times) is μακάριος (*makarios*), which means happy or fortunate. The second most-used word (used thirty-four times) is εὐλογέω (*eulogeō*) which means to praise, give thanks to, speak well of, or act kindly toward. With these definitions in mind, if one says, "God bless America," does God view this statement as legitimate? Does God make America, or any country, happy or fortunate? The happiest people I've met in my travels live outside the US.

Using the second word, does God praise, or give thanks to, or speak well of, or act kindly to America as a nation, when the New Testament is clear with words used to describe blessings as directed only toward individuals? There is no record of Jesus ever blessing a nation. I believe many people who make the statement "God Bless America" are not asking but are instead making the statement as if it were a fact based solely on the made-up benefits the country supposedly enjoys.

Are Americans misguided in their so-called patriotic belief when God promises that he does now, and always will, bless and care for us as individual Christians? I do not recall seeing a poster or T-shirt with, "God, please bless America." When Christians ask for blessings, what do we usually have in mind? A spiritual or a material blessing? My first response to the question is that many Americans, living in a so-called free, capitalistic society, pray that God blesses America in a material way, which, it is hoped, will lead to world economic domination, solid retirement funds, and then to happiness.

Why do farmers pray for rain? So that crops will grow. Why do they want crops to grow? So they can be harvested and sold. If a farmer lives in an area with regular seasonal rains, as evidenced by historical weather records, and if God tells us to not worry about the needs of life, does the farmer really need to pray for rain? There are those more educated than I who have clearly analyzed and discussed the fact that money does not buy happiness, yet I still hear Christians praying for rain on their land. Recently, during a period of local drought in our area, many people prayed for rain because their crops and animals were suffering. Several months later when the drought was broken and flooding resulted from the high amount of rainfall, I heard no prayers for the rain to stop. The question seems to be one of whether asking God to change the natural laws he set in motion during the creation is a valid prayer, if the end result is to make some money.

God set in motion physical laws when he created the universe. Those laws were impacted by the flood but are still in place and will be until the end of time. The hydrologic cycle that produces rain has not changed, the shifting of the earth's crust that results in earthquakes has not changed, and the Coreolis effect that results in warm and cold fronts, and high and low barometric pressures has not changed and cannot be impacted by prayer because that would cause God to go against what he created. His creation was finished on the sixth day, was deemed complete and good by God, and it is still complete. There is neither scripture saying creation is an ongoing process, nor is there any indication that new physical laws are being created or old laws changed.

During the 2011 drought that affected most of the state of Texas, many Christian farmers prayed for rain, but in the same breath mentioned they were thankful for government crop insurance. The question is, "If God is a loving God and hundreds of Christians are praying for rain, but not receiving any, why isn't God answering prayers the way they want?" As with many "unanswered" prayers, it is important for Christians to think about why they are praying. A better prayer might be specifically asking for rain so money can be made to do God's work by helping widows and orphans. Money does not bring happiness and is not a blessing. It is only a convenience.

Doesn't God Bless Us Because We Are Free?

Some will argue that America is blessed by God because we have *freedom*. The obvious questions become, "Given the current discussions on electronic surveillance, torture, secret prisons, holding of American citizens in Guantanamo Bay without charges or access to their attorney, airport-security pat downs, are we really free? Do we have true liberty? Are we independent?" I argue that people are blessed for being Christians, not for being citizens of America, or any other country for that matter.

With thousands of rules and laws in place at the local, state, and federal level, perhaps we can argue that most of what we do on a daily basis is out of requirement. Each day we are faced with some type of coercion to vote for a certain politician or buy a certain product. We are constrained in choice by the lack of intelligent, open, honest, and unbiased programming on radio and television (both local and satellite). Slavery is alive and well in America as evidenced by immigrants forced to work to pay off their *fees* for being brought into the country and the increasing numbers of women and children sold into sexual slavery each year. One estimate by the US Department of State is as high as 30,000/year, or over eighty-two children sold each day, in the US. The abuse of presidential privilege seems to be the opposite of "liberty." It seems as though we may not be as free, or as *blessed* as we think we are, on a national level.

In the Old Testament there were many blessings of a material nature (food, land, success in battle, possessions, children, etc.) while in the New Testament, most blessings are of a spiritual nature. As a note, New Testament blessings are referred in the present tense because they are still relevant! Old Testament law served its purpose for the children of Israel until the birth, death, burial, and resurrection of Jesus, and establishment of his New Testament Church, at which time the old law became void. The Old Testament is useful in that it provides a background and outline of the heritage of Jesus's coming birth and life on earth.

Is It Time To Think About Your Treasures?

On a personal level, Christians should have a difficult time with the concept of demanding that God bless America, or any country for that matter, in any material way. Why? A few simple words from Jesus will explain. In the New Testament book of Matthew, Jesus describes why Christians must focus on treasure that is in heaven not on all the *stuff* we have here on earth.

> Do not store up for yourselves treasures on earth, where moth and rust destroy, and where thieves break in and steal. But store up for yourselves treasures in heaven, where moth and rust do not destroy, and where thieves do not break in and steal. For where your treasure is, there your heart will be also. The eye is the lamp of the body. If your eyes are good, your whole body will be full of light. But if your eyes are bad, your whole body will be full of darkness. If then the light within you is darkness, how great is that darkness! No one can serve two masters. Either he will hate the one and love the other, or he will be devoted to the one and despise the other. You cannot serve both God and Money
>
> Matthew 6:19-24

There is a big difference between serving God and serving money. This does not mean Christians cannot work to make a living, pay bills, feed and clothe families, etc. This does not mean Christians cannot save and invest for retirement. It does mean Christians are to be good employees and good keepers (stewards) of finances. There is a big difference between greed and wise budgeting, spending, and investing. We must, as a matter of spiritual life and death, clarify who our master is.

But I Need My Stuff!

The key question always is, "What and where is your treasure?" Sadly, countless Americans own so many things they can no longer find space for them in their homes or garages. Most

American cities have hundreds of storage units for rent. On any given day it is not uncommon to drive by and see people storing all their stuff – items they do not have room for in their already overcrowded garages at their homes. Who is the master here? Now, a few tidbits from *Mother Jones* magazine:

> Since the 1970s, the average US home has grown by 80%. Yet Americans face a "storage crisis," according to UCLA researchers.

> The self-storage industry is only 35 years old. It took 25 years for the first billion square feet of storage space to be built. The second billion was built in just 8 years. 1 in 11 households rents storage space – 1 million more households than two years ago.[7]

Several years ago, I called a plumber to replace a water heater. When he arrived, I let him in through the garage, and he stopped in amazement when he noticed we actually had cars in the garage! He could not comprehend a home where the garage was not filled with stuff, and the cars are parked in the driveway. Where is our priority? Is it on the grace of God, which was given to us, or our stuff (*which takes money*)? What causes such a level of insecurity that some feel they have to buy more than they can ever use then store it in a locked storage unit? Could it be a lack of knowledge about a lack of trust, and a lack of faith, in God?

> Therefore I tell you, do not worry about your life, what you will eat or drink; or about your body, what you will wear. Is not life more important than food, and the body more important than clothes? Look at the birds of the air; they do not sow or reap or store away in barns, and yet your heavenly Father feeds them. Are you not much more valuable than they? Who of you by worrying can add a single hour to his life? And why do you worry about clothes? See how the lilies of the field grow. They do not labor or spin. Yet I tell you that not even Solomon in all

his splendor was dressed like one of these. If that is how God clothes the grass of the field, which is here today and tomorrow is thrown into the fire, will he not much more clothe you, O you of little faith? So do not worry, saying, 'What shall we eat?' or 'What shall we drink?' or 'What shall we wear?' For the pagans run after all these things, and your heavenly Father knows that you need them. But seek first his kingdom and his righteousness, and all these things will be given to you as well. Therefore do not worry about tomorrow, for tomorrow will worry about itself. Each day has enough trouble of its own.

Matthew 6:25-34

Demanding that God bless America for material gain is in direct contradiction to Jesus's teaching that Christians must not collect "treasures" during our short stay on earth. He clearly states, "pagans run after these things." (The December 2008 trampling death of a Walmart worker by customers running in to take advantage of Christmas sales comes to mind.) His statement that our hearts will be where our treasures are is quite clear in our society today. Apparently our hearts are locked in storage units. Maybe this feeling of wanting so much carries over into other possessions as well.

Greed versus Need

When was the last time you saw a massive, four-wheel drive vehicle covered with mud and scratches from being driven in the wilderness? Rarely, if ever. Is the need of such a vehicle because the driver lives in an area without roads? Rarely, if ever. Does the driver have to drive through deep water to buy groceries? Rarely, if ever. Is there a legitimate need for a vehicle with an engine so powerful it gets only a few miles per gallon of gasoline or diesel fuel? Probably not. Where is the priority (and the heart) of the driver? Perhaps it is in possessing the biggest and most expensive toy so his neighbors and friends might be impressed. Is it not more logical and spiritual to drive something much smaller and less expensive, building up spiritual treasures in heaven instead?

Several years ago, one of the deacons serving the congregation I attended decided to buy a new car. Cost was not a factor as this person was quite wealthy. His primary reason for buying the car he did was made crystal clear when he stated, "I will look good in that car." Could he have driven to work in a less flashy and less expensive car? Yes. But, he would not have looked as good to others (at least from an earthly, narrow-minded, ego-driven viewpoint). He was a corporate executive, and one way he could show off his wealth was to drive the latest and most expensive car in the neighborhood. He was also the only person I've known who said he would look good in a car.

Some Christians who understand what Jesus says may fall into the trap of believing we are the only ones who understand the concept of the thoughts in Matthew 6. Think again! The following quote is Osama bin Laden's reply to President Bush commenting on what terrorists want and what drives their behavior: "… we shall still have Allah to take care of us; livelihood is sent by Allah, we shall not want."[8] The words sound familiar, and they should. The Koran was written hundreds of years after the New Testament, so it is likely that one of the sources of the Koran was the Bible. How interesting that a non-Christian terrorist understands concepts from the book of Matthew, "we shall not want!"

Greed and ego also manifest themselves by the actions of those who feel they must have the latest fashions, most recent cellular phones, most up-to-date computers, latest cameras, latest whatever. Then, once they own the latest of everything they can get their hands on, they go shopping for presents to give others! A 2010 Gallup poll stated, "Americans currently predict they will spend $714 on Christmas gifts this year."[9] "Washington, September 20, 2007 -- The National Retail Federation today

JOSEPH ALAN REDMAN

released its forecast for the upcoming 2007 holiday season, predicting that sales will rise 4.0 percent this year to $474.5 billion."[10]

For my current family this breaks down into $89.25 per person. Is this amount good or bad? Do we not have a right to buy gifts for our families at Christmas? While Christians do believe in the birth, death, burial, and resurrection of Jesus, he was not born on December 25, and there are no scriptures commanding the celebration of the Christmas holiday, which was originated from a pagan holiday many years after the resurrection of Jesus.[11] While not related to the modern Christmas tree, the following verse from Jeremiah does address what are called "customs of the peoples", customs which led to idolatry.

> For the customs of the peoples are worthless; they cut a tree out of the forest, and a craftsman shapes it with his chisel. They adorn it with silver and gold; they fasten it with a hammer and nails so it will not totter.
>
> Jeremiah 10:3-4

Granted these verses are talking about idols, which are not to be worshipped or used as a replacement for God, but are some customs of modern day people, such as the materialistic side of Christmas along with massive, expensively decorated trees, being used as a replacement for God?

So what is the problem with celebrating the birth of Jesus by giving gifts to everyone at Christmas? Some argue it shows our love of family. I believe it shows many have fallen into the out-of-control capitalistic trap that the only way love can be shown is to buy things, and give them away. It shows many have fallen into the out-of-control capitalistic trap that *things* bring happiness. If Christmas were a celebration of the birth of Jesus, would it not be more significant if we dedicated our lives to serving others each day of the year instead of only one specific holiday?

I have a cartoon taped to the door of the refrigerator. The first frame is labeled January, February, and March, and shows a homeless person sitting on the sidewalk as a man walks by, ignoring the homeless person. The next frame is labeled April, May, and June, with a jogger running by, also ignoring the homeless person. In the July, August, September frame a man reading a newspaper walks by, ignoring the homeless person. In the October and November frame a woman with a shopping bag walks by, again ignoring the homeless person. In the December frame a man stops and gives the homeless person some money. The final frame is January, and a man with a cup of coffee walks by, ignoring the homeless person.

Each Christmas season there are accelerated efforts to gather food, clothing, money, volunteers, all in the so-called spirit of giving. My question is, considering Galatians 6:10 tells us to do good to all men as we have an opportunity, why are we not as loving and generous every day of the year? Why do we accept that celebrating the birth of Jesus, something never commanded in the New Testament, receives more publicity and seems to have more value than the taking of communion, something commanded and designed to help us remember and celebrate the death, burial, and resurrection of Jesus? The idea of setting aside the ornate, the costly, and the selfish may be offensive to some. To restate the purpose of this book, I want the reader to move from being startled, angry, and skeptical, to a state of introspection, thoughtful questioning of personal motives, and deep prayer, as priorities are shifted from the physical to the spiritual.

A Few Critical Questions

A critical question for each person must be, "What am I doing to actively demonstrate my faith in God and my love for my family, so that what money I spend on gifts can be given to the poor

JOSEPH ALAN REDMAN

instead?" How would families react if they heard, "There will be no gifts this year. Instead, we are buying food for several families, so they can have something to eat this week?" Would most families readily give up the annual give–me–more-stuff holiday? The attitude of wanting more only gets worse. Because of how our society functions, greed driving the desire to buy more means, "…we spend more on shoes, jewelry, and watches ($80 billion) than on higher education ($65 billion)." [12] "I may not be able to read, but I look good in my neighborhood!"

The June/July 2010 issue of *Reader's Digest* printed an article titled "BEST of America – From the most benevolent boss to the tallest Great Dane, our annual celebration of the people, places, and ideas that make us great." [13] Other items included: Best Trekker, Best Impersonators, Best Street Name, Best Wildlife Watchdogs, Best Grief Therapy, Best Offbeat Holiday, Best Quartet, Best Swimming Lessons, Best Home Store, Best Roadside Attraction (Yes, the twelve-foot -high ball of twine was listed here!), Best Big Dog, Best Dream Team, Best Blogs, Best Irresistible Ice Cream Flavors, Best Crowd-pleaser, Best Workout, Best Ballpark Food, Best License Plate Slogan, Best President with a Little-Known Talent, Best Anti-Ponzi Scheme, Best Math Tool, Best Recycler, Best Road Trip, Best Lawn Guys, Best Chain Reaction, Best US Patent, Best Festivals, Best Town Names, Best and Weirdly Popular Baby Names. There were multiple entries on some items, resulting in a total of one hundred. Notice anything missing from the list?

What about best version of the New Testament? Best minister? Best Christian? Best contribution? Best faith-based act? The word "God" and the word "church" were not listed anywhere in the article. Some people on the list were nice, and some items on the list were fun and entertaining. The questions are, "Are these the things we are proud to say are the best things in America? Are these things for which God would bless us? We may be in trouble, because my favorite ice cream was eaten in Switzerland!

As a child, I remember having three pairs of shoes. The best pair were reserved for Sunday when we went to worship. The second best were for school, and were my old *Sunday shoes*. The worst pair were for play, usually my old *school shoes*. Many times one of my parents would remind me to put on my *play shoes* before going outside. It wasn't until seventh grade (1957 – I think!) that I was required to have a pair of *gym shoes*. Today I have at least several pair: cowboy boots, steel-toed work boots, sandals, jogging shoes, and one pair of clown shoes. Many of the Tibetan people with whom we played and entertained had no shoes. Most of the children in the tent cities in Haiti I saw after the 2010 earthquake had no shoes. Every news or humanitarian video segment I have seen of children all over the world shows children and adults with no shoes.

A question for the reader – How many pairs of shoes do you own? (You will see this question again!) Realistically, cowboy boots, slippers, jogging shoes, or business-casual work shoes are not essential. I could easily get by on sandals, work boots, and clown shoes. Why do we have shoes we do not need? Why do we have so many shoes when we can only wear one pair at a time? One reason is large egos driven by a sense of greed based on the view that "I deserve it. I am living the American dream!" My cowboy boots are second in comfort only to my clown shoes, but at present, wearing clown shoes to worship is not appropriate for me. I could wear work boots, but there is still a small ego-power part of me that says, "I must look my best when I go to worship." (A weak lesson taught by my parents.) I believe God will not judge me on my appearance (See Galatians 2:6), but my ego still gets in the way when it comes to how I look, at least for now.

I refuse to wear an expensive watch. In fact, I wear no watch at all. This practice gives me an excuse to talk to people by asking them for the time. My *jewelry* consists of a wedding ring, a brass Montagnard bracelet from the Rhadé tribe in Vietnam, a multi-colored hand-woven bracelet from my hospital clown friends in

Guatemala, and a stone bracelet made in Tibet. The bracelet from Vietnam is a reminder of the struggle of the Montagnard people and their strong and close sense of community. The bracelet from Guatemala is a reminder of the unconditional love and sense of joy shared by the hospital clowns there. The bracelet from Tibet is a visual reminder of the poverty and the joy of loving play we experienced. It is somewhat amusing to see a television commercial asking people to send in their junk-gold jewelry for cash. Junk gold. That is exactly what it is in the sight of God.

My wife and I have come to the point where we no longer want or need presents for our birthdays, anniversaries, or the superficial Christmas holiday. We give each other a card, and may go out for dinner. I have tried to convince my children to donate to their favorite charity any money they originally planned to spend on presents for me and my wife. Why? To back away from the concept that to be happy we need material things, which is one of the driving forces of the out-of-control capitalism today.

The Wrong List of What Is Best

As Christians our first priority must be as a child of God living in His kingdom. The fact that we live in an imaginary and temporary democracy is irrelevant. Winston Churchill said, "It has been said that Democracy is the worst form of government except all those other forms that have been tried from time to time."[14] Mr. Churchill was on the right track – there are no good human governments. Some may be better and more effective than others, all are determined by God, but if humans are involved, they are all most likely driven by greed and ego-power. What is the result? "Greed becomes culturally admired as competence and false or unrealistic promises as cleverness."[15] There are many television and radio interviews of people who are known for making hundreds of millions of dollars. Each year, several news organizations publish a list of the ten richest people in the world. People all over the country interview and quote these rich people as if they were the only source of legitimate information on how to live. Why do we not publish a list of the ten most spiritual people in the world? How about the ten poorest? The ten happiest? Should we include a list of the most loving and compassionate? Why are we so obsessed with the rich and their money? Are we that insecure in our faith in God?

Take A Look At C-SPAN

The quote above mentions greed as being admired and false promises as being clever. Many Americans do not believe our politician's false and unrealistic promises are clever, but one example of how American politicians conduct their business may help to clarify this point. The US senate begins each business day with a prayer read by the senate chaplain. On most days, the only people present are the acting senate president and the staffers. After the chaplain reads his professionally printed prayer, he closes the leather cover and leaves the floor. The chaplain does not close his eyes, bow his head, or offer anything other than reading the pre-printed prayer. Most senators are in their offices, unaware of anything spoken by the chaplain. Is it clever for senators to willingly be absent from the start of business each day, disregarding the prayer? Why would God bless this behavior when he instructs us to be constant in prayer?

Many evening news programs refer to polls on what Americans think about their elected officials. One frequent comment is that politicians at all levels will say, promise, and do almost anything to become elected and re-elected. One technique legislators use to gain votes is to include amendments that add projects (pork) benefiting their respective local communities. As a result, all legislation is filled with unnecessary spending requests that exemplify the love of wasting the taxpayer's money. The 2008 bailouts of various financial institutions come to mind. Love of money is everywhere in America, something God abhors. Here is one example from the insurance industry, a large lobbying force targeting Congress. "...critics of the insurance industry maintain that rising premiums are owing less to claims than to insurance companies poor returns on their investments ..."[16] Because of the collapse of community as a way of life in America, many have fallen into the trap of needing insurance to cover their lives and massive homes.

Self versus Other

Gone are the days when the people of the community helped rebuild a home burned by fire. Gone are the days of community in general. Americans do love their homes. On a global scale, by comparison, American homes are large. While visiting a cancer hospice in China in 2000, I chatted with an elderly man, a former Chinese army officer who spoke English, about homes. I showed him a photo of our home at that time, a small, one-bedroom log cabin in New Jersey that was built in the 1930s. When I told him that in America our home was quite small, he quietly replied with a slight smile that in China it was quite large. I understood exactly what he was saying to me. Never underestimate the wisdom of our elders, no matter their nationality. In New Jersey, housing costs soared higher and higher to the point where our small lot and a one bedroom log cabin that was built in the 1930s cost nearly $150,000 in 2001. "In the 1990's, when 70% of nuclear families had two working heads, the average house cost more than six times their average joint income."[17] Using this simple formula, a couple earning $100,000 per year could easily be living in a $600,000 home, on average. In October

2004, the reported average cost of a home in the United States was $264,540.

How does this compare to the annual personal GDP of a few select countries (data compiled from 2002-2005 approximately; from the US Department of Labor website, showing earned income without housing costs)? What kinds of homes does one usually see in these countries? How many of them have an average cost as high as America, for the *average* family?

Afghanistan	= $165	or $0.42/day.
Bangladesh	= $421	or $1.15/day.
Brazil	= $8,400	or $23.01/day.
China	= $1,200	or $3.29/day.
Iraq	= $870	or $2.38/day.
Israel	= $19,500	or $52.42/day.
Russia	= $4,000	or $10.96/day
United Kingdom	= $27,700	or $75.89/day,
United States of America	= $34,142	or $93.54/day.

The figures for the US do not include cash wages paid to illegal immigrants who are paid well below the minimum wage. The exact amount for each country is not important. What is important is Americans are the some of the richest people on the earth and may be the least happy and most selfish at the same time. Why?

Money, Happiness, and Health

Money does not and cannot buy happiness. Greed and the desire to get more money so we can get more stuff frequently leads to stress-induced illness. Almost seventy-five percent of visits to doctors are the result of stress-induced illness.[18] There are also reports stating that around 70% of the *illnesses* for which people visit a doctor will go away on their own without any intervention by the doctor, and without the use of any prescription medications.[19] Those who watch television are bombarded all day long with advertising by pharmaceutical companies for medicines that can only be obtained through a doctor's prescription. We are told, "Ask your doctor if this medicine is right for you." Because we live in an out-of-control and greed-driven society, pharmaceutical companies continually work to develop ways to increase sales, often at the expense of valid scientific testing and at the expense of patients who are injured or die as a result. Each year dozens of medicines previously approved by the FDA are recalled because of faulty research results or poor manufacturing practices. It must be noted that the US and New Zealand are the only two countries that allow pharmaceutical companies to market prescription medications directly to the public. In all other countries, pharmaceutical companies cannot promote their products by television, radio, or print advertising. The information can only be presented to health care professionals. What better way is there to market and advertise *medicines* than to create a sense of fear in a person that they just might need this new medicine for this newly created *disease*!

Need longer eyelashes? Take a pill. Need more manly stamina? Take a pill. Can't sleep? Take a pill. There is even a pill advertised that will help you with the other pill you are already taking! The end result is people rushing to their doctors to ask for these new miracle medicines. Amazingly, doctors just happen to have some free samples to give patients while they write a prescription for the same. One dismal outcome from this marketing attack is, "The reduction of soul to economic psychology has made the world sick."[20] Somehow this doesn't seem like how Jesus as the great physician approaches sickness.

Some claim we are a country without soul. As a point of spiritual clarification, and separate from the use of metaphor, a country cannot have a soul. People have souls. Because individual American souls are at the depressing level of being obsessed by money and possessions, the result is a country with rapidly diminishing moral values, houses and storage units filled with junk we do not need, closets full of clothes we do not wear, children with hundreds of toys never played with, and billions of dollars spent on unnecessary prescriptions for medicines prescribed by doctors who show little interest in identifying and caring for the true, complete physical, emotional, and spiritual needs of the patient, all while funding the largest war machine in the history of the world. God bless America?

Shocking Life-expectancy Facts

In spite of all this, many still believe they must stand and sing nationalistic songs when their *wonderful* way of life is threatened by imaginary weapons of mass destruction. If our way of life is to be an American, the threat is not from weapons of mass destruction, but from a jealous God who expects his children to be dedicated to him. Just as we cannot serve two masters (remember the scripture on serving either God or money?), our way of life cannot be equally focused on two lifestyles. We either believe the entire Bible, or we do not. We are either Christians or we are not. We either follow God or we do not. Our citizenship is in heaven or it is not. Whether or not we are Americans does not matter. Whether or not we are Christians does matter. I challenge any reader to find one Bible verse that implies God will bless America.

But wait – there is much more exciting news about being a *blessed* American!

If we take the African American male population in, say, the District of Columbia, St. Louis City [sic], New York, or San Francisco, we find that they fall behind the Chinese or the Keralan at a remarkably early age. And this despite the fact that in terms of income per head, which is the focus of attention for standard studies of growth and development, the African Americans are much richer than the poor population with whom they are being compared in terms of survival patterns."[21]

Think about what this quote says. The full article states that African Americans in the United States of America fall behind children (die at an earlier age) in China and the region of northern India called Keralan in spite of the higher level of income and standard of living in the US. Those who believe God blesses America over other nations might argue that point based on our apparent higher standard of living than those *foreign* countries. Yet in China and Northern India, areas Americans typically condemn or criticize for being behind the US, life is better than one thinks it could possibly be. Christians living in America must be cautious about making hasty judgments about those living in other countries without knowing factual information, especially if one has never traveled to another country. Simply believing we are blessed and better than others does not make it happen.

One telling set of statistics may help change this narrow-minded viewpoint. First, look at the following table that shows life expectancy information for a group of selected countries: QuickStats: Life Expectancy at Birth, by Sex --- Selected Countries, 2001*

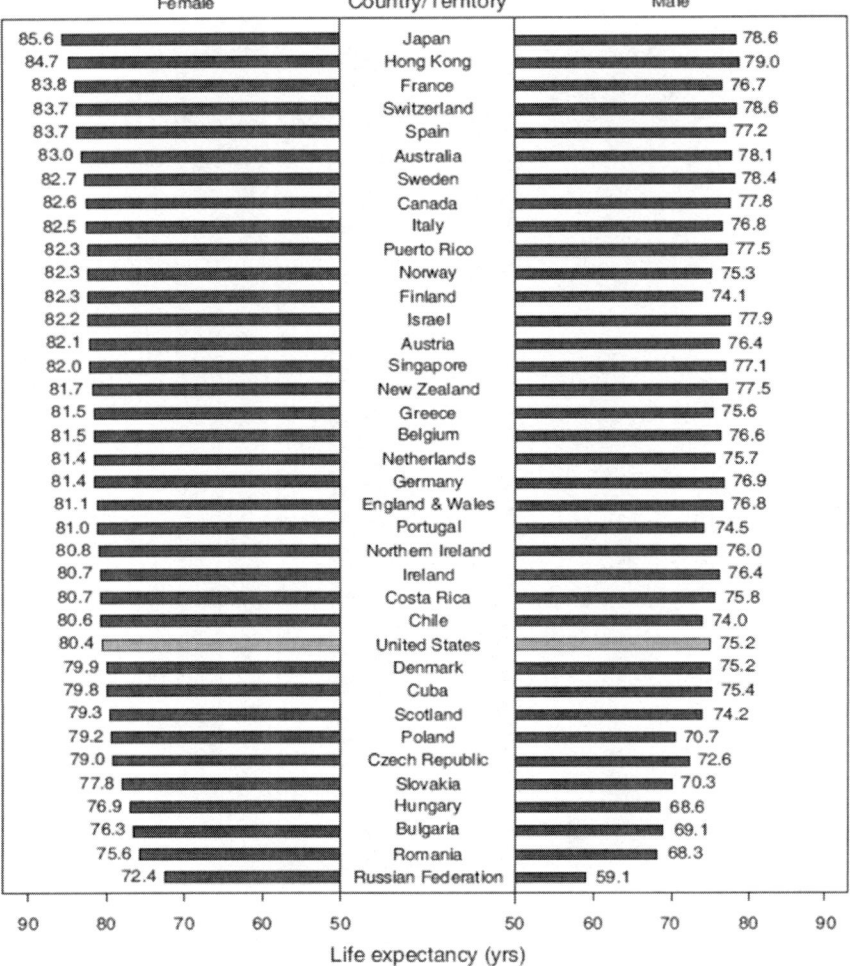

Female	Country/Territory	Male
85.6	Japan	78.6
84.7	Hong Kong	79.0
83.8	France	76.7
83.7	Switzerland	78.6
83.7	Spain	77.2
83.0	Australia	78.1
82.7	Sweden	78.4
82.6	Canada	77.8
82.5	Italy	76.8
82.3	Puerto Rico	77.5
82.3	Norway	75.3
82.3	Finland	74.1
82.2	Israel	77.9
82.1	Austria	76.4
82.0	Singapore	77.1
81.7	New Zealand	77.5
81.5	Greece	75.6
81.5	Belgium	76.6
81.4	Netherlands	75.7
81.4	Germany	76.9
81.1	England & Wales	76.8
81.0	Portugal	74.5
80.8	Northern Ireland	76.0
80.7	Ireland	76.4
80.7	Costa Rica	75.8
80.6	Chile	74.0
80.4	United States	75.2
79.9	Denmark	75.2
79.8	Cuba	75.4
79.3	Scotland	74.2
79.2	Poland	70.7
79.0	Czech Republic	72.6
77.8	Slovakia	70.3
76.9	Hungary	68.6
76.3	Bulgaria	69.1
75.6	Romania	68.3
72.4	Russian Federation	59.1

Life expectancy (yrs)

* Rankings are from the highest to lowest female life expectancy at birth, as published in *Health, United States, 2005* (HUS 2005). Life expectancy at birth represents the average number of years that a group of infants would live if the infants were to experience throughout life the age-specific death rates present at birth. Data are reported by countries. Because calculation of life-expectancy estimates varies by country, comparisons should be made with caution. Certain life-expectancy estimates were revised and differ from those published in HUS 2005.

In 2001, life expectancy (LE) at birth ranged from a low of 59.1 years for Russian males to a high of 84.9 years for Japanese females. LE for males in the United States ranked 26th among 37 countries (74.4 years) and for females ranked 25th(79.8 years). The greatest difference in LE between sexes was observed in Russia (13.2 years). The smallest LE difference between sexes was in Costa Rica (4.3 years). SOURCE: National Center for Health Statistics, Health, United States, 2005: with chartbook on trends in the health of Americans. Hyattsville, MD: US Department of Health and Human Services, CDC, National Center for Health Statistics; 2005.

If God blesses America more than other countries, why are we not at the top of the list? Let us look at a shorter table, again looking at life expectancy.

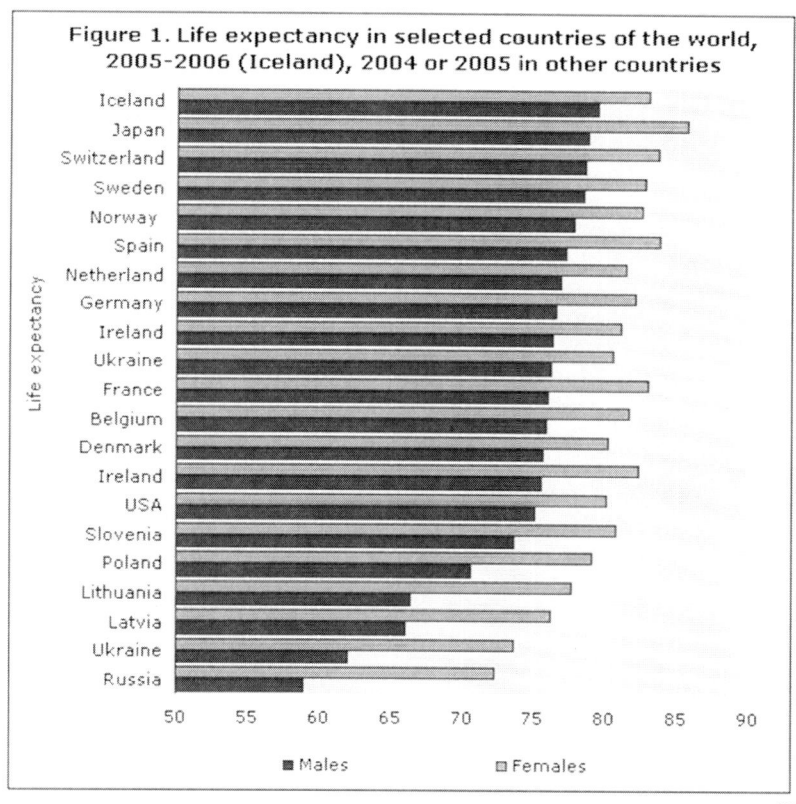

Figure 1. Life expectancy in selected countries of the world, 2005-2006 (Iceland), 2004 or 2005 in other countries

22

Hmmm. It looks like we may have a problem here. When it comes to living a long life, is God blessing other countries more than he blesses America? If God blesses America, why aren't we highest on the list? Based on this data, one could argue those countries with better numbers must be more Christian than the US, or, more logically, could there be something to the argument that God only blesses people and not countries?

Where Are The Christians?

Many denominational congregations have signboards mounted in their auditoriums showing the previous week's attendance and contribution and frequently the amount of the weekly budget. A member can easily determine if the money contributed exceeds or is smaller than the budgeted amount. I often wonder if visitors to the worship service believe the most important items of value to that congregation are money and number of people in the pews.

Weak logic would state that, if God does bless America, attendance would be growing. Not true. In the small town of about 6,500 people where we attend worship services, there are over thirty-five different denominational congregations. In most the average attendance on Sunday morning is between thirty and fifty people. And the number of people attending is falling each year. The following is but one example of what is really taking place in America, Canada, and Britain.

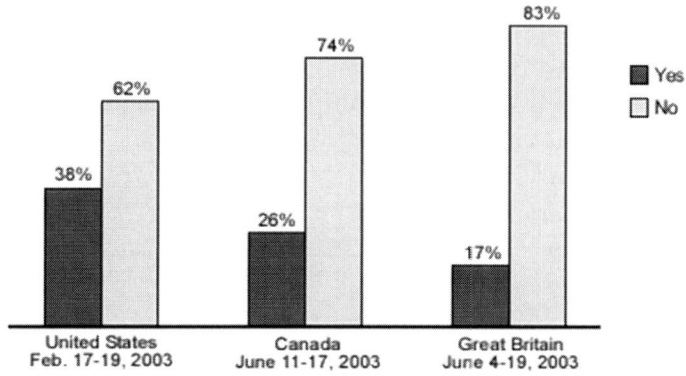

Church Attendance in the U.S., Canada, and Great Britain

(United States) Did you, yourself, happen to attend church or synagogue in the last seven days, or not?

(Canada/Great Britain) In the last seven days, did you, yourself, happen to attend a religious service at a place of worship, or not?

■ Yes
☐ No

United States
Feb. 17-19, 2003

Canada
June 11-17, 2003

Great Britain
June 4-19, 2003

23

The results of this Gallup poll state well more than half of Americans did not attend a religious service within the past week. By itself, this statistic is not conclusive. From 1992 through 2007, the table below lists American's responses to this question: "How often do you attend church or synagogue -- at least once a week, almost every week, about once a month, seldom, or never?"

How often do you attend church, synagogue, or mosque?

	% At least once a week	% Almost every week	% About once a month	% Seldom	% Never	Sample size
2010 (Jan-May)	35	8	11	25	20	146,355
2009	35	8	12	25	20	353,849
2008	34	8	12	26	20	311,591

Gallup Daily tracking

GALLUP

24

These data indicate well less than two-thirds of Americans attend a weekly religious service. If God blesses America over all others, why do we not attend the very religious services we claim are so important to our culture, history, and personal lives? What are we doing instead of attending religious services? Sleeping? Watching television? Sports? Shopping? Working to make more money? Christians must be on guard against worldly influences that gradually pull us away from the lives each must live. Even the illusion of God blessing America, found in the confusion of what is called patriotism, is distracting Christians from the love-driven and faith-based actions so necessary in our daily lives.

All during America's short existence, children have been taught to sing nationalistic songs, recite the pledge of allegiance, and ask God to bless the country, so we can continue living in peace and freedom, enjoying all the material things Americans enjoy. We do not know peace (read our history!), and the freedoms we enjoy are limited and do not come close to the freedom Christians have in God. The freedoms given by man through laws can and are being taken away. If we are the kind of people we claim to be by wearing the title "Christian," then by default we obey all human laws and should not be concerned when they change because the freedoms Christians have in the kingdom of God are permanent. Instead, because of our misdirected focus is on being patriotic, we are not interested in anything in the rest of the world unless it threatens our excessive comfort. As a society in general, we truly do not care about the rest of the world.

Where In The World Are We?

Many Americans cannot locate other countries on a world map and have no idea where they are in relationship to North America. In March of 2007, after returning from a hospital clown trip to Venezuela, I was asked if Venezuela was where "they have those gondolas in the canals." I politely informed the questioner that gondolas were in Venice, Italy. In September of 2008, after returning from a trip to North Korea, when I mentioned to an acquaintance that the roads were lined with beautiful flowers throughout the country, she replied, "That's what I've heard about those tropical islands." In September of 2010, after returning from a humanitarian clown trip to Vietnam, I was asked, "North or South?" A friend asked if Canada was, "…over by Seattle." Another asked if Haiti belonged to the United States. While sharing stories about a clown trip to Costa Rica in August, 2011, the person I was talking to said, "Doesn't Costa Rica belong to the U.S.?" She thought it was a U.S. territory. This apparent ignorance of global geography is spread across the country. "Results from the 2006 NGS [National Geographic Society] survey include:

> 20 percent of young Americans think Sudan is in Asia (it's the largest country in Africa).
>
> Despite the US invasion in March 2003, 63 percent of young Americans cannot find Iraq on a map.
>
> 70 percent cannot find North Korea on a map.
>
> Half of young Americans cannot find New York on a map. [25]

If we are to go into the world and baptize all people for the forgiveness of their sins, how can we go when we don't know where we are going? How can Christians claim to be part of a global family of Christian brothers and sisters without knowing where they are?

I believe it is safe to presume we are concerned with ourselves instead of thinking about those who do not know God's grace, love, and forgiveness. Many really do not care that we have fat stomachs from too much food while others have bloated stomachs from malnutrition and disease. Many do not care that we spend exorbitant amounts of money for bottled water when most people around the globe do not have any access to any safe drinking water. There is a line from an old worship song that goes,

> This world is not my home, I'm just a passing through. My treasures are laid up, some where beyond the blue; The angels beacon me from heaven's open door, and I cannot feel at home in this world anymore.[26]

I feel there are only few American Christians who sing this song in worship services with the mindset of actually believing the words of the song. People love their possessions! Some love their possessions so much they are willing to fight and kill to keep them safe. Some are even willing to fight for possessions that are not theirs. A sign at a protest in England read, "What is our oil doing under their sand?" (Middle Eastern oil comes to mind.) Looking beyond the humor, it is easy to see why many really aren't interested in heaven but hope to find complete satisfaction here on earth.

I Want More!

As Christians, we even allow our greed to find its way into our worship songs. In the song titled "Mansion over the Hilltop" written in 1949 by Ira Stanphill, can you find any greed in the lyrics? "I want a gold one (mansion) that's silver lined. I want a mansion, a robe, and a crown."[27] Selfish arrogance at its best – demanding through the words, "I want..." to a God who already promises us everything we need. Who do we think we are, telling God, "I want! I want! I want!"

Our love of wealth and power regularly causes problems around the world when it comes to others views of America. Blatant arrogance with our wealth is only one cause of hard feelings around the world toward America. "...the extent of our wealth and strength will always breed resentment."[28] I do not recall ever reading or hearing a statement like, "The reality is that the extent of American poverty and weakness will always breed resentment." Children understand the difference between a child showing a new toy and a child bragging about a new toy. The main difference usually has something to do with sharing instead of gloating. Gloating always results in resentment. We resent other countries that have natural resources that we think we deserve because, after all, God blesses America! A March 2007 newspaper and website commentary from the office of Texas senator Kay Bailey Hutchison ended with a comment about us (America) *losing South America*. Since when is South America *ours* to lose? Her comments were based on the out-of-control capitalist view that Venezuelan oil somehow belongs to America, and if Hugo Chavez does not sell it to us at reduced prices, then he is an enemy, and we must do everything we can to take him out of office, even though he was democratically elected more than once by internationally validated elections! Hugo Chavez and the country he leads are not alone in being the target of America's desire for control of natural resources and peoples under the banner of democracy and capitalism.

> While decrying subversion, the United States overthrew independent governments in Iraq, Iran, Guatemala, Chile, South Vietnam, Grenada, Panama, Nicaragua, and El Salvador and abetted the overthrow of regimes in Brazil, the Congo, Dominican Republic, Indonesia, and many other nations. While fulminating against Communist dictatorships, American leaders supported brutal pro-Western dictatorships in scores of Third World nations.[29]

Who do we think we are? It is no wonder the rest of the world is tired of our "Christian" interference in their internal affairs.

Extreme inequality breeds violence. This is really the crux of it all. This has been true throughout history.

Have you ever heard of a peasant revolt? The dark ages were full of them. What inequality is really good at is creating resentment, and the perception that one is receiving less than his or her fair share.[30]

Evidently some in Congress and higher offices believe America is being treated in a way that is not equal to other countries needing oil, so we are justified in attempting to violently overthrow other legal governments. The rest of the world knows we use and waste more resources than any other nation on the planet, and that rising tide of inequality is breeding violence against America around the world. Is this the result of proclaiming we are "one nation under God?" If we truly are a nation under God, shouldn't he simply give us what we need from resources on the earth? Why do we have to invade or overthrow other governments to get what we want? Could it be we have forgotten the difference between want and need? Could it be we have forgotten that God provides all we need? Forgetting what God does for us each day causes unrest in the population who wants more and more from the government and the world.

Will we see a violent revolution against the American government in our lifetime? Possibly. In the spring of 2006, hundreds of thousands of illegal immigrants marched in the streets of several large, American cities to demand a quick process for obtaining documents so they could legally work in America. The marches were peaceful. At the same time, several retired generals voiced their opinion in support of then secretary of defense, Donald Rumsfeld, stepping down, something that finally did take place late in 2006. Their comments were peaceful, and no revolt took place within the ranks. If the central thesis of the book *Pathologies of Power* is correct, it is only a matter of time before a violent revolution takes place in America. Why could this happen? In a word, inequality. In the first months of 2011, throughout the Middle East, thousands of protestors were in the process of over-throwing their governments. Why? Inequality between the rich and the rest of the country. Should this be a concern for the US? I believe the real concern is our fear that the oil supply will be interrupted, and we will have to do something drastic to get "our" oil back. All the while, in the middle of this unrest, aid groups struggle to deliver aid to all who are in need. As discussed elsewhere in this book, governments come and go. They always have and always will. We must remember that God sets the places and times for earthly governments to come and go, and each is to be a reminder that no human government will *ever* compare to the kingdom of God.

One tragic example of how our involvement in other countries causes problems is as close as Haiti. Shortly after the 2010 earthquake in Haiti, the US government sent thousands of soldiers, airmen, sailors, and marines to help with the relief effort. Fully armed soldiers became a police force and took control of the civilian airport in Port au Prince. Flights with humanitarian aid were turned away, so more military troop flights could land. Many flights were instructed to fly to the Dominican Republic, the other half of the island, with instructions to transport their relief supplies by truck into Haiti. This unnecessary take-over of the airport did little to provide help in the first few days of the crisis. But, our involvement in Haiti goes back much further than 2010. I strongly recommend the book *The Uses of Haiti* by Paul Farmer for anyone interested in how the history of the poorest, and one of the oldest democracies in the western hemisphere, was directly impacted by American policies going back as far as our revolutionary war.

Let's Talk Power

America is known around the world for its use of guns and repression in all situations long before any consideration is given to addressing the root causes of hunger, illness, poverty, and racism. If we are a nation who *trusts* in God for all we need, and if God is love and filled with compassion and peace, and if we are a country supposedly based on Christian principles and values, and if we are a nation that advocates peace, why is it that American presidents insist on flying all over the world in military aircraft? Why do American presidents continue to use military honor guards to stand and salute them at the bottom of the steps to their helicopter? Why would anyone want a twenty-one gun salute with highly polished, chrome-plated howitzers?[31] Why do we have marines dressed in their dress uniforms stationed at the White House to open doors? Why are all visiting heads of state presented with military parades, honor guards, and cannon fire? Could it have anything to do with our history of war? Could it have anything to do with our inability to work for peace without the use of weapons? Could it have anything to do with the greed running rampant in the defense industry and the open door policy available to them when approaching the president's office? Are their no other options?

Imagine a president who flew in a coach seat on a commercial airline. Imagine her talking to the people around her about what their needs were. Imagine the head of state from another country arriving at the White House and being greeted by civilian volunteers showing their art works. Imagine no twenty-one gun salutes. Instead, imagine the president simply shaking hands with the head of state and walking quietly through the White House gardens before meeting for business. These may not seem realistic given the culture of fear and hatred we seem to enjoy. It is not beyond reason to imagine no formal ceremony at all during the visit from an official from another country. Will it ever happen? No. Why? For many, their love and devotion is misdirected toward the idols of our time and away from the influence of God and His Word.

Christians are in an out-of-control capitalist country with an economy driven by a gigantic, military-industrial complex, and that type of economy is not healthy for a nation supposedly blessed by God. As Christian taxpayers, it is important that we understand how America spends tax monies. The following is a breakdown of defense spending for America as of April 2005:[32]

Military and defense = 21% (*We spend as much on the military as all other nations combined - $527 billion in 2005!*)

Social Security = 20% (*$519 billion in 2005*)

Medicaid and Medicare = 20% (*$521 billion in 2005*)

Other = 19% (*$200 billion in 2005*)

National Debt Interest = 12%

Major Social Aid Programs = 8% (These include: unemployment monies, food stamps, supplemental security income, veteran's medical costs, low-income household help, and educational grants.)

Some other costs include: [33]

$1.2 billion for the US secret service to protect the president, vice president, their families, and visiting dignitaries.

$225 million to maintain the executive office of the president.

The president receives a salary of $400k plus allowances for "extra travel" of $100k, "personal" expenses of $50k, and "unanticipated" expenses of $1 million! (*My exclamation point. Imagine what humanitarian good could be done with $1,550,000!*)

During World War II, many American manufacturing plants converted from civilian manufacturing to military, such as converting from producing tractors to tanks. After the war, factories converted from making implements of war back to civilian products. Today, hundreds of thousands of employees work at single-product manufacturing plants, producing only military equipment, with no provisions to convert to civilian products. As a result, we have sadly moved to a point where the American economy would fail if military spending were either dramatically reduced or stopped entirely. (I refer the reader to this website where President Eisenhower's speech outlines the danger of uncontrollable military spending: http://coursesa.matrix.msu.edu/~hst306/documents/indust.html)

God, the heavenly father of Jesus, teaches Christians to turn the other cheek and to love and feed our enemies, something many continuously fail to do beyond a token effort. Therefore, in light of the verse mentioned earlier about the love of money, why would God bless the American or any other military-driven economy, for example, China, Russia, or North Korea? As a voting taxpayer, the military budget is not where I want my taxes to go. I do not want my taxes to fund organizations such as:

American Center for International Labour Solidarity (ACILS)

American Institute for Free Labor Development (AIFLD)

Central Intelligence Agency (CIA)

Center for the Service of Popular Action (CESAP)

Center for the Publication of Economic Knowledge (CEDICE)

Nicaraguan Democratic Coalition (CDN)

Defense Intelligence Agency (DIA)

Development Alternatives, Inc. (DAI)

Embassy Political Office (POLOFF)

Federal Bureau of Investigation (FBI)

Free Trade Union Institute (FTUI)

Initiative for the Construction of Confidence (VICC)

International Military Education and Training (IMET)

International Republican Institute (IRI)

National Democratic Institute for International Affairs (NDI)

National Endowment for Democracy (NED)

National Security Agency (NSA)

National Security Council (NSC)

Office of Transition Initiatives (OTI)

United States Agency for International Development (USAID)[34]

I strongly encourage the reader do research into these organizations to identify their true purposes. One may be surprised to learn most are designed to increase American involvement in the internal affairs, typically through spying, including overthrowing legitimate governments of other countries. Perhaps a better system would be a tax system allowing citizens to select where they want their taxes spent. If most citizens do not want most of their taxes to be spent on *defense*, then those funds would be reduced. If citizens want an increase in education funds, then those funds would be increased. As it stands now, citizens have no say at all about where their tax dollars are being spent. Eva Golinger's book, *The Chavez Code*, is an excellent and in-depth look at how some American tax monies are being spent often with little or no public knowledge.

The influence of American greed is also felt in countries where tourist dollars drive the economy. Hotels are plentiful anywhere in the world tourists flock to during their vacations, even in developing countries. But what about the availability of hospital rooms?

> Hospital beds per thousand people: Number one in the world is Switzerland, with 18.3 beds/1000 people. The US is 27th, with 3.6 beds per thousand people. Mexico is 29th, with 1.1 beds per thousand people. The weighted average for all countries in the survey was 7.3 beds per thousand people.[35]

In the US, that country blessed by God, the land of opportunity, the number is 3.6 per 1000, only two places above Mexico and well below the average for all countries. The message seems to be one of *come visit but don't get sick*. Greed, instead of caring for people with love and compassion, drives this behavior. This practice is so remote from what the New Testament teaches.

What's Wrong With This Picture?

The Bible teaches that what a person thinks in his heart is what he is. Following this logic, if one is filled with greed, selfishness, and complete disregard for others, and if that greed leads to stress, then this will lead to physical and emotional illness. Why would any logical human being want to live under this model? Why would any Christian want to live under this model? Why do we continually demand that God bless this model instead of acting as loving Christians to affect some changes?

Those who think they are in high and powerful positions demonstrate their on-going lack of concern for the poor of all countries by routinely voting to spend money for weapons and weapons research while tossing a few scraps into the let–us–help-others pot. America's interest seems to be in developing a better landmine or cluster-bomb than in identifying causes and treatments for serious illness and disease. One result? "… wealthy societies driven by social inequality have poorer health indices than societies in which comparable levels of wealth are more evenly distributed."[36] America is one of the richest nations on the planet, yet our healthcare indices show we do not provide for health needs of the poor, the elderly, or those without insurance. Granted, hospitals do provide *charity care,* but unwillingly and with the mindset those patients are not worthy of the highest quality of care. An increasing number of people in the US struggle with essential health needs and frequently will go to the emergency room instead of waiting a few days for a doctor's appointment because their insurance, if they have any, will cover the ER but will require a deductible or co-pay for an office visit. For example (bold in original text),

> In 2005 ... more than 40 million people—reported that they needed and **did not receive one or more of the following services in the past year because they could not afford them:** medical care, prescription medicines, mental health care, dental care, or eyeglasses.[37]

This one statistic covers almost everything one can think of when it comes to health care. From the same report,

> In 2005, about 12% of adults 18 years of age and over reported that they **did not receive needed dental care;** 7% did **not purchase needed eyeglasses,** and about 9% **did not purchase needed prescription drugs due to cost.**[38]

It is frightening when anyone can do research and find dozens of reports showing the same results, over and over again. There are even more examples,

> Almost all **adults 65 years of age** and over have Medicare coverage. Despite this health insurance coverage, in 2005, 4%–6% of those with income below or near the poverty level **did not get needed medical care** during the past 12 months, 6%–9% **delayed their medical care,** and 9%–12% **did not get the prescription drugs** they needed due to the cost.[39]

> In 2005, 19% of people under age 65 years of age who were uninsured for all or part of the preceding year **did not receive needed medical care** in the past 12 months **due to cost,** compared with 2% of people covered by health insurance for the full year.[40]

The Bible tells us that pure religion is to care for orphans and widows. Adding them to a Sunday morning prayer without follow-up action does little to change the results of these surveys and polls. The underlying cause of many of our healthcare problems is the illusion of the need for money to do medical research which causes all prices to increase. This illusion is frequently driven by the need to make more money for the company.

The 2007 National Center for Health Statistics Report Executive Summary includes this statement:

> Yet, even as progress is made in improving life expectancy, increased longevity is accompanied by increased prevalence of chronic conditions and their associated pain and disability. In recent years, progress in some areas has not been as rapid as in earlier years, or trends have been moving in the wrong direction. Moreover, improvements have not been equally distributed by income, race, ethnicity, education, and geography.[41]

From the birth of the nation until today, we continue to face the reality of inequality of many services when it comes to income, race, ethnicity, education, and geography. If the Bible is true when it states that God is not a respecter of persons but treats everyone equally, then is this how God blesses America, with inequality? The message Jesus delivered was presented for all humanity for all time. Anything contrary to that approach is not going to be blessed by God, no matter where it originates. Once again we must seriously consider that blessings are for individual Christians not countries.

From January 1968 through August 1969, while serving as a medic in Vietnam, I accompanied teams of doctors, nurses, and medics visiting Vietnamese civilian hospitals to give them much needed supplies and patient care. The hospitals were open-air facilities with plain concrete floors and concrete-block walls painted in green and white (when paint was available). Many patients were on thin, blood-stained mattresses without sheets or blankets. There were no screens on the windows and only a few fans to move the hot air. Few beds had mosquito nets over them. Today, one would think those were primitive conditions. Yet in 2000 and 2004, when visiting China and Tibet, and again in Haiti in 2008 and 2010, I found almost identical conditions in the hospitals used by the common citizen.

When in China we were also allowed to visit the newer hospitals that were obviously planned for the elite Communist party members and their families, but for most Chinese, hospital conditions did not contribute to good patient care. Hospitals for the elites and rich tourists were modern, air-conditioned, with clean linens, bathrooms with western fixtures, more than enough staff, and well-stocked hospital pharmacies. In 2005, while visiting hospitals in Russia, our humanitarian clown group observed hospital pharmacies with inadequate supplies, nursing staff that had not been paid for months, and conditions from which many Americans would turn their heads. Yet the nurses still showed up for work, hoping to get paid, but more concerned for the welfare of their patients.

In Haiti in 2008, I noticed *all* intravenous fluids being administered in the hospitals we visited were at least two years out of date! I also noticed a pile of broken medical equipment that looked like it came from a junkyard. When I asked the nurses why this was, they replied that all the IV bags were donated from American hospitals. In other words, if it is out-of-date, send it to another country where there is no recourse if a medicine is out-of-date and causes complications with the patient. After all, it's the Christian thing to do, you know, helping others. Can we expect God to bless a country who routinely sends expired medical supplies and broken medical equipment to poor countries under the false umbrella of charity? In any country, when hospitals focus on making money instead of serving everyone, regardless of need, insurance availability, or the color of their skin, only the administrators, pharmaceutical companies, and insurance companies win. Are there other options?

During a March 2007 trip to Venezuela, our humanitarian clown group met with Venezuelans from all walks of life, from the rich to the poor. Part of our journeys into the various neighborhoods of Caracas and the surrounding areas included lengthy bus rides. During these rides we discussed health care with our Venezuelan guides. We learned there are around 4,400 clinics in neighborhoods all over Venezuela. This is a photo of one.

42

The small clinic occupies the ground floor and the doctor's apartment occupies the top floor. Over 22,000 doctors and nurses staff these clinics in both urban and rural Venezuela. Basic medical care and preventive medical education is performed for anyone living in the neighborhood, free of charge. Many of the doctors come from Cuba. Both Cuba and Venezuela have a joint, physician-education program agreement where one desiring to become a doctor can commit to serving in one of these clinics for a predetermined time, usually a few years, then their medical education will be paid for by the federal government. One question is, "How is this program funded?" Part of the program is funded by oil revenues and the rest is funded with tax revenue. Each resident of Venezuela pays an equal percentage of income into this *social security* program. The poor pay a little, the rich pay much more, both pay the same percentage, and everyone benefits.

Part of the preventive medicine program includes frequent physicals performed by the doctor on the citizens of the local community. Based on the results of the physical, an individual may receive instructions on how many calories are needed to either lose weight in the case of one being overweight, or to gain weight in the case one suffers from malnutrition. The food prepared in community kitchens is not sophisticated by American standards. Black beans, rice, plantains, arépas (a round, cornmeal pan bread), shredded beef or chicken, and fresh fruit make up the meal, and the food is filling, healthy, and tasty! [43] We also clowned in a new pediatric cardiac hospital in Caracas that was equipped with the latest state-of-the-art equipment and supplies. Children with heart problems from Venezuela, and from all other South and Central American countries, were treated free of charge. Free health care in Venezuela is the norm while in America, free health care is an rare oddity.

The whole point of my discussion of this supposed emerging *third-world* country is that America can learn from others, regardless of the false and misdirected propaganda and hatred being spread by presidents, other political leaders, and the wide variety of *intelligence* agencies. The winners under this health care system are the people, the patients, and their families, not highpaid administrators and giant pharmaceutical companies. How many Americans are denied health care because they do not have insurance? While the Cuban and Venezuelan healthcare systems may not be perfect, they are worth studying.

There is a healthcare system in central Texas from which this next example of ego-power is taken. The organization was always struggling with finances and placed their hopes on a new CEO hired to bring the hospital back into the black financially. One of the first steps he took was to reduce housekeeping, dietary, and other support staff through layoffs, under the guise of saving money, followed by a six-figure upgrade of his office and adjoining board room. Anyone who works in a hospital knows the value of the housekeeping staff. They are the first-line of defense, after hand-washing, between the patient and infections. Reducing the number of housekeepers means those remaining staff have to work faster to clean rooms and equipment between patients, increasing the risk of residual bacteria/germs that can be passed on to the next patient. Reducing the number of dietary staff equals a similar reduction in the quality of the food presented to the patient, the staff, and to family members. The CEO's ineptness was further demonstrated by the fact he redecorated his office again in less than a year, because he was not satisfied with how it looked. (He said the carpet looked different once it was installed than it did in the store.)

In the meantime, people were being eliminated, and jobs were combined forcing people to do two or three times the work at the same pay level. Considering this hospital was supposedly a "church" hospital, how did the focus go from the patient to the carpet and board room under the direction of a large board of *Christian* directors? To this day, I am amazed at the money wasted on healthcare facilities across America instead of investing in patients and good medicine. Talk about extremes! On a personal note, when studying the Bible, I find no instance of Jesus receiving money for healing others. I realize my comments seem harsh, but when it comes to love of money over love of people, I become quite unsympathetic to those executives, especially when they claim to be good Christians!

As a humanitarian clown visiting hospitals and nursing homes in my community, I recently experienced yet another example of putting money ahead of the needs of patients and the community. One small hospital had an out-patient clinic for seniors (and others) in need of psychiatric support due to stress, anxiety, sadness, fear, or other emotional needs, usually as the result of the loss of a family member. Patients met in both group and private sessions with a social worker and a psychiatrist. On Wednesdays, I ate lunch with the group and clowned with them while they waited for their individual meeting with the doctor. The program was staffed with a visiting doctor/psychiatrist, a registered nurse, a social worker, a secretary, and a driver (patients came from all over the county). Because the program was not "paying for itself," the board decided to close the program and give the office space to another local doctor. The RN and the secretary were placed in other departments, and the driver was switched to part-time. The social worker was terminated. From a financial view, the small salary of one social worker was saved.

Who won? Obviously not the patients. Paul Farmer states: "the prosperity of the few cannot be based on the poverty of the many."[44] Paraphrased, his statement might read, "the prosperity of the hospital cannot be based on the poverty of the patient." Many times, after the program was cancelled, I met some of the patients and their families in restaurants and the grocery store. Without exception, they all said they missed the help that was provided them by the program, and they were sad it ended. Once again, welcome to misdirected, out-of-control capitalism. These are high-paid officials in board rooms and high-level administrative positions, who frequently demonstrate they care only about making more money for themselves and their stockholders. I understand the need to balance the budget, especially in a hospital. I spent many years working in hospitals all across the country.

The question often overlooked is, do the benefits of the program outweigh the costs? And if they do, can we identify true waste in spending and remove it instead of cutting valuable programs from a human perspective?"

> Some 37 million Americans, mostly working people and members of their families, carry no health insurance, but earn just enough to be disqualified from receiving publicly funded medical care. As budgetary pressures mount at all levels of government, the "safety net" of public health programs is rapidly unravelling, [sic] and millions of poor people are falling through the giant holes that have developed in the system. Such problems invite a basic question about this tangle that we call the health care system—is it ethical?.[45]

God offers his love without concern for how rich or poor we are. Why can we not follow His model of care? It is a sad state of affairs when the first question caregivers ask after, "What is your name?" is, "Do you have insurance." Good healthcare is available in America, for the right price. The modern lyrics of an old worship song would probably now read, "The Great Physician now is near, the sympathizing Jesus, VISA or MasterCard please."

"Hello. I'm your doctor for today. What prescription medicine do you want?"

Along with hospitals, the pharmaceutical industry only adds greed to the process. Doctors' offices are flooded with samples of the *newest* and *best* drugs available, and deals are cut whereby these medicines are easily made available to the patient. How do patients learn about these new and improved medications? By watching television and reading magazine advertising. On the web page nofreelunch. org, information is provided about pharmaceutical companies wooing doctors with samples of their newest medicines:

Many doctors provide samples to patients who lack prescription drug coverage or out of convenience. In fact, many doctors will say that obtaining samples is the primary reason they see reps. Drug companies spend ½ their promotional dollar (more than 10 billion dollars in 2002) on these samples. And for good reason: Samples are an extremely effective marketing "tool." Samples get patients, and doctors, "hooked" on the sampled drug. But, not surprisingly, the "Sample Closet" is filled with the newest, most expensive medications, in brightly colored promotional packaging reminiscent of the supermarket cereal aisle. Though receiving a sample from your doctor may often seem convenient (and may also save you money in the short run), it may also result in you ending up on the wrong medication, and in the end costing you even *more* money, and maybe even worse.

"Do you have a problem? Ask your doctor about (insert the latest 'disease' here)." We do love our medicines. It is almost a badge of honor to be taking several prescription medications! Time and time again I talk to nursing home residents and ask them what they would like to change about their current lifestyle. Most say they would like to stop taking so many pills! There have been many times where the family will change doctors, and the new doctor will immediately reduce the number of medications the nursing home resident is taking, because they are causing more problems than they are helping. But, for some still walking the streets under their own power it can also be a badge of honor to be *suffering* from any number of newly discovered *diseases* and *illnesses*.

Baldness seems to be more important than the rapid increase in malaria, tuberculosis, and HIV/AIDS cases in the world. Baldness was never considered an illness until the past several years, and now the message is, "If you are bald or losing your hair, you will never be attractive, sexy, and you are *sick*!" If losing one's hair was not enough, now we must deal with the global epidemic of erectile dysfunction! Oh my! What are we to do? I know – take more drugs! What happened to candlelight, music, flowers, dinner, and the line, "Let me go change into something more comfortable?" What happened? The capitalistic greedy mindset that says, "I have to work all this extra time each day, so I can make more money to pay for all the stuff I want, so I can keep up with everyone else and get high blood pressure from stress, which will cause my sexual desire to fail when I want it to work. And even if that causes me to believe I do not have time to woo my wife and do all those things we first did when we were married, then let me go to a doctor for a ten minute visit, so I can get me some drugs to take care of the problem!" Whew!

But, if you have malaria or tuberculosis, diseases affecting millions of people worldwide, there is a problem. Pharmaceutical companies invest a higher percentage of their research and development time and money into producing drugs to treat what I call *designer* illnesses such as Restless-leg Syndrome and Chronic Fatigue Syndrome. These drugs cost much more than they should thanks to a change in the laws governing approval of new drugs. The new focus of drug companies is on diseases that are very rare and have been given the title *orphan diseases*. Prior to 1993 they were not a high priority for pharmaceutical companies. In 1993 the Orphan Drug Act was created allowing pharmaceutical companies to bypass the typical approval pathway for drugs affecting much larger populations. The intent was to provide tax and approval incentives so that pharmaceutical companies would recover investments in research and manufacturing these low volume medicines, known as orphan drugs. One example is Cerezyme, used to treat Gaucher, an inherited genetic condition that causes fatty deposits to build up in organs and bones. The interesting thing about this orphan drug is that Gaucher disease affects less than 10,000 people worldwide. There are almost seven billion people on the planet, so the number of people suffering from Gaucher disease is so small a percentage, most small calculators can't compute a number that small.

> If you're going to develop an orphan drug, you're going to have to charge a substantial price for the drug in order to make it worthwhile," said Matthew Geller, analyst for CIBC World Markets. Genzyme charges up to $200,000 a year for Cerezyme treatment, according to Genzyme spokesman Dan Quinn. But insurance companies are willing to pick up the costs because of the drug's efficacy, said Quinn.[46]

So, the drug works and is paid for at the cost of $200,000. Could this money for research that affects such a small percentage of the world's population be better invested in finding new drugs for malaria and tuberculosis, drugs typically costing much less than orphan drugs? Inequity in drug research so more money can be made is only one problem for the poor.

Water for small farms in developing countries is a serious problem. A small, simple pump that costs thirty-three dollars can irrigate three-quarters of an acre allowing small farmers to improve the crop yields of their fields. This cheap solution could impact millions of farmers around the world. Instead of finding ways to get pumps to the world for a few dollars, big we're-here-to-help-everyone-get-better companies focus on making money for the stockholders and company officers, not on developing medicines or machines to reduce or eliminate global sickness. As one radio talk show host states, it is time to wrap one's head with duct tape to keep the brain from exploding! Have we gone crazy? No. We are simply filled with a misguided love of money and things. We have fallen into Satan's trap of loving the things of the world over loving the spiritual things of God. Remember, "For we brought nothing into the world, and we can take nothing out of it." (1 Timothy 6:7)

When pharmaceutical companies invest in hair and erectile-dysfunction drugs, or drugs that may help such a small percentage of humans on the planet, instead of cures for malaria or tuberculosis, solely for the purpose of making more money, then:

> In the name of cost-effectiveness, we cut back health benefits to the poor, who are more likely to be sick than the nonpoor [*sic*]. We miss our chance to heal. ... In the name of expedience, we miss our chance to be humane and compassionate.[47]

While Americans have great difficulty showing humane and compassionate behavior toward other humans, on the other hand (or paw) we do treat our pets quite differently. If you have one or more pets, think about how you treat them in comparison to how you treat other humans. Look for more on this later!

It is frightening to me to see people taking better (more *humane*) care of their pets and farm animals than they do for their elderly relatives locked away in nursing homes. My heart aches when I see health-care staff who complain when a hospital patient or nursing home resident uses the call light, hoping for a quick reply to their need. It is sad to see and hear nurses who obviously have no desire to care for others in need, doing everything they can to avoid patient contact. Many claim to be active Christians. Sometimes I wish humanitarian clowns had the authority to fire people! Granted, there are some in the health care industry who actually care for their patients and are happy to do so. I know of many nurses who've not had a salary increase in many years, yet they still are willing to work two back-to-back shifts to take care of their patients, not because of the money, but because of their dedication to caring for others. Sadly, they seem to be in a very small minority in America.

We have no record of Jesus going only to rich neighborhoods to cure people. We have no record of him asking for insurance cards before he performed a miracle. We have no record of Jesus building a new medical facility in the *nice* part of Jerusalem, so he would not have to deal with the poor. We have no record of Jesus redecorating his office and board room, twice. We have no record of Jesus encouraging his followers to focus on reducing their staff, so he could operate the church more efficiently and make more money. If Jesus was like a modern American executive, we probably would read about the six apostles. We have no record of the corporate miracle sales representative giving Jesus free miracle samples for him to use. The reason we do not have a record of these things is because his model of dealing with people is based on demonstrating love, compassion, and care for all, regardless of social or political standing. Why do we not get it? Could it be that we love our stuff more than we love humanity?

"Who are you wearing today?"

Frequently, our stuff includes clothing endorsed by *famous* people. Fashion designers, Hollywood stars, musicians, NASCAR drivers, and other sports personalities seem to top the list of buy-the-product-with-my-name-on-it people. Here is an interesting comment on those items and the workers who put them together for us.

That means," Brubaker wrote, "a Haitian woman can earn anywhere from 40 cents to one dollar for every dozen baseballs she stitches. It can take from 5 to twenty five minutes to sew the two covers of a baseball together. (Each baseball has 108 double or 216 single stitches.) "Using a 15 minute average, and a 70 cents per dozen pay scale, a woman could expect to earn $2.80 a day if she worked for eight hours without a break." Carrying out the calculations further, in 1977 an employee of a baseball factory in Haiti, if she worked six days a week could earn as much as $769.60 in a year. Meanwhile in the US the minimum wage for MLB players was $60,000. Today it's about ten times that.[48]

Here are a few thought questions for the reader. If *professional sports* (a true oxymoron!) vanished, would the world end? How much money would be available to care for the poor? If Disney vanished off the face of the earth, how much money would be available to care for the poor? If NASCAR stopped racing, how much money would be available to care for the poor? (Not to mention an increase in gasoline supplies!) How much medicine could be given to those who have no money? How many children could be given clean water, soap, toothpaste, and brushes, clothes, and school supplies and books? Neither professional sports nor Disney provide anything of spiritual value to any human. The sole purpose of both is, through temporary entertainment, to make money for a few people, nothing more. On my desk I have two photos. One is of our granddaughter standing beside Cinderella at Disney in Florida. She is wearing her Cinderella dress and is obviously happy she got to meet the *real* Cinderella. Next to that I have a photo postcard from a friend. The photo is of two children in Bali, Indonesia. They are squatted down alongside a muddy, water-filled road wearing no clothes and are covered with one conical straw hat. It is pouring rain, and the look on their faces is one of complete fear and concern for their future. The photograph was taken by Steve McCurry in 1983 and can be seen at www.flickr.com/photos/marja2006/3766379422/. My point for having these two photos is to remind myself of the incongruence between our imaginary world and the real world. It is also a reminder for me always be aware of the actions I take when doing my humanitarian clown activities.

The Bible tells us Christians will be held accountable for their actions. There is no record in the Bible of Jesus, during his ministry, endorsing the latest sport sandal, newest jogging robe, or third-world-made silver cross to hang around one's neck on gen-

JOSEPH ALAN REDMAN

uine *Corinthian* leather necklaces. In fact, we find he had almost no personal possessions other than the clothes on his back. Jesus told us the truth. "Merely telling the truth, of course, often calls for extensive research."[49] Throughout the Bible, we are instructed to study, study, study. That means much more than reading alone. It means reading, thinking, asking questions, searching through references, and formulating beliefs based on faith in God, then taking that faith and reinforcing it with love-based action.

Corporate Greed

After spending so much time on the topic of greed, it is essential to consider other factors involved in wanting more than we need. "Greed and moral indifference define the corporate world's culture, which is why…business is booming."[50] Notice the addition of the words "moral indifference" to "greed." Obviously the two are strongly connected. If one is morally indifferent, he does not care what the result of his actions may be, and he does not care about his impact on others. The person who is greedy and has moral indifference cares only about how many things she can accumulate, how good she can look and feel, and how much ego-power she can wield. When we think of those who are greedy it is seldom the destitute or poor that come to mind. While they can be just as greedy as the next person, we usually think about those who are already wealthy as being greedy when they want much more than they need. Not surprisingly, some of those people are CEO's and politicians.

> But when the average CEO in today's America makes 531 times as much as the employee with the lunch pail, what does that say about the country this nation has become, one that, more than any other nation in the world, seems to be losing the ability to distinguish between its needs and its greeds?[51]

In my local community, a waitress with a good job earns eight dollars per hour. Based on the previous numbers, a typical CEO would make $4,240 per hour. I do not discount the fact CEOs are responsible for many jobs in their companies, and they are responsible to their boards to make money for the shareholders. In America, in spite of fancy corporate vision statements and hours of customer service training, the purpose of the corporation is to make money at any cost. Period! Let me say that again – *the purpose of the corporation is to make money!* The problem comes when a CEO is only interested in power and money at the expense of the hourly employee. Almost once a month, another CEO is raked over the coals for extravagant spending for personal items and violation of tax laws. The problem does not stop there.

Do We Have To Obey The Law?

Beyond making money, "…the corporation feels no moral obligation to obey the law."[52] Because corporations feel no moral obligation to follow the law, and because corporations offer millions of dollars used by lobbyists to influence all members of Congress, can we assume Congress does not care about the law either? How many times are members of Congress called to appear before a committee challenging their ethics, and the end result is a mild slap on the hand? Why is it ethical to ignore overtime laws that apply to the rest of the country by not applying those laws to the regular employees of the Congress? I can only imagine the thought process in Congress when passing new legislation, but it may go something like, "If I pass this legislation it will make a certain friendly lobbyist happy, and since that lobbyist represents a company that has given my re-election campaign a lot of money, they will give me more and ensure I get re-elected." Jesus never became involved in politics other than commanding we obey the law and pay our taxes. I think I can see the reason why.

When reading new laws passed during the past several years, one seemingly common thread is the amazing number of words used to describe what the law entails. It is almost as if the wordier the bill, the fewer people will read it. I guess the logic is one of overwhelming others, who are already pressed for time, into voting for the bill without considering whether or not the details could do harm to the voting public. The Ten Commandments contains 322 words. The Bill of Rights is stated in 516 words. Lincoln's Gettysburg Address contains 272 words. A recent federal directive to regulate how growers of cabbage are insured contains 3,589 words. I have no idea how many cabbage growers are affected by the insurance law, but it seems some bill-writers have too much time on their hands. Using data from various tables on the US Senate website, the total number of laws passed from 1947 through 2004 equal 28,091, or an average of 492 per year. In 2010, the senate was in session for 158 days, with senators averaging 6.8 hours of work each day. And during the 2010 session, 258 new laws were passed down from the average of 492. Some investigative reporters spend their time finding those laws that are passed but never enforced due to lack of funding. The question is, for those un-enforced laws, what was the financial and/or political gain for passing these laws? One wonders how many laws are on the books that will never be enforced. For Christians, this would be comparable to saying we do not need to obey the laws of God that we aren't interested in. Ignoring its own laws is a dangerous practice for a country, and it is even more dangerous for an individual to ignore God's law.

In addition to ignoring some of our own laws, we also ignore other documents to which we have placed our nation's autograph. During World War II, a liberty ship blew up while waiting off the coast of Italy to unload passengers and cargo. The explosion was kept classified for many years, and most thought the sinking of the ship was caused by a German U-Boat.

> The fifty-year secrecy blackout expired in 1993, and the magazine had picked up on the newly released information. Under the headline 'Mustard Gas Horror at Bari' it revealed that one of the ships moored in Bari harbour, a US Liberty ship named *John Harvey*, had been carrying a top-secret cargo of two thousand 100 pound mustard bombs.[53]

The saga continues. "The mustard gas had been brought from the United States to back up President Roosevelt's promise that if poison gas was used against American troops, he would reply in kind."[54] As of the end of 1997, the US maintained over one million rounds of munitions containing mustard gas in storage sites across the US. The use of mustard gas was outlawed at the end of World War I, at the insistence of the United States. We insisted mustard gas be outlawed, yet we still maintain an enormous stockpile of mustard-gas munitions. I think the proper word for this behavior is *hypocrisy*. In other words, we are deliberately ignoring international law. If the US is truly blessed by God, does this mean he pays no attention to his own laws found in the Bible, those stating we are to obey the laws established by the leaders of the nation? God is not a kindly, grey-bearded grandfather who lives in a cabin and smiles down on our ignorance of the law. God loves us, but he is also a God of vengeance when it comes to those who deliberately ignore his law.

In 1947, following World War II, the United Nations wrote a document titled, *The Universal Declaration of Human Rights*. The US signed the document then proceeded to ignore it completely. One example can be found in Article 5 of the declaration. "No one shall be subjected to torture or to cruel, inhuman or degrading treatment or punishment." America signed this document in 1948 – immediately after World War II, during which torture was a common practice by several nations. It is ironic that America is now a leader in the use of torture around the world. Why is it that after World War II the American legal system prosecuted, convicted, and executed former Japanese officers for water-boarding American prisoners, and during the Vietnam war, American soldiers were prosecuted, convicted, and jailed for water-boarding Viet Cong prisoners, while in 2008 it is an accepted form of interrogation that can be used by Americans on their prisoners? Please read this amazing document we have chosen to ignore. A copy can be found at Appendix B. In May of 2010, former President Bush admitted he supported the water-boarding of prisoners and said he would do it again. In his auto-biographical book titled *Decision Points*, Bush readily admits he approved water-boarding as an interrogation method for use on suspected terrorists. I fail to see the difference between water-boarding in World War II and today. Torture is torture. We create new laws while ignoring the old.

Do we really need more new laws? Corporations pay lobbyists to sell Congress on laws they want, so they (the corporations) will be able to make more money for their CEO's and shareholders.

> If corporations and governments are indeed partners, we should be worried about the state of our democracy, for it means that government has effectively abdicated its sovereignty over the corporation.[55]

There is no *if*. Corporations and the American government are partners, and democracy in America is a myth with no real spiritual value. The modern democracy we have in America has been transformed into a life philosophy of "get as much money/power/possessions as you can." Once more, the role of the corporation is to make money. (Repeat this sentence three times, click your ruby wingtips together, then jump out of the window with your golden parachute on your back, all while saying, "There is no place like one of my four, multi-million dollar homes.") The role of the corporation is not to care for employees, the environment, the community, or any other non-corporate-related group. The corporation makes money. Period! (Yes, I know I said this before. It is important to remember this!) Out-of-control capitalistic governments are driven by money-earning-over-all-else corporations. Therefore, the statement that the government has abdicated sovereignty over corporations is true. (Other words for sovereignty are: authority, power, rule, and control.) However, since trusting in America doesn't really matter, the sovereignty we must recognize is that of God. He is in control of the lives of Christians, and they are individuals he blesses. As individuals blessed by God, we must think about our actions and the words we speak each day, analyzing them as either being right or being wrong. There is no middle ground when it comes to sin. It either is, or it isn't. Regrettably, as a society,

> We have now circled back to the world where people argue, not about right or wrong, but whether something was done the right way. Bureaucracy, founded to liberate government from process, does almost nothing else.[56]

What is the best example of intelligent people afraid to make a mistake spending much of their time arguing about processes? Human governments in action.

Where Are We And Where Are We Going?

C-SPAN broadcasts live proceedings from the House of Representatives and the Senate and most senators make a feeble attempt to follow parliamentary rules, so they will present the image of organized decorum. The image they present is one of complete disinterest in the American people; one of so much emphasis on the procedural rules that the process is excruciatingly slow, cumbersome, wasteful, childish, trite, boring, filled with the non-involvement of the senate as a body; one of large egos; one of avoiding important issues and instead filling time with empty speeches designed to ensure re-election. The American government is far from being effective or efficient, and is not an example for anyone or any country to follow. The American government is an embarrassment to peaceful, loving, and compassionate Christians. The American government does not operate under the words of the pledge, "under God" and like everything else on earth, is a quite temporary entity.[57]

The following quote was supposedly written by a gentleman named Alexander Tyler. Further research indicated the quote may have been written by Alexander Fraser Tytler instead. Even further research shows the quote has no known source, so I will attribute it simply to Alexander. Who wrote this text is not important. The content, however, is vital:

> A democracy cannot exist as a permanent form of government. It can only exist until the voters discover that they can vote themselves money from the public treasury. From that moment on the majority always votes for the candidates promising the most money from the public treasury, with the result that a democracy always collapses over loose fiscal policy followed by a dictatorship.
>
> The average age of the world's greatest civilizations has been two hundred years. These nations have progressed through the following sequence: from bondage to spiritual faith, from spiritual faith to great courage, from courage to liberty, from liberty to abundance, from abundance to selfishness, from selfishness to complacency, from complacency to apathy, from apathy to dependence, from dependence back to bondage.

The logic used makes complete sense, and the question is: *Where is America in this pattern?* America seems to be somewhere close to selfishness, complacency, and/or apathy, and no matter how formal senators think they are perceived to be, they are temporary and bogged down in trivialities designed to support their ego-power. In my many conversations with both hospital patients and nursing home elderly, one common comment they share when we discuss their view of what is taking place in the country is that their elected representatives seem to be busy but don't really know what is going on in the small communities, and they just don't seem to care one way or the other what the people's real needs are. Many of my elderly friends who are still able to vote have given up on the process and refuse to vote anymore. There is a general feeling that human governments are cumbersome, slow to act, and filled with waste. One example is "…in 1994, the Defense Department spends more on procedures for travel reimbursement ($2.2 billion) than on travel. ($2 billion)"[58] Effective? Efficient? Worth the money? Give me a break! In a civilian corporation, if a department was caught spending more to process travel than the cost of the travel alone, someone would lose their job. This fact makes one wonder how difficult it can be to set up a procedure for travel reimbursement.

Another complaint from my wise friends is their observation of what is called the welfare state. They share amazing stories of very difficult lives on farms and in small communities where every penny earned was important and nothing was free or came easy to them and their families. Considering my friends are confined to a nursing home, they are quite up-to-date on political happenings in their community and at the federal level in Washington, D.C. They often comment that in their day, people helped each other when there was a need. If a family needed food or clothing, other families and congregations in the area helped provide what was required. Because everyone helped in whatever way they could, the concept of handouts did not exist as a key part of society. There was the occasional hobo making his way through the area, but for the most part, needs of the community were met by the community. Everyone shared with no expectation of reward or recognition. Since the 1960s, with a dramatic increase in federal handouts, the percentage of people who vote in national elections has dropped to where the annual average runs around forty-eight percent. The mindset seems to be one of "why should I do anything different when I can get what I need from the government?"

> On the other hand, some critics from very divergent perspectives explain the current decline in democratic involvement by contending that the welfare state curtails active citizenship and promotes passive dependency.[59]

If this is true, we may also see signs of this shift by the facts of a population filled with fat from junk food, living in over-priced *I-can-get-rich-in-real-estate* apartments and mini-mansions, million-dollar recreational vehicles, condos, houses, and mobile homes filled with electronic equipment that encourages dependency and passivity – television, DVD players and recorders, VCR's, cellular phones, beepers, walkie-talkies, laptops, and on and on and on. It is truly a strange and unique event to see two people actually talking face-to-face! When technology attempts, or is allowed, to replace face-to-face contact between two people, there will be a proportional increase in miscommunication and a decrease in mutual understanding. John Naisbett said, "The more high technology around us, the more the need for human touch." Jesus spent his short life on earth engaged with others through his physical presence and his loving touch. We are quickly moving away from the model he left us in scripture.

Look! A Squirrel! (And Other Diversions)

Americans (and others) are notorious for their love of electronic gadgetry. Those with excess money have an excess of gadgets. All classes have their gadgets, but there still remains a distinct upper class, something the New Testament teaches against, and a group definitely off the list of *Those Whom God Blesses*. Many upper-class workers seldom need to *clean-up* at the end of their work day, unlike mechanics, gardeners, housekeepers, etc. Who are the upper class, the elite? "Non-industrial upper-class occupations may be roughly comprised under government, warfare, religious observances, and sports."[60] This text, written in 1899, is strikingly similar to America today. Think about these categories for a minute: Government; Warfare (the military); Religious observances (pseudo *reverends and pastors*, television evangelists, *religious holiday* celebrations); Sports (*professional*, college, high school, and children's organized sports activities). The amount of money wasted in these areas is probably uncountable. I do, however, want to draw the reader's attention to the following table listing discretionary funding by major American government agencies for 2010:

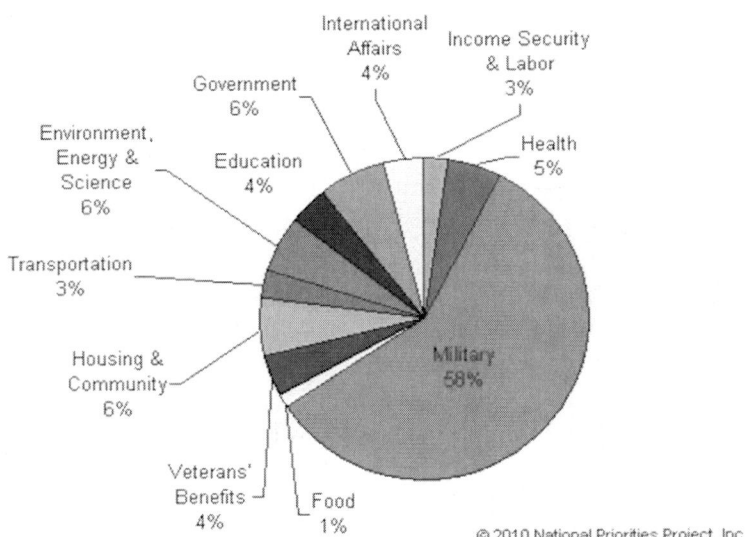

Discretionary Spending, FY 2010

© 2010 National Priorities Project, Inc.

Stewardship

More money is spent by the American government on warfare (the *defense* budget) than any other category. Almost forty-nine percent of the discretionary spending budget funds people, processes, and equipment designed to wound or kill others. The following pie chart shows military spending by America in comparison to the rest of the world. We spend $711 billion dollars compared to $379 billion for the rest of the world combined!

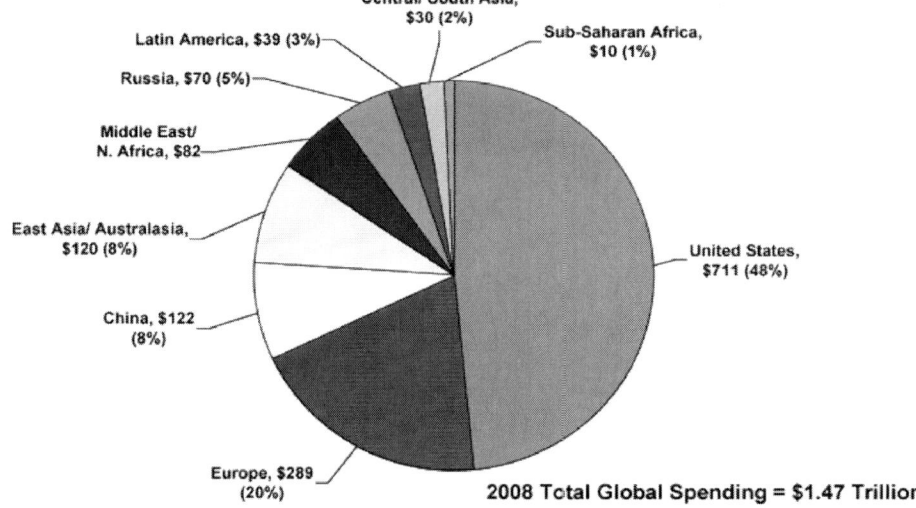

U.S. Military Spending vs. The World in 2008
(in billions of U.S. dollars, with % of total global)

Central/ South Asia, $30 (2%)
Sub-Saharan Africa, $10 (1%)
Latin America, $39 (3%)
Russia, $70 (5%)
Middle East/ N. Africa, $82
East Asia/ Australasia, $120 (8%)
China, $122 (8%)
Europe, $289 (20%)
United States, $711 (48%)

2008 Total Global Spending = $1.47 Trillion

NOTES: Data from International Institute for Strategic Studies, *The Military Balance 2008*, and COD. The total for the United States is the FY 2009 request and includes $170 billion for military operations in Iraq and Afghanistan, as well as funding for DOE nuclear weapons activities. All other figures are projections based on 2006, the last year for which accurate data is available.

62

Is this what the Bible means by commanding us to love our enemy and to turn the other cheek? Is this considered good stewardship? Is this an example of a "Christian" nation's wise use of money?

Looking at the remaining groups listed by Veblen as non-industrial upper-class occupations, specifically religious observances and sports, he continues, "…the characteristic feature of leisure class life is a conspicuous exemption from all useful employment."[63] Veblen was not referring to Christian ministers preaching and teaching without concern for grandeur in their buildings and enormous salaries. He is referring to those who abuse the name of God for their own glory, publicity, and ego. Television evangelists who preach the coming judgment with charts and maps supposedly proving Jesus will return in a matter of months then close their programs with a sales pitch to buy their latest book on the topic are laughing all the way to the bank. If they were sincere in their efforts to help convince people to believe and have faith in God, does it not make sense that they would give their books away as fast as they could, for free? If their efforts were truly based on Scripture, why do they reprint *revised* editions of their books every year? Are these people truly usefully employed? I do not recall reading anywhere in the New Testament where Jesus charged for his services. Even Paul, commenting on preachers being allowed to be paid for their services, stated that he never accepted money for preaching the Word of God. As an aside, all money raised by the sale of this book goes directly to support orphans in Haiti, through the Mercy & Sharing Foundation.

One who is usefully employed provides a product or service that helps others live in a healthy and safe environment, is loving and compassionate in their daily lives, and is also one who follows the commands of God. Those in the leisure class engaged in predatory occupations (see quote below) do not fit this category.

> So, those offices which are by right the proper employment of the leisure class are noble*, such are government, fighting, hunting, the care of arms and accoutrements, and the like – in short, those which may be classed as predatory employments.[64]
>
> (*as in *aristocratic*)

They are not convincing human beings in the sense that, even when claiming to be a Christian, their actions typically suggest otherwise. The author's use of the word "noble" may have been a little tongue-in-cheek. Living a life of love and compassion just does not seem to fit the label of "predatory." When thinking of a predator, imagine a lion stalking its prey with one intention – to kill. Is not this also one of the New Testament descriptions of the devil? Perhaps if there was a way to eliminate those jobs, shift the money wasted there to caring for the poor and homeless in the world, and place all these "professionals" and others in the truly noble professions such as in jobs genuinely helping others, there could be a different result than what we currently see with the poor and homeless in the world. But for some reason, I doubt many of those would give up their multiple mansions, cars, and jewels. To do so would remove them from being (at least in their minds) more powerful than others. Our society is still one filled with bias toward those we feel are *below* our level economically, personally, emotionally, or spiritually. By subconsciously judging others, we place them above us so we can hate them for what they have or below us so we can feel better about where we are in relationship to them. "The pervading norm in the predatory community's scheme of life is the relation of superior and inferior, noble and base, dominant and subservient persons and classes, master and slave."[65] These categories seem to be out of sorts with the Bible and out of sorts with Christian behavior. We either have forgotten or never really understood that when we became a Christian, we became a new creature. We moved from being only physical to being purely spiritual with a short-lived physical attachment called the body. Paul reminds us:

> You are all sons of God through faith in Christ Jesus, for all of you who were baptized into Christ have clothed yourselves with Christ. There is neither Jew nor Greek, slave nor free, male nor female, for you are all one in Christ Jesus.
>
> Galatians 3:26-28

In America, the gap between the rich and the poor grows by leaps and bounds, continuing the model of superior, noble, dominant, and master. Those who know their New Testament can finish this sentence: "It is easier for a camel to go through the eye of a needle than for a rich man to ..."

Jesus tells us our physical needs will be taken care of if we seek the kingdom of God. In other words, we will have food, shelter, and clothing to sustain us while we are alive. The problem facing many Americans is the desire to want more than just the basics, because we actually believe we are invincible as a nation and will live forever. In fact, many believe it is their right to take more than they need to live. Isn't that the American dream? Many are infected with greed thanks to the myth of the wonders of capitalism and advertising. We see those of the noble class on television, in movies, in magazines, in the news and feel angry and frustrated we are not just like them. Our hopes and wants are to look like the imaginary heroes created by the media, to dress like them, to own the same things they own, and to live like them every day. What happened to the idea of living simply for God and wanting to be Christ-like by allowing Christ to live in us?

We are not a Christian country. We never have been. We are not a country that believes in God. We are not a country blessed by God. We are a country driven by need for ego-power and an increasing appetite for material things. Placing "In God We Trust" on our money does not demonstrate any Christian belief found in the New Testament. Christians must stop saying "God bless America" and instead ask, through prayer, for a better understanding of the New Testament and the word of Jesus so that we can glorify God.

JOSEPH ALAN REDMAN

Chapter One Thought Questions

1. Do your actions demonstrate a greater love of God or of money? How would your friends answer this question about you?

2. What do you worry about? Why?

3. Do you buy a new vehicle every one or two years? Why?

4. How much do you spend each year on presents for family and friends? Why?

5. How much do you give (money, time, supplies, etc.) to a congregation or other charitable organization each year?

My Challenge Tasks

1. List ten ways you are blessed without listing money, possessions, or things.

2. Collect everything you do not really need and give those things to someone or to an organization that can distribute them.

3. List the last five books you have read. Were they fiction or non-fiction? Spiritual or earthly? Why do you read what you do? Is the Bible on your reading list?

4. List the magazines to which you subscribe or buy each month. Why do you read these magazines? Can you eliminate them without impacting your spiritual life?

5. List how much time you spend reading those items in #3 and #4, then compare that time with the amount of time you spend reading and studying the Bible.

WHO CAN GIVE
A BLESSING?

It is more blessed to give than to receive.

Acts 20:35

This chapter will be short in length because the following are those who can give either spiritual or physical blessings: God and Humans.

You cannot get much simpler than that! But, because most Americans easily relate to monetary figures, let us look at a few monetary examples of how poor a job Americans do when *blessing others* with material gifts. As you read through the list, look for examples of selfishness, lack of knowledge, deception, waste, double-standards, pre-judging, or any other behavior that goes against what the Bible teaches. The following examples come from *Mother Jones* magazine:[66]

1. In 2002, Americans deducted $654 million for cars they donated to charity – 7 times what the cars were actually worth.

2. On average, Americans think that 24% of the federal budget goes toward foreign aid. Only 0.9% actually does.

3. Because aid agencies are forced to buy from US companies at inflated prices, historically, America has effectively taken back 70% of the aid it donated.

4. The average American family throws away 14% of its food.

5. The typical American child receives 70 new toys a year, most of them at Christmas.

6. Americans spend $8 billion on Christmas decorations, almost 4 times what they give to protect animals and the environment.

7. US Donations made thus far per victim of 9/11, Katrina, and the tsunami, respectively: $736,771, $2,827, $1,173.

8. Gift bags for Academy Award presenters contained $100,000 worth of freebies.

9. 18 hours after the 1906 San Francisco earthquake, the first trainload of relief supplies arrived. Within a week, nearly every military tent was pitched in the city. Within three weeks, 10% of the Army was on hand.

10. FEMA's website listed Operation Blessing, Pat Robertson's faith-based organization, second on its list of charities that would speed relief to Katrina victims.

11. Last year, Operation Blessing gave half its donation - $885,000 – to the Christian Broadcasting Network, of which Robertson is chairman.

12. (From a chart on page 17) In 2003 the average donation to charity by those earning $200,000 and over was 3.4%. The average donation to charity by those earning $15,000 and under was 26%

While one human can give another human a blessing, it appears wealthy Americans do not grasp that concept when it comes to sharing with others! I think I prefer God's design for giving and receiving blessings. I recommend reading Wendy Smith's book titled *Give a Little: How Your small donations Can Transform Our World*. This happy book is filled with information about organizations that are making a big difference in the world all through small donations from individuals. From clean water to growing, healthy crops, there are literally dozens of ways to help change the lives of those we consider less fortunate than us. During my many travels as a humanitarian clown, I've found that while others outside the US may not have the financial wealth we take for granted, they often have a profound sense of optimism and happiness lacking in many Americans. It is time for Christians to back away from only asking God for things and, instead, begin thanking him for what he's given us. It is also time to stop the greed and excessive want for more, and time to give, give, give to those who have real needs.

Chapter Two Thought Questions

1. How are you a blessing to others? How do you know? How do they know?

2. How many days worth of food do you have stored in the refrigerator and in cupboards? How much of the food in your refrigerator looks like a bacteria-growing science experiment?

3. How are others a blessing to you?

4. How is it more blessed to give than to receive?

5. How many pairs of shoes do you own? Why?

My Challenge Tasks

1. When buying groceries, use the Feed the Hungry coupons usually found near the register.

2. Go to the United States Institute of Peace website at www.usip. org, read their mission and recent activities, then write politicians at all levels encouraging them to create a Department of Peace! Ask them to add the Department of Peace to the president's cabinet , giving them legitimate power and authority to encourage global peace-making actions at the federal government level.

3. Spend a day not eating until your stomach growls with hunger. Try it for one day a week. Four or five days a month. Fifty-two days a year! If you do this, you will not begin to approach the hunger millions of people feel each day of every week, month, and year. Think about it then do something about it.

4. At the Thanksgiving holiday, buy a complete meal then invite an individual, a couple, a family, or a student away from home to share the food with you. Make enough for them to have leftovers! If you will not do that, find a local food bank and donate a lot to it every month.

5. Write and visit an elderly person or an orphan as often as possible. Read, play, hug, and tell them they are loved. Bring cookies.

WHO CAN RECEIVE
A BLESSING?

Believe on him and receive eternal life.

1 Timothy 1:16

Who can receive a blessing? Note: Keep in mind the definitions of the word blessing as used in the New Testament. Several verses from the book of Revelation are used, and I accept there are many views of how the book should be interpreted. Some of the references I used to help me develop my views of scripture as related to this book are:

The NIV Application Commentary by Craig S. Keener

Revelation by Wayne Jackson

Revelation through First-Century Glasses by W.B. West, Jr.

The People's New Testament Commentary by Barton Warren Johnson

A Commentary on the Book of Revelation by John T. Hinds

Those chosen by God:

Praise be to the God and Father of our Lord Jesus Christ, who has blessed us in the heavenly realms with every spiritual blessing in Christ. For he chose us in him before the creation of the world to be holy and blameless in his sight.

Ephesians 1:3-4

JOSEPH ALAN REDMAN

Here we learn that God has blessed us in the heavenly realms (where we live) with every spiritual blessing in Christ, for (or because) we were chosen before the creation to be holy. Even though God exists outside of everything he created, he still provides every spiritual blessing we need through Christ. Why? Because Christians have made the decision to follow Him making us holy and blameless in His sight. There does not seem to be any mention of America or any other nation here in this passage. Accurate interpretation of the New Testament shows God chooses individual people, not nations, as recipients of blessings. This is even more important when we realize America, like any other nation in history, is temporary, while the souls of individuals are eternal. Money does not choose humans to bless. We choose it and think of it as a blessing when, in fact, is usually is a curse. However, God did choose us to bless. It is critical to our salvation that we accept the blessing he offers.

Those who do not turn away from Jesus:

> Blessed is the man who does not fall away on account of me.
>
> Matthew 11:6

When we face those who criticize us for being a Christian, and we do not fall away or turn our back on Jesus and our faith, we are considered blessed. A nation can neither be blessed nor fall away on account of Jesus. The key word in this verse is "man." The verse does not say, "Blessed is the man and his country." It is an individual act. Because the American government is known for greed, war, waste, and political corruption, one logical conclusion is those whose actions can be described by the adjectives at the beginning of this sentence (greed, war, waste, political corruption), have chosen to move away from Jesus and his teachings. I sadly believe this describes many Americans. I do accept there are Christians who have matured and moved beyond greed and ego concerns. I sincerely believe they are in the minority.

Those who believe:

> Blessed is she who has believed that what the Lord has said to her will be accomplished!
>
> Luke 1:45

> So those who have faith are blessed along with Abraham, the man of faith.
>
> Galatians 3:9

It is important to note that both women and men can be blessed. One of the simplest human tests of faith is when a mother or father opens their arms and tells the child standing on the edge of the porch to, "Jump!" Jesus is telling us to jump without fear, so our faith will grow. The result is an individual blessing to either a woman or a man, not the blessing of a nation.

Many Christians, whose faith is still developing to where their level of trust is unshakable, struggle to comprehend the concept that when God forgives a sin, he also forgets it. Jesus covered our sins by his death, burial, and resurrection. When Christians repent and ask God for forgiveness, he blesses us by a promise to never count that sin against us. Once again, this is an individual relationship between a human and God, not between God and nations.

Those to whom sins are forgiven and those to whom God gives justice without works:

David, quoted here in the book of Romans, says the same thing when he speaks of the blessedness of the man to whom God credits righteousness apart from works:

> 'Blessed are they whose transgressions are forgiven, whose sins are covered. Blessed is the man whose sin the Lord will never count against him.' Is this blessedness only for the circumcised, or also for the uncircumcised? We have

been saying that Abraham's faith was credited to him as righteousness.

Romans 4:6-9

In other words, Christians can do no work, or task, or activity to gain a blessing from God – it is a gift, based solely on our expressing faith in God. Once a person (not a country because, the last time I checked, a country cannot be circumcised) accepts Jesus as their Savior and puts him on spiritually through the act of baptism, they have a responsibility to live a life filled with daily demonstration of love and compassion for all. Just as they can choose to accept the gift of salvation, they can also choose to walk away from it. The important idea here is that God offers his blessings to individuals, and only to individuals. As a reminder, under the Old Covenant with Israel, God did bless them as a nation. That blessing ended with the coming of the Messiah, Jesus Christ.

Those who endure physical, emotional, and spiritual difficulties for Christ:

> Blessed are you when men hate you, when they exclude you and insult you and reject your name as evil, because of the Son of Man.

Luke 6:22

On the rare occasion, the mainstream news covers a story with true global implications, such as the Iranian man threatened with death in 2006 for refusing to renounce his Christianity, or a woman, also in Iran, jailed in 2010 for being a Christian, we see this verse in action. Many American Christians have not yet been blessed to meet a person who has faced death for being a Christian. Many Americans have also never met a man who wanted to kill them for their faith in Jesus. If they are ever placed in that situation, the choice is simple. When and if they are faced with that situation and they continue demonstrating faith in

Jesus, they will be blessed, whatever the outcome. I remember reading a short story about a woman who was questioned about being afraid to die. Her reply was that if she died, she would be with Jesus. If she lived, he would be with her. For me personally, the closest I ever came to suffering for what I did was while serving as a helicopter ambulance (DUST OFF) medic in Vietnam. All crewmembers who flew together understood the red crosses painted on the nose and doors of our helicopters were used as targets by the enemy. We were not targeted for our beliefs. We were targeted because the Viet Cong and the North Vietnamese Army were ordered to shoot us down. Daily I consider myself blessed by God to have survived that illegal and unnecessary war.

Those who study and obey the word of God:

> But the man who looks intently into the perfect law that gives freedom, and continues to do this, not forgetting what he has heard, but doing it—he will be blessed in what he does.
>
> James 1:25

> But blessed are your eyes because they see, and your ears because they hear.
>
> Matthew 13:16

> Blessed is the one who reads the words of this prophecy, and blessed are those who hear it and take to heart what is written in it, because the time is near.
>
> Revelation 1:3

> Behold, I am coming soon! Blessed is he who keeps the words of the prophecy in this book.
>
> Revelation 22:7

What can Christians do to *hear* the word of God? The verse in James gives us a clue – look "intently!" This excludes the pre-set, daily reading calendar that ensures reading the entire Bible in a year if the goal is only to read without studying and thinking. Simply reading, without looking intently into the perfect law through self-regulated, detailed study of the Bible is only reading enough to place a checkmark on a calendar. We must look intently, using our eyes and ears, taking what we learn to heart, and then we are blessed. Once again, there is no evidence nations will be blessed by studying the Bible, only individuals.

Those who are baptized for forgiveness of their sins:

> Blessed are those who wash their robes, that they may have the right to the tree of life and may go through the gates into the city.
>
> Revelation 22:14

Here we have a clear statement of the importance of baptism. Washing one's robes is a metaphor for New Testament baptism commanded by Jesus. By being baptized into Jesus, the result is the right to the tree of life and permission to enter through the "gates into the city" which is the New Testament Church. No nation universally practices the act of baptism. Governments are not baptized. Parliaments are not baptized. Congressional committees are not baptized. Being blessed by God, through baptism, is an individual relationship activity from God for the benefit of the individual, regardless of nationality.

Those who hunger and thirst after righteousness:

> Blessed are those who hunger and thirst for righteousness, for they will be filled.
>
> Matthew 5:6

The spiritual metaphor is one of the most powerful tools in communicating sacred concepts to humans. At the time of this writing, it is estimated there are in excess of twelve million Americans who go to bed hungry each night. They hunger and thirst for food and drink. Their stomachs make noises, and their faces show their dire situation. Jesus tells Christians to feel the same symptoms spiritually when we look for righteousness. In other words, to receive the blessing of being filled spiritually, we must make that our daily priority, just as our want for food and drink. The formal government structures of nations do not eat or drink. Individuals living in those nations do.

Those who keep on going when dealing with suffering:

> Blessed is the man who perseveres under trial, because when he has stood the test, he will receive the crown of life that God has promised to those who love him.
>
> James 1:12

How simple does this need to be? Blessed is the man not the nation. And, in reference to spiritually receiving a crown, the queen of England individually wears the crown not the country. By persevering as a Christian during our short time on earth, the spiritual crown of life will be our blessing from God. Asking God to bless America simply does not fit the model he has designed for us as individuals. As a reminder, Satan tempts while God tests.

Those who remain constantly vigilant:

> Behold, I come like a thief! Blessed is he who stays awake and keeps his clothes with him, so that he may not go naked and be shamefully exposed.
>
> Revelation 16:15

This verse does not mean we must take a shower with our clothes on in case the judgment day takes place early tomorrow morning. Again, this is a metaphor describing how we must always be spiritually aware of our state of mind and our surroundings. Our being awake means total focus on God each day knowing judgment can come at any moment. Being naked means spiritually isolating ourselves from God, not having to take a shower with our clothes on! Spiritually ignoring God is thinking, "I can do this by myself." As a country, America cannot stay agreeably focused on anything, much less collectively waiting for Jesus to return. Individual Christians can.

Those who lose their life for God as Christians:

> Then I heard a voice from heaven say, "Write: Blessed are the dead who die in the Lord from now on." "Yes," says the Spirit, "they will rest from their labor, for their deeds will follow them."
>
> Revelation 14:13

Simple. Accepting Jesus and dying while living fully the Christian life equals being blessed. Nations do not die in the Lord, only individuals. The difference is when nations die, as they all do, that is their end. When Christians die in the Lord, they then shift to living spiritually for eternity.

Those who have part in the first resurrection:

> Blessed and holy are those who have part in the first resurrection.
>
> Revelation 20:6

As Christians, having faith in Jesus and having been baptized, we are participants in the first resurrection, the rising of Jesus from his tomb three days after his crucifixion. How can a nation do this? A nation cannot.

The pure in heart:

> Blessed are the pure in heart, for they will see God.
>
> Matthew 5:8

In Matthew 19, Jesus scolded his disciples for preventing children from gathering at his feet. He reminded us the way to heaven was to become like children in heart. By their nature, being created in the image of God, children are pure in heart. So, if we desire to see God, a pretty remarkable blessing to look forward to, we must become like a child – loving and compassionate and pure in heart, and always in awe of the power and love that is God. If we refuse to love all others unconditionally, and with no concern for anything in return, our Christianity is called into question, especially by those who observe our actions every day.

The poor in spirit:

> Blessed are the poor in spirit, for theirs is the kingdom of heaven.
>
> Matthew 5:3

To be poor in spirit is to recognize that as a human, we can do nothing without the love of God. By accepting the love of God, growing our faith in him, being baptized, and living a Christian life, the kingdom of heaven is ours. To be poor in spirit is to realize the damage false Christians can do in the world, and to realize loving, faith-based action is the only cure.

The meek:

> Blessed are the meek, for they will inherit the earth.
>
> Matthew 5:5

Meekness is associated with being humble not with being fearful. Meekness is associated with gentleness not arrogant and loud behavior driven by one's ego. Meekness is being compliant with the desires of God. Jesus is the perfect example of the quiet strength of a meek man. Nationalism and patriotism are concepts based on a statement of military strength and economic power in the world and are fueled by a desire to always engage in armed conflict with some other country on the planet. Has there ever been a meek nation? Only a human individual can be meek, and it is a choice driven by love.

JOSEPH ALAN REDMAN

The merciful:

> Blessed are the merciful, for they will be shown mercy.
>
> Matthew 5:7

How much more plain can this be? Bombing civilians and labeling it *collateral damage* is not a demonstration of a merciful option. Hoarding national food surpluses when people are hungry is not God's idea of being merciful. Imposing sanctions against other countries, resulting in children being deprived of food; medicine; clean water; safe housing; and schooling, is not merciful by any stretch of the imagination. Spending more money than all other nations combined on improved technology, the only purpose of which is to kill others, all under the guise of *defense*, does not fit God's definition of mercy. Torture can in no way, shape, or form be considered showing mercy. Showing mercy is serous business for all Christians.

Jo Wilding, a humanitarian clown, visited and lived with Iraqi friends from February 2003 to May 2006. She wrote about conversing with Iraqi citizens.

> There was always a delicate balancing act between self-censorship and putting other people in danger. If you talked to Iraqis, asked what they thought or went to their homes, it might cause suspicion to fall on them. If you didn't, then, like the mainstream media, you risked silencing them altogether.[67]

In one conversation with a friend, an Iraqi doctor, he stated the following,

> "All we want is to live in peace."…Jalal said, "If we want to change some things it's our business. It's not for America to come and tell us we have to change, we have to have a different government. …yet still they want to attack us."[68]

This conversation took place in February-March of 2003. Here is a clown having a conversation, just prior to the war deemed necessary by President George W. Bush, a conversation that was apparently not held by our *diplomatic experts* with anyone in Iraq. Jo's book is written from the viewpoint of one who lived with Iraqis during the first several years of this war, and she clearly understands and explains the true definition of *collateral damage*. It is important to note that she was one of one-thousand women worldwide nominated for the 2005 Nobel Peace Prize.

Throughout recorded history, nations emerge, grow, and die. I am amazed at the number of Americans who act as though America will be here forever, ignorant of the signs showing fatal failure may be closer than we think. Many hold the view that America is the world's only superpower; how naïve and egotistical. America is only one of hundreds of empires that will be recorded in history books. As with any politically defined nation, it has both good and bad characteristics. But, from a spiritual point of view, America has no power at all. God is the only spiritual power in all creation. Therefore, any person failing to show mercy to others will suffer the consequences.

The generous:

> But when you give a banquet, invite the poor, the crippled, the lame, the blind, and you will be blessed. Although they cannot repay you, you will be repaid at the resurrection of the righteous.
>
> Luke 14:13-14

During visits to nursing home residents in my community, my clown character teases the residents when they receive their lunch trays by pretending to steal their desserts, especially chocolate brownies! It is always heart-touching that these wonderful people, struggling through their last days on earth, still enjoy laughing and playing as much as little children. (Hmmm – see the connection here?) Without exception, they will offer me their dessert. Without exception! As a caring clown, I play the fool and do what I can to encourage laughter and silliness with the residents, without eating their dessert. And yet, even while we are playing, they continue to willingly offer their chocolate brownies to me, week after week. My reply is to kiss them and give them a hug, week after week.

Where does this immediate display of generosity originate? The answer is simple – their parents. Time and time again I find those who have little are the most generous when it comes to sharing with others, and they learned that lesson from caring, involved, and loving parents.

A brief interlude with an anecdote about food: My wife recently attended a business conference, and I accompanied her to the dinner. The amount of food presented was enough to feed twice the number in attendance. Why? When we dine at our favorite little restaurant near our home, we are stunned by the amount of food people consume from the buffet line. Ordering from the menu, then acknowledging the portion sizes are much too large for one meal, we take half of our food home for lunch or dinner the next day. There are those, however, who will eat five or six completely full plates of food from the buffet. I watched as one woman actually took three pork chops, wrapped them in a paper napkin, and put them inside her purse, then returned to fill her plate again. Granted, the cost is cheap, even for the area, but these are people driving giant trucks, expensive SUVs, and they do not appear to have ever missed a meal, ever!

Going back to Luke 14, are we guilty of not inviting anyone listed in these verses to dinner? Do we rationalize this away by convincing ourselves we contribute money to the church, and to a few charitable organizations that we hope will take care of this for us? Perhaps we can all improve in this area.

The peacemakers:

> Blessed are the peacemakers, for they will be called sons of God.
>
> Matthew 5:9

Looking for ways to start a war is not peace-making. Setting up corrupt governments driven by the same greed we experience in our government is not peace-making. Spending massive amounts of money to develop more effective weapons systems is not peacemaking. Arresting and detaining people for years without allowing them access to some form of legal process is not peacemaking. The one example we have in the New Testament, Jesus, the one Son of God, is the example we must look to for direction. His example, when placed on trial and beaten, was to silently turn the other cheek. His example of peacemaking was to die for others. Children, when faced with a challenging, interpersonal situation, deal with their initial anger a few minutes later by making up – peacemaking – and resuming their play. Adults go blow up the other person. Here's another question – How do *peacekeepers* differ from *peacemakers*? It would seem obvious that *peacekeepers* around the world seem to always carry weapons. Does this not seem a little incongruous?

Mourners, the hungry, and those who cry:

> Blessed are those who mourn, for they will be comforted.
>
> Matthew 5:4

One can assume the disciples mourned the death of Jesus, as many modern Christians do symbolically when they eat the Lord's Supper (communion). The disciples and apostles in the New Testament (and Christians today) did and should receive comfort and rejoice knowing Jesus was raised from death, which is the foundation of Christianity. During most of my life as a Christian, taking communion was a somber, quiet, sit-still-and-do-not-do-anything-but-bow-your-head ceremony. I agree we must be in complete awe and honor when we are in the presence of God during any part of the worship service. However, rarely do I hear a song leader select a song of hope as a preface to taking communion. I do not accept the tradition of sad, gloomy songs about the death of Jesus when we should be celebrating the fact he is alive and at the right hand of God. Personally, communion should be a celebration of the resurrection of Jesus, not a somber ritual that is performed more from habit than thankful and joyful hearts. This can be done by a preface of joyful songs and spoken comments of hope and excitement about our eternal future.

I want to continue this thought by discussing funeral and mourning traditions in America. I have conducted funeral services but, when at all possible, I avoid attending them. I once read a book describing the first cause of family and community breakdown in America. I cannot remember the book but the premise was that before *professional bereavement counselors*, families, communities, and local congregations helped the family through the grieving process. Funeral services were conducted at home and the dead were buried in the family plot behind the garden near the barn.

A traditional Christian funeral today is held either in a funeral home or a worship building. The night before the funeral people come to visit the family and look at the body, often making uncomfortable remarks like, "She looks so good. They did a good job with her." When I hear those comments I bite my tongue instead of saying, "She looks dead." People sit and do their best to comfort the family, commenting that she is in a better place now, which makes them the judge of their life, something only God has the power to do. Those attending the service wear somber colors, usually black or gray, as if anything colorful would offend either the dead person or a family member. A eulogy is presented, providing details of the person's life that will be duplicated in the newspaper later in the week. Following the preacher's comments, everyone will parade by the casket, usually open, dabbing a tear here and there, then either go home or go to the cemetery for the graveside service. I could go on but I think most know the routine. My question is, if the dead person was a Christian, and if the dead person lived their life in full view of the world and seemed to fulfill love in action and complete faith in God, why do we not become happy and joyful knowing they have left this miserable lump of rock hurtling through space, and quite possibly are at home with God? I believe it is because for some, their faith in the Bible and God is not as strong as others. All Christians must be mindful of the following verse written by Luke.

> Blessed are you who hunger now, for you will be satisfied.
> Blessed are you who weep now, for you will laugh.
>
> Luke 6:21

As evidenced by the disciples hungering after Jesus's knowledge and love, and crying at his death, Christians today have the *food* of the Bible to fill our spiritual hunger, and we can laugh at death because of both Jesus's resurrection and our promise of resurrection on judgment day. Separate from the concept of being happy with death, before one becomes a Christian, they may feel an emptiness, a hunger in their life. They may cry with the sadness of not knowing why they exist. They may anguish over the meaning of their life. Once one becomes a Christian, the spiritual hunger can be filled by the Word of God. They then can laugh with joy knowing they were created for God to love.

Faithful Christians at judgment day:

> Then the King will say to those on his right, 'Come, you who are blessed by my Father; take your inheritance, the kingdom prepared for you since the creation of the world.
>
> Matthew 25:34

Here we find the result of our being blessed by God – heaven.

Those who eat in the kingdom of God:

> When one of those at the table with him heard this, he said to Jesus, "Blessed is the man who will eat at the feast in the kingdom of God."
>
> Luke 14:15

> Then the angel said to me, "Write: 'Blessed are those who are invited to the wedding supper of the Lamb!'" And he added, "These are the true words of God."
>
> Revelation 19:9

Christians are invited to the wedding supper, which is joining with Christ on judgment day, the ultimate blessing an individual can receive.

I have listed twenty-two categories of those who can receive blessings, and they are all individuals, not nations. Let us return to "God Bless America." In the New Testament, there are no examples of God giving a blessing to a country. God blessed, and continues to bless, individuals and small groups of Christians. Period. So, who can receive a blessing? Any faithful Christian.

In America today, especially at public sporting events, people claim God is for their cause. In America today, during chaplain's prayers for soldiers going into battle, some claim God will take care of them and bring them back safely. I do not believe for one moment God really cares about which pit-crew will change their tires faster than the next, resulting in one driver winning a race. I do not believe for one moment God takes sides in any war. It seems...

> Our task should not be to invoke religion and the name of God by claiming God's blessing and endorsement for all our national policies and practices – saying, in effect, that God is on our side. Rather, Lincoln said, we should pray and worry earnestly whether we are on God's side.[69]

Chapter Three Thought Questions

1. Set aside time, and list all your blessings again. Compare them with the list you created in Chapter One. Do you notice any changes?

2. Do you sing "God Bless America?" Why? Have you analyzed the words of the song in comparison to what the Bible says about giving and receiving blessings?

3. When were you last criticized for being a Christian?

4. When were you last persecuted for being a Christian?

5. As a forgiven Christian, is God your loving Father or a frowning parent waiting to punish you? Why do you believe the way you do about God?

My Challenge Tasks

1. Make a list of your current faith-supporting love actions and a list of those you want to add or improve.

2. Visit a Bible bookstore, and make a Bible study wish list. Buy, read, and study at least four books for the first year (one every three months) then increase to at least one per month in future years. Then share the books with someone.

3. Set aside time to read the Bible aloud to your family or friend(s).

4. Make a list of five ways you can show mercy to others then do them!

5. Invest in quiet time each day in prayer thanking God for his blessings and asking God for strength to be a conduit for his love.

6. The next time you are in a restaurant, look around and identify someone or some family you do not know. Before you leave, tell the waitress or cashier that you want to pay for their meal without them knowing about it. Leave and think about the reaction they will experience knowing their meal is free!

CHRISTIANS AND PATRIOTISM

You'll never have a quiet world till you knock the patriotism out of the human race.

George Bernard Shaw

Keeping with the thought that Christians cannot serve two masters and must make a choice between serving God or serving man, I will discuss five patriotic traps that are easy for a weaker Christian to fall into possibly causing confusion when it comes to individual Christian priorities. These are:

1. The Pledge of Allegiance
2. The American Flag
3. Military Service
4. The Concept of *Country*
5. The American Government and Greed

Part 1 The Pledge of Allegiance

The pledge of allegiance states:

I pledge allegiance to the flag
of the United States of America,

and to the republic for which it stands,
one nation,
under God,
indivisible,
with liberty and justice for all.

Nice sounding words that, in truth, do not apply to Christians. Why? Once again, let us turn to the 1930s dictionary for some definitions.

> Pledge: anything placed as a security or guarantee; pawn; hostage; a health in drinking: to give as security or guarantee; deposit in pawn; drink to the health of.

These definitions do not seem to fit our use of the word in the pledge of allegiance, so looking at a newer dictionary (1996) we find,

> Pledge: 6a: a binding promise or agreement to do or forbear (to do without.) *(Notice this definition is the sixth definition of the word – hardly something one would use routinely in daily conversation.)*

> Allegiance: the tie or obligation of a subject to his sovereign or government; fealty; fidelity to a cause or person.

What does the Bible say about one's allegiance?

> No one can serve two masters. Either he will hate the one and love the other, or he will be devoted to one and despise the other. You cannot serve both God and money.
>
> Matthew 6:24

The United States is driven by out-of-control capitalistic corporations influencing state and federal legislators to make laws beneficial to the same corporations, especially their stockholders, boards of directors, and CEOs. To pledge allegiance to the United States is to pledge allegiance to out-of-control capitalism and greed, not spiritual freedom. We are not one nation under God. We are a diverse nation under greed and the gods of many religions. Our government honors the pope, the Dalai Lama, and other so-called and often self-labeled religious leaders while allowing fringe legal groups to argue, at the level of the Supreme Court, against so-called Christian symbols. We are not indivisible, as evidenced by the War Between the States (Civil War), the childish name-calling and superficial bickering seen during election-year debates, and the hostile arguments every day in the House of Representatives and the Senate.

The blatantly childish behaviors demonstrated daily by both groups is amazing. Senators talk for hours with no one listening other than the recorder who walks around with an antiquated, hand-operated recording machine. It is a sad commentary that one senator, recently assigned to perform the duties of the senate president, spent the time signing autographs on his photos then asking the senate parliamentarian what to do from a parliamentary point of view after another senator finished his remarks for the record. Both sides submit, in essence, the same bills and amendments. Both sides show their disdain for each other by false courtesy and use of empty adjectives such as "the distinguished senator from…" and, "my esteemed friend from…" Facial expressions and body language verify many senators could not care less about the outcome of a bill, unless it affects their personal or state bank account. Career politicians are driven by a sense of *duty* to bring as much money into her or his state as possible, thereby ensuring re-election, with little concern about issues that matter most. Why would any intelligent Christian pledge themselves to this kind of fruitless, human system? Does it not make more sense to pledge oneself to God and His perfect kingdom?

Contrary to popular belief, there is limited liberty and justice in America for those who are either poor or not a celebrity. (Think back to the categories of the noble class – government, fighting, hunting, the care of arms and accoutrements, and the like.) Man-made liberty and justice are frequently reserved for those with powerful lawyers and lots of money. (Recent *celebrity* murder trials come to mind.)

Part 2 The American Flag

To pledge allegiance, or loyalty, to a flag is to ignore the words recorded in the New Testament about worshipping idols. If Christians are to love, honor, and serve God, they cannot love, honor, and serve the flag of any country. (Remember Matthew 6:24.) Tradition states the flag of the United States, with fifty stars and thirteen stripes, stands for purity, innocence, hardiness, valor, vigilance, perseverance, or justice. There has never been any *official* designation of the stars, stripes, background, or colors of the US flag. Does anyone believe America can be defined as either pure or innocent? If we are so pure and innocent, why are there more lawyers listed in the phone directory than any other profession? If we are so pure and innocent, why do we have so many people in prison?

Recently, I was speaking on humor and health at a local civic organization's lunch meeting when a woman dressed in a blue business suit entered the meeting room unannounced, apologized for interrupting, then proceeded to distribute a booklet titled *Our Flag*. She was a volunteer for the US Congressman from the area and said he wanted these booklets to be distributed to as many voters as possible. It did not matter that she interrupted the presentation. It did not matter, because she represented a Congressman and because of that, she could do whatever she wanted! The audience sat stunned, with their mouths open, until she left.

The forty-eight page booklet she forcefully distributed provides the history of the American flag, examples of early American flags, drawings of the flags of all the states and territories, flag laws and regulations, information on Flag Day, a description of the great seal of the United States, a map of Fort McHenry, the pledge of allegiance, the *American's Creed*, school projects, further reading, and the lyrics to *The Star Spangled Banner*. All this information is already freely and readily available in encyclopedias, local libraries, and federal and state government websites. Yet this specific publication has a *special* purpose. This document, H.Doc 107-145, was printed by authority of House Concurrent Resolution 244, 107th Congress, 2001. The resolution, submitted by Mr. Dodd, reads in part as follows:

> *Resolved by the House of Representatives (the Senate concurring),*
>
> SECTION 1. PRINTING OF REVISED EDITION OF "OUR FLAG".
>
> A revised edition of the publication entitled "Our Flag", revised under the direction of the Joint Committee on Printing, shall be printed as a House document.
>
> SECTION 2. NUMBER OF COPIES.
>
> a) IN GENERAL – Except as provided in subsection (b), there shall be printed a number of copies of the publication described in section 1 as follows:
>
> 1) 250,000 for the use of the House of Representatives, distributed in equal numbers for each Member of the House and each Delegate and Resident Commissioner to the Congress.

2) 51,599 for the use of the Senate, distributed in equal numbers to each Senator.[70]

3) 2,000 for the use of the Joint Committee on Printing.

4) 1,400 for distribution to the depository libraries.

5) ALTERNATE NUMBER. – If the total printing and production costs of the number of copies provided under subsection (a) exceed $150,000, there shall be printed the maximum number of copies of the publication described in section 1 for which such total costs do not exceed $150,000, with distribution allocated in the same proportion as in subsection (a).

How many hours of intense discussion were conducted on the floors of the house and senate on this *critical* piece of legislation - all for information already available from dozens of sources, for free? These self-serving, pseudo-patriots wasted tax-payer money, so their volunteers could interrupt private meetings to show America how patriotic they are. According to the quantity amount listed in Section 2. (2), each senator would receive 515.99 copies of this booklet. Why? The populations of each state are not the same, yet each senator received an equal number. How can 515.99 copies be evenly distributed? There does not seem to be any logic in the publication and printing of this booklet – none! Patriotism is man-made and leads to a false worship of flag, country, and politicians instead of the sole worship and praise of the living God. According to Webster, a patriot is "one who loves his or her country and supports its authority and interests." Some believe, as I did in 1966 and again in 1974, that patriotism can easily be demonstrated by serving in the military. I was wrong.

Part 3 Military Service

In America, men, not women, must register for the draft when they reach age eighteen. The following map shows the percentage of compliance to the registration law. If we are such a blessed and patriotic nation, why are there states with less than one hundred percent registration rates?

State-by-State Selective Service Compliance Percentage Rates

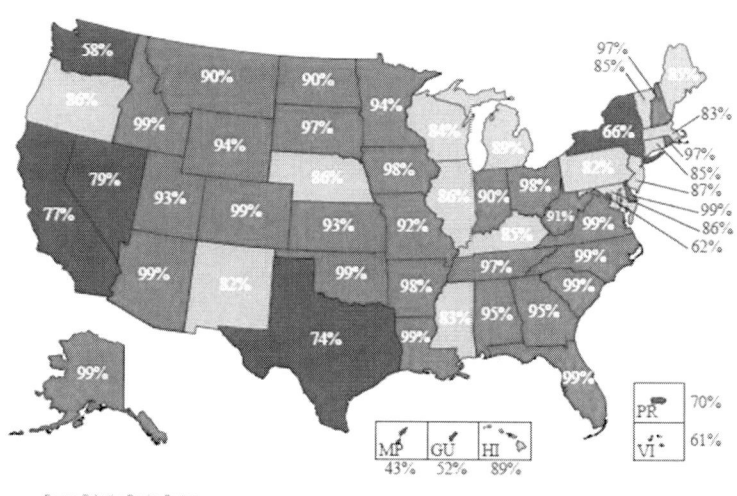

Source: Selective Service System

71

Even Texas, the home state of former President George W. Bush, is among the lower compliance states. Both enlisted men and commissioned officers are required to take an oath of office upon their enlistment or commissioning ceremony. Here is a chart showing the development of the military oath of office:

Key Variations of US Military Oaths

Date/ Statute	Oath	Comments
1 June 1789 1st Cong., 1st sess., statute 1, chap. 1	Officer Oath: I, A.B., do solemnly swear or affirm (as the case may be) that I will support the Constitution of the United States.	The very first law of the United States identified the requirement for government officials to take an oath or affirmation according to Article 6 of the Constitution.
29 September 1789 1st Cong., 1st sess., statute 1, chap. 25	Enlisted Oath: I, A.B., do solemnly swear or affirm (as the case may be) to bear true faith and allegiance to the United States of America, and to serve them honestly and faithfully against all their enemies or opposers whatsoever, and to observe and obey the orders of the president of the United States of America, and the orders of officers appointed over me.	This statute separated the military oath from the oath for other public officials. It also created an oath for enlisted personnel distinct from the officer's oath, with an allegiance to the United States rather than the Constitution and a requirement to obey the orders of their chain of command. The officer's oath mirrored the oath specified in statute 1, sec. 1 for members of Congress.
30 April 1790 1st Cong., 2d sess., statute 2, chap. 10	Officer and Enlisted Oath: I, A.B., do solemnly swear or affirm (as the case may be) to bear true faith and allegiance to the United States of America, and to serve them honestly and faithfully against all their enemies or opposers whomsoever, and to observe and obey the orders of the president of the United States of America, and the orders of the officers appointed over me, according to the articles of war.	This statute, passed as the means to continue the military establishment, required both officers and enlisted personnel to take the same oath. On 3 March 1795, the last phrase changed to "according to the rules and articles of war." Each new Congress would repeal the previous Congress's act and pass a new statute creating the military establishment, including a section on the oath. In 1815 (13th Cong., 3d sess.), Congress no longer duplicated the previous military-establishment act and identified changes only to previous law establishing the military.

JOSEPH ALAN REDMAN

2 July 1862 37th Cong., 2d sess., chap. 128	Officer Oath: I, A.B., do solemnly swear (or affirm) that I have never voluntarily borne arms against the United States since I have been a citizen thereof; that I have voluntarily given no aid, countenance, counsel, or encouragement to persons engaged in armed hostility thereto; that I have neither sought nor accepted nor attempted to exercise the functions of any officers whatever, under any authority or pretended authority in hostility to the United States; that I have not yielded a voluntary support to any pretended government, authority, power or constitution within the United States, hostile or inimical thereto. And I do further swear (or affirm) that, to the best of my knowledge and ability, I will support and defend the Constitution of the United States, against all enemies, foreign and domestic; that I will bear true faith and allegiance to the same; that I take this obligation freely, without any mental reservation or purpose of evasion, and that I will well and faithfully discharge the duties of the office on which I am about to enter, so help me God.	The intent of this Civil War statute was to ensure that government officials were not supporting, or had not supported, the Confederacy. This "Ironclad Test Oath" greatly expanded and contained more detail than previous oaths. The statute also separated the officer oath from the enlisted oath, once again making the officer oath consistent with the oath of public officials.

11 July 1868 40th Cong., 2d sess., chap. 139	Officer Oath: I, A.B., do solemnly swear (or affirm) that I will support and defend the Constitution of the United States against all enemies, foreign and domestic; that I will bear true faith and allegiance to the same; that I take this obligation freely, without any mental reservation or purpose of evasion; and that I will well and faithfully discharge the duties of the office on which I am about to enter. So help me God.	This statute was the first post–Civil War change to the oath. The new oath deleted the "background check" of the 1862 version and established the exact wording of the current officer's oath. Future legislative changes addressed the application of the oath but not the wording.
5 May 1950 81st Cong., 2d sess., chap. 169 (Public Law 506)	Enlisted Oath: I, ___, do solemnly swear (or affirm) that I will bear true faith and allegiance to the United States of America; that I will serve them honestly and faithfully against all their enemies whomsoever; and that I will obey the orders of the president of the United States and the orders of the officers appointed over me, according to regulations and the Uniform Code of Military Justice.	This statute was the first post–World War II legislation on the oath, establishing the Uniform Code of Military Justice to unify, consolidate, revise, and codify the Articles of War, the Articles of Government of the Navy, and the Disciplinary Laws of the Coast Guard. Section 8 identified a standard oath for all enlisted personnel.
5 October 1962 87th Cong., 2d sess. (Public Law 87-751)	Enlisted Oath: I, ___, do solemnly swear (or affirm) that I will support and defend the Constitution of the United States against all enemies, foreign and domestic; that I will bear true faith and allegiance to the same; and that I will obey the orders of the president of the United States and the orders of the officers appointed over me, according to regulations and the Uniform Code of Military Justice. So help me God.	This legislation was enacted to make the enlisted oath more consistent with the officer oath, using the phrase "support and defend the Constitution" and adding "So help me God" at the end. This was the last legislative change to the wording of either oath. Subsequent legislation on the oath addressed administrative issues.

Notice the difference between the original oath when compared to the oath currently being used. There have been many changes through the years, which indicates there may be future changes to the oath as the country changes. It is also interesting to note the phrase, "So help me God," was not introduced until 1862 during the War Between the States. It almost seems that God was an after-thought when the country was being torn apart by the war. Historical records show both the north and the south fought with the belief God was on their side alone. Today, each new soldier swears/affirms that he or she will bear true faith and allegiance to the constitution of the United States then closes their oath by stating, "So help me God." If we are such a God blessed and Christian nation, why is there no mention of bearing true faith and allegiance to God and the Bible in these oaths?

Once new soldiers and officers complete their training, they are assigned to various units stationed around the globe. The following map shows locations of American troops and bases around the world. World War II ended over sixty years ago, and we continue to keep troops and bases in many NATO countries. In early 2010, President Obama approved the increase of special forces operations around the world, expanding operations into over sixty countries.

Map 3:

The US Military Footprint on the World

U.S. Navy
Pacific Fleet:
5 Aircraft Carrier
Strike Groups
37 Attack Submarines

U.S. Navy
Atlantic Fleet:
8 Aircraft Carrier
Strike Groups
40 Attack Submarines

● countries with
established US sites and bases → offshore US sites and bases ● countries with
proposed US sites and bases

— · — typical ground tracks of US space-based survelliance and proposed weapons systems

Source: US Department of Defense, *Base Structure Report, 2008.*

73

If we are a nation blessed by God, why do we believe we must keep a military presence around the world? Could it be linked to the defense budget, and the way it keeps the economy somewhat stable? It is time for Christians to put down their swords and back away from being involved in any military service. It is time to realize patriotism and nationalism are man-made idols designed to stir superfluous emotions that stroke the ego. If you don't believe ego is involved, look at the ribbons, pins, and badges that fill the uniforms of those in the military, especially the generals. Napoleon Bonaparte said, "A soldier will fight long and hard for a bit of colored ribbon."

Part 4 The Concept of *Country*

If we are to comply with the command of God to love all humanity, Christians must do all that is humanly possible to eliminate war. As I am writing, the United States is supposedly at war against terrorism. The implication is we are good, and they are evil. We are right – they are wrong. You are either with us, or against us. We are regularly reminded the attacks on September 11, 2001 were against America, that *Christian* country. Former president Bush indicated God talked to him and that God is on our side. I assume he uses *our* to mean Americans. In one of his presidential speeches, Bush said, "By invoking God on our side…'We believe in human rights and the human dignity of every man, woman, and child on this earth.'"[74] Oh really? And does ordering torture also fall under this belief?

We never turn the other cheek as one would expect a truly *Christian* country to do. We never immediately reach out to feed and show love to our enemy as commanded in the New Testament. In fact, we do nothing remotely close to any command found in the New Testament on how to deal with an enemy. Instead, our reaction is to reach out with massive weapons and large numbers of troops, so that we could fight terrorism all over the world beginning with Afghanistan and Iraq. Our actions were titled *Shock and Awe!* So much for our *Christian* response! Besides, terrorism is only one of many tactics. We may as well have declared a war on a right-flanking movement!

Much of our reaction was the fault of a media empire focused on the *big story*. "The actions of terrorists and the spectacular nature of their attacks are designed to make good television coverage. The media then become tools for terrorists to spread fear."[75] We are conditioned by watching television *news* programs, eagerly staring glassy-eyed at the screen, waiting for the next *breaking news* item. Recently one of the *major* news channels covered (for several hours!) a breaking story about a commercial 747 airplane that was in the process of returning to the airport after one of its four engines was shut down by the pilots. Immediately, *experts* were testifying the airplane could take off, fly, and land with three engines without any possibility of a problem. The news stations were so involved in gathering as many *experts* as possible to discuss this *situation* that they completely missed covering the landing of the airplane only realizing their error fifteen minutes after the plane landed safely. Our focus is pulled toward tragic statistics that are indeed sad but pale in comparison to additional statistics that make the news only once a year, if then. Consider this comment about the attacks on September 11, 2001:

> Three thousand casualties was an appalling figure, but in a country that experienced 30,000 suicides, 16,000 homicides, and 15,000 deaths from falls in the same year, a more moderate reaction might have been expected....The difference in reaction is due partly to the spectacular effect of terrorist atrocities, which is magnified by the media with their compelling stories of heroism, chance, and tragedy.[76]

Instead of placing all our attention on the overly dramatic news, let's consider an alternative version of shock and awe, something other than millions of dollars of so-called precision munitions fired under the watchful eye of pre-positioned news cameras.

When Jesus was approached by his captors in the garden, Simon Peter pulled his sword to defend him. John records the incident:

> Then Simon Peter, who had a sword, drew it, struck the high priest's slave, and cut off his right ear. The slave's name was Malchus. Jesus said to Peter, "Put your sword back into its sheath. Am I not to drink the cup that the Father has given me?"
>
> John 18:10-11

I can only imagine that those present were shocked and then awed by Jesus's reaction. When Jesus was *attacked*, he turned his other cheek, repeatedly, and was killed for his beliefs. His concern was for his followers and completing his mission by doing the will of God. America's response after being attacked was to attack, killing civilians, including many women and children, all for concern about love of money, love of country, love of flag, love of stuff, ego-power, oil, imaginary weapons of mass destruction, patriotism, nationalism, and total lack of love for humanity. One estimate (Spring 2007) exceeds 500,000 Iraqis killed in our war on terror, so far. Millions have been displaced and are now homeless – refugees in their own country. What a kind, loving, and compassionate country we are. As we saw in the last chapter, there is nothing here that qualifies for a blessing from God.

America, as a country, is currently made up of fifty separate states and a variety of territories, most represented in Congress by the more wealthy members and predominately *white* members of the society. Each Congressman or Congresswoman fights in Congress for federal funds for their respective states, so that they can be re-elected, often under the guise of bringing or keeping jobs. The short-term focus on projects adding little or no value to the poor and helpless of the community is rampant. The day to day operation of Congress is so far from being effective or efficient. It is an embarrassment.

While writing this book, I spent many hours watching the senate on C-SPAN in an attempt to get a feel for how the day-to-day business of the senate is conducted, at least as presented on C-SPAN. E-mails and letters were regularly written to my senators, their web pages were read, and I kept track of their voting records. On many occasions, debate on the floor of the senate consisted of one person talking to the senate support staff and the poor senator appointed to play the role of the acting president of the senate during the session. Rarely were any other senators present. Then, after both sides presented their arguments, a vote was taken. There were times the vote was taken after relatively few remarks from either side, (and immediately following the remarks) meaning unless a citizen happened to be watching C-SPAN and e-mailed or called a senator immediately after the close of the remarks, there was no opportunity for input from the constituents of the senator on the issue. Is this how we define *representation*? Can't we see how different this is from the kingdom of God where we can talk to God immediately, any time we want?

There were other times in the House of Representatives where a timed vote was announced, usually a fifteen minute vote, and the vote was held open for more than an hour. On one occasion, at the end of the fifteen minutes, the vote was decidedly against the bill being considered. But, after more than an hour, the vote changed to be for the bill (by two votes!) Congress routinely creates law after law after law with little or no real input from voters, frequently violating their own rules of order, with no provisions for enforcing those laws. Are we supposed to be patriotic and pledge our allegiance to a piece of fabric or a paper document a little over two-hundred years old represented daily by an incompetent Congress? I think not. As Christians, we must place our allegiance and trust in a timeless and eternal person and document over two-thousand years old – Jesus and the Bible.

A few of my e-mails were answered with letters mailed to my home address. My impression was each letter contained a boilerplate opening and closing sentence, and a cut-and-paste paragraph as the body of the letter, depending on the topic. There were times where I asked something specific, and the answer received was still the generic paragraph related to the general topic. One specific e-mail had to do with the approval of a Combat Medic's badge for DUST OFF medics who flew in Vietnam. The letter I received in return thanked me for my input on the "*military and defense spending legislation and support for the military*," neither of which was mentioned in my e-mail!

Several weeks later, I received another letter on the Combat Medic's badge, and the reply stated the bill was in committee, and because the senator was not on that committee, it was *not her concern*. The reply was interesting, because the bill was out of committee, was approved by the house, and was part of the senate defense bill being debated. (Ultimately the wording was dropped from the bill and never brought to a vote.) It was quite obvious the staffer had not done adequate research into the topic.

On another occasion, I wrote expressing my concern for the unsuitable candidacy of Harriet Myers for the Supreme Court and received a two-page letter from one senator explaining why she supported Ms. Myers and why Ms. Myers was the best choice for the position and why she (the senator) was going to vote for her confirmation to the Supreme Court. The letter was dated three weeks after Ms. Myers withdrew her name from consideration! E-mails to other representatives were only answered with a generic *thanks-for-sending-an-e-mail* statement in a return e-mail with no letter or other comment indicating any interest in my thoughts. Living in one of the poorest counties in Texas may have something to do with who gets a real reply and who gets a boilerplate reply!

So, in my case, because I am not wealthy, connected, and powerful, as perceived by my Congressional representatives, my voice is not heard and my resulting perception is that there is no true government of the people as originally laid out by the wealthy, white land and slave owners of the 1700's. (Remember, perception is often reality.)But, as a Christian, we are free to follow the laws these ego-powerful politicians generate each year, such as paying taxes (as commanded in the New Testament), unless those laws contradict the Bible. But, given the fact the American Congress continues to pass hundreds of new laws each year, who ultimately benefits? "Millions of people have been victimized by disastrous development policies…which in the end have developed little but the ruler's own fortunes and powers."[77]

If the American Congress continues to create laws which benefit only those at the top of the economic food chain (many of which are somehow amazingly present in Congress!), are those laws really necessary? When those laws cause wars to take place "…in spite of the enormous differences among political systems today, so many seem to share a fervent desire to wipe modern culture off their respective maps."[78] In the late 1960s or early 1970s, I recall seeing a black and white cartoon showing a devastated city and one, lone man, walking glassy eyed through the streets with a television in one hand and the electrical cord in the other. He seemingly was looking for an electrical plug for the television. Are we coming to a point where we no longer care about the people who make up culture, civilization, society, way of life?

Throughout America's short history, as evidenced by war memorials across the country, we seem bent on fighting more than making peace, in direct contradiction to the New Testament teachings. Jesus instructs us to pay our taxes and pray for our leaders, so that we may live in peace. Voting is one method a citizen has to try making change in the government. Also allowed is communicating one's opinions and suggestions to members of Congress, by phone, mail, e-mail, or face-to-face meetings. However, as evidenced by my many e-mails and letters written to members of Congress, those receiving communication from citizens can easily choose to avoid any reply at all.

> Electronic media may at times facilitate communication, but they can also block communication with a new effectiveness: it is now possible for the state to simply not answer, to be more elusive than ever, to let its subjects ring forever without response.[79]

Sending e-mails to senators is one way of offering suggestions and presenting a Christian voter's view on topics being discussed on the floor. One senator regularly replies with a cut-and-paste letter sent through regular mail, even though I specifically

JOSEPH ALAN REDMAN

requested no paper mail be sent. Encouraging her staff to save paper and postage, I asked that no regular mail be sent in reply to my e-mails adding that my review of her voting record would indicate how my concerns were being addressed. Instead, written replies are always sent in the mail, when there is a reply. Not being politically interested enough to use a telephone to reach the senator's office, I have no interest in speaking to a staffer, especially if it is the one who cuts and pastes an answer using a different font size and different margins from the first and last sentences of the reply. (This actually happened!)

My conclusion is, senators have a total disinterest in anything from a regular voter with no money to donate to their re-election funds.

On a more specific note, one of the topics I have written about to my senators is the environment and the permanent damage that will result from drilling for oil in Alaska. The replies received indicate the Congressional mindset is similar to their oil company lobbyists and CEO friends. Extreme environmental views can range from those views supported by legitimate science, to the following:

> The CEO and most officers of one of the major American mining companies are members of a church that teaches that God will soon arrive on Earth, hence if we can just postpone land reclamation for another 5 or 10 years it will then be irrelevant anyway.[80]

The New Testament tells us that even Jesus does not know the time of the final judgment. Apparently the CEO's have a more direct line to God!

Americans have an inaccurate opinion that America is the only real-world power on the earth, and an inaccurate opinion that America as a country will last forever. In what other ways are Americans ignorant of the real world?

> "In a survey of 819 Americans, only 12% knew that Canada was the largest buyer of American goods and services. The other top responses included Japan, China, the United kingdom and Mexico. Only 1% of Americans cited Canada as the leading source of oil and natural gas for the US market. Saudi Arabia, Iraq, Venezuela, Kuwait, Mexico and Iran received much higher percentages. In fact, Canada is the largest supplier of oil to the United States and provides the vast majority of all US natural gas imports."[81]

Why is this statement important? We share a long border with Canada. Does it not make sense that Americans would want to know something about Canada (a true neighbor) other than they have not attacked us during our lifetime? Why do Americans look at the rest of the world as being inferior and in existence only to support us? Why do we not read and study, so that we are more knowledgeable about the rest of the world? Ego, driven by greed. It seems the attitude is one of, "Why do we need to know anything about our *servants* and *slaves*?" (i.e., the poor adults and children in China and other countries who produce the junk we think we must have.) Americans seem to be more interested in filling their homes with personal possessions instead of actively participating in the electoral process that would replace greedy politicians with those who are driven by a true Christian purpose of serving God.

> Declining voter turnouts and increasing disdain among polled members of the public for politicians…are evidence that people in a number of Western countries have concluded that voting is a waste of effort.[82]

Human governments do not work effectively or efficiently; never have; never will.

Part 5 The American Government and Greed

If America doesn't matter, does voting matter? Probably not. In small, local elections, our votes might mean the success or defeat of someone like the county treasurer, a school board member, or the county sheriff. But, as a Christian who follows the law, pays taxes to support the schools and other needs of the community, should we really care about who gets elected? Are we to not be anxious about the concerns of the world?

At the state level, group-think often prevails, and people vote along party lines. When I used to vote, I voted issues versus party platform, so I was already in a minority when I voted. State legislators will do whatever it takes to make money for themselves and their favorite special-interest groups, and if we are truly Christians not really interested in money, will our one vote in a state election make any difference? Not as often as some would hope. At the federal level with the Electoral College still in place in America, and with increasing levels of technology to fuel voting fraud, there is little need to vote at all. There are those who will disagree with me on the value of a single vote, and that is fine. As a Christian, my *government* must be the kingdom established by Jesus not some country or society that has only been here a few hundred years and may or may not be here ten or fifteen years from now. We are spiritual beings here on earth for a very short time. Our true eternal citizenship is in heaven, not on earth. As C.S. Lewis so accurately observed, "You do not have a soul. You are a soul. You have a body." We are not defined by our passport or voter registration card. We must be defined by our faith-based actions not by how much we own, what kind of car we drive, or for whom we vote. "We are what we purchase…"[83] If this statement is true, most Americans are living metaphors for Chinese junk, over-priced diamonds and gold, and living on too much food. Knowing I have a soul, and knowing I only have one life to live on this planet, it only makes sense that I must focus on that which is eternal and not that which will not be here in the future.

Collectively, Americans in general, and many Christians specifically, demonstrate little concern or care for anything that doesn't affect them directly. They guard their personal wealth, their egos, and little else. What a country! As a hospital clown, when asked, "Where are you from?" I reply, "Earth!" For me, it is sad I cannot have a *Citizen of Earth* passport for international travel. Having said that, my true eternal citizenship is one of being a Christian with a future home in heaven. Yes, I repeat myself several times in this book. Repetition means it is important to every Christian! "My eternal citizenship takes precedence over every aspect of my life and informs my cultural, societal and national identity, not the opposite. (This is also another way of saying that God is neither Democrat nor Republican, and there is not now - nor will there ever be - an American flag flying in Heaven)."[84] This concept is difficult for many Americans who claim to be Christians. Patriotism, love of country, family, and materialism get in the way of a Christian's allegiance to the church, Jesus, and God. I remind the reader:

> Whoever loves father or mother more than me is not worthy of me; and whoever loves son or daughter more than me is not worthy of me;
>
> Matthew 10:37

Before greedy, non-Christian lawyers came onto the political scene, it was common for the Bible to be read in school, prayers to be said at the beginning of the day actively mentioning God and Christianity without fear of a lawsuit. Because of fear and political correctness, and because we are moving toward becoming an apathetic nation, we quietly accept what happens and over time and, as Satan does his work, we fall into the trap of letting our faith fade away. "When religion is regulated merely to the

JOSEPH ALAN REDMAN

private sphere, it becomes vulnerable to the charge of being 'soft' and therefore irrelevant to public life."[85] With the increase in insane lawsuits, Christianity is now something many Americans avoid all together. Those who still actively practice Christianity as defined in the New Testament are no longer considered normal citizens. Instead, we are religious radicals who are arrested and jailed for our beliefs and actions. A Google search for "Christians arrested in the U.S." will show dozens of stories where Christians have been arrested for exercising their so-called free speech rights in public places. From reading the Bible in public, to handing out religious literature to pedestrians, Christians trying to spread the word of God can face difficult times. The anti-religion lawyers are driven by a mindset of *legal violence* with the desire to neutralize Christianity in America. Whether physical or legal, violence does not fit the model of Christianity outlined in the New Testament. Instead, we are to be defenders of the faith.

> "Extraneous and gratuitous violence pervades every aspect of our North American culture: movies, television - including children's programming - newspapers, fiction, etc. Wink says, Violence seems to be what works. If a god is what you turn to when all else fails, violence certainly functions as god. What people overlook is the religious character of violence. It demands from its devotees an absolute obedience unto death. The myth of redemptive violence is the dominant religion in society today."[86]

This goes right back to our history of violence and preponderance of monuments and memorials to war.

Getting back to the original discussion, our desire to provide over a trillion dollars to the *defense* budget instead of using those funds for the good of humanity across the earth is one reason why I can no longer recite the pledge of allegiance. My allegiance is to God alone. Why would a Christian want to pledge allegiance to a country whose historical and projected path is filled with the glorification and perpetuation of physical conflict and war?

> Those who use Hiroshima to defend nuclear weaponry are forced to adopt a sort of celebratory triumphalism about the massive, indiscriminate killing of civilians, which contravenes every principle of Christian just war theory.[87]

After serving in Viet Nam and later in West Germany during the Cold War, I have come to the conclusion there is no such thing as a just war. Growing up in an army family I was indoctrinated that normal people carry weapons and wear uniforms. After beginning my humanitarian clown activities and realizing I was wrong, I am now completely comfortable being just a Christian. My clown character, Fungus A. Mungus, is known for the slogans on his t-shirts. One recent addition that has been well received by almost everyone, including TSA staff and customs officers in other countries, is one that says, "UNARMED, NONVIOLENT, HUMANITARIAN CLOWN."

I now look solely to Jesus as my guide. When faced with his trial and murder on the cross, he spoke very little and offered no resistance. Because the entire Bible is the perfect message of God's love for humanity, wanting all to come to His perfect love, how can any Christian justify any armed conflict? The one argument I hear over and over is that of protecting the country from foreign and domestic enemies. I cannot find any verse supporting that logic in the New Testament. I can only find verses supporting total love for God, self, others, neighbors, and enemies. God will protect His Church. How else could it have survived for over two thousand years? My job is to keep close to God through study and prayer so that my faith is protected. There was a time when I was willing and ready to launch nuclear missiles toward former communist forces. That time has passed.

This is a critical piece of evidence Christians must think about as they look toward the future. The Bible tells us God is love –

plain and simple. Everything in the New Testament leads me to believe all actions taken by those who claim to be Christians must be to glorify God, not to satisfy the ego or wallet of the individual. Budgeting trillions of dollars to support the military industry and their quest to build more *sophisticated weapons* is the same as turning one's back on God, not glorifying Him. Who in their right mind wants to design and/or use these weapons? How is this cluster bomb an example of love toward humanity?

In addition to current and proposed massive expenditures for weapons, the American government, in the past, also spent millions of dollars to actively use torture to gain information from alleged *insurgents*. The frightening thing about torture is what superficial Christians think about its use.

> It shows that currently, more than six-in-ten white evangelical Protestants (62%) say that the use of torture against suspected terrorists in order to gain important information can be often or sometimes justified. This is significantly higher than the number of white mainline Protestants (46%) and religiously unaffiliated (40%) who say torture can be often or sometimes justified. Additionally, those who attend religious services at least once a week are much more likely than those who seldom or never attend religious services to take this view (54% vs. 42%). But there are only small differences across religious groups in the number saying that torture can often be justified, and among every group there are relatively few people who say torture can never be justified. [88]

> Where the US government did violate fundamental principles and behave in a manner wholly unworthy of the country's tradition was in the decision that the Geneva Conventions do not apply to the war on terror and the indefinite detention and mistreatment of suspects that resulted.[89]

For me, torture is one of the most controversial subjects on the minds of many people I meet. To read that such high percentages of *Christians* say torture might be ok for use seems to indicate that those of that opinion have not studied much of the New Testament. It seems they do not understand what the Bible says about love. Or, possibly, they are ignoring what the Bible says, because it is easier to hate others who seem different. The story of the Good Samaritan, found in Luke 10:25-37, comes to mind. Please take time to read and think about what Paul says in the book of Romans.

> Do not repay anyone evil for evil. Be careful to do what is right in the eyes of everybody. If it is possible, as far as it depends on you, live at peace with everyone. Do not take revenge, my friends, but leave room for God's wrath, for it is written: "It is mine to avenge; I will repay," says the Lord. On the contrary: "If your enemy is hungry, feed him; if he is thirsty, give him something to drink. In doing this, you will heap burning coals on his head." Do not be overcome by evil, but overcome evil with good.
>
> Romans 12:17-21

Both former President Bush and Vice-president Cheney said they authorized and supported the use of torture on our *enemies*. Their logic was that of terrorists supporting the different governments of the *Axis of Evil* were evil and had harmed us. Romans 12:17 is very specific when it tells us not to repay evil for evil. I agree there are those who want to kill me because I am an American and a Christian. Romans 12:18 tells me that as far as it depends on me, I must live at peace with everyone I possible can. If there are those who want to kill me, it is my choice to place myself where I am in danger, or to avoid travel to that country. If I am harmed, I must not take revenge, which is exactly the opposite reaction our leaders and military took when invading Iraq and Afghanistan.

JOSEPH ALAN REDMAN

Given the opportunity, Christians must provide food and drink to any enemy, foreign or domestic.

In Romans 12:20 we find an interesting metaphor for helping an enemy. On the surface, heaping burning coals on one's head sounds like torture, but the opposite is true. Restating Proverbs 25:21-22, Paul refers to an Old Testament practice of sharing burning coals with a neighbor whose cooking fires had gone out. Tradition tells us a special insulated container designed to be balanced on the head was used to share burning coals from one house to another. So, if I provide food and drink to my enemy, in effect I am sharing my most valuable resource with him. Regrettably our government and military continue to ignore Romans 12:21. Using torture is not overcoming evil with good. That practice has never worked and never will. Many accounts written by former prisoners of war during World War II, the Korean war, and Viet Nam validate the fact that torture doesn't work. I believe this is why the New Testament is so crystal clear on the issue of dealing with enemies. It begins to look like we are not a Christian nation blessed by God after all.

> Deploring, for instance, the Bush administration's decision not to follow international law in the area of torture and the rights of terrorist defendants at their trial, retired general Wesley K. Clark, formerly the supreme commander of the North Atlantic Treaty Organization, said, "It was America that led the creation of the Geneva Convention, and now we're walking away from it…"[90]

For an American president to ignore the Geneva Convention on illusory legal technicalities indicates greed and ego-power are driving his behavior as opposed to being guided by the example of the perfect teacher – Jesus.

Another example favoring the use of sophisticated weapons over what is right from a biblical point of view is the recent accepting of a proposed treaty requiring the elimination of stockpiles of cluster bombs/munitions by the year 2016. Cluster bombs, often painted in bright colors and resembling toy balls, are one of the most horrific weapons ever designed by humans. Cluster bombs that do not detonate can easily be picked up by children, struck with a stick, or driven over with a vehicle, causing them to explode. Of the 111 countries to sign the treaty, there were only five who opposed the ban and did not sign the proposed treaty. "The US, along with Israel, Pakistan, China and Russia, who are among the main producers and stockpilers [sic] of the weapons, have opposed the ban."[91] These weapons do not always function correctly.

> Their recent use in the conflict between Israel and Hezbollah last summer was another wake-up call to the havoc they wreak. In the last three days of the fighting, 4 million cluster bombs were dropped. At least one in every four did not explode. The ones that remained caused 161 casualties among civilians, including 19 deaths, by Christmas -- initially at a rate of three accidents a day.[92]

These cluster bombs were sold to Israel by America. During my visit to the West Bank in the Spring of 2009, Palestinian farmers showed our group boxes of munitions remnants that had been used against unarmed protesters including many with the "Made in America" stamp still legible. Why would God bless a country that designs, manufactures, and sells weapons with the sole purpose to intentionally and indiscriminately wound, maim, and kill unarmed men, women, and children? Knowing the high percentage of failure of these weapons to function the way they were designed, what rational, loving person would continue working for the companies that manufacture them?

> Whoever sheds the blood of man, by man shall his blood be shed; for in the image of God has God made man.
>
> Genesis 9:6

This Old Testament statement of truth was updated for us by Jesus in the New Testament when he stated that if one hates another person, he is subject to judgment. This brings to mind the statement of President George Bush when he stated he wanted Osama bin Laden, dead or alive. In fact, the president's agreement with the Central Intelligence Agency (CIA) plan to assassinate bin Laden was crueler than his simple "dead or alive" statement. Quoting Cofer Black in September 2001:

> Gentlemen, I want to give you your marching orders, and I want to make them very clear. I have discussed this with the president, and he is in full agreement.[93]

> I want bin Ladin's head shipped back in a box filled with dry ice. I want to be able to show bin Ladin's head to the president"[94]

> It was the first time in my thirty year CIA career that I had heard an order to kill someone rather than to effect [sic] their capture and rendition to justice.[95]

When any president tells the world his goal is to capture someone and he does not care if the person is killed in the process, exactly what *Christian* message of compassionate love for all is being sent? The answer is simple – none. In addition to the fact that God is love, God is also much more patient than we. We are reminded of this:

> The Lord is not slow about his promise, as some think of slowness, but is patient with you, not wanting any to perish, but all to come to repentance.
>
> 2 Peter 3:9

If God wants all of humanity to come to repentance, it is the simple task of any Christian to do all that is possible to patiently fulfill that task. If God wants no one to perish, who are we to take the life of others thereby depriving them of His want?

The president's (George W. Bush) impatient drive to go to war at any cost under the false guise of fighting terrorism led to the killing of thousands of innocent people, which in turn made America a terrorist country, not a country of God. Even before the war, we strong-armed the United Nations assembly into establishing and implementing damaging sanctions.

> 500,000 children under the age of five died between 1991 and 1998 in Iraq due largely to the impact of the sanctions.[96]

> Western state terrorism, as in the "sanctions of mass destruction" employed against Iraq from 1990 into 2000, the massive and deliberate bombing of Serbian civil society in 1999, and the terrorism of Western client states such as Indonesia, apartheid South Africa and the "National Security States" of Latin America in the 1970s and 1980s, has been vastly more deadly than the retail terrorism that has preoccupied the Western media. Such state terrorism has all been functional, serving to protect Western interests in establishing and maintaining hegemony in areas with restive populations and effectively justifying the West's terrorism as mere "retaliation" and "counter-terror".[97]

> The wars fought by foreigners are not like ours. They kill women and children.[98]

The last quote about foreigners killing women and children was made by Shaka, emperor of the Zulu nation, when he described how the white men (British) fought in Africa, all in the name of peace. Is it logical to say one is *fighting* for peace? A better option is *loving* for peace. But, here in America, most proudly beat their drum of democracy, patriotism, and out-of-control capitalism, gradually and blatantly moving away from a government of the people to an overbearing government driven by greed and ego and power. We are told by America's leaders that we are fighting the war so that we can bring peace to the world. As A. J. Muste wrote, "There is no way to peace. Peace is the way." Instead of glorifying God through faith-driven actions of prayer and compassion, America's leaders do everything possible to ignore the people of the country. From ignoring e-mails and letters to holding private meetings behind closed doors then rushing to conduct a vote when there has been absolutely no input from the American people demonstrates failure of a democratic system of government listen to the people. "To glorify democracy and to silence the people is a farce; to ignore discourse on humanism and to negate people is a lie."[99]

Do we glorify democracy? In 2005, while eating breakfast at a restaurant co-located with a country-style store, I bought a copy of a paperback book titled, *The Good Citizen's Handbook – A Guide to Proper Behavior.*[100] Here are a few astonishing excerpts from the book, which was noticeably biased in that almost all drawings were of *Caucasian* people. Of the 140 pages, there were only three or four with drawings of other than Caucasians including one of what appears to be Hopi dancers on the title page of the chapter, "7. Good Citizenship in the World." (I did not realize the Hopi were *foreigners*!) My comments will be *italicized* and in brackets – [ ].

From the list titled, "A Good Citizen Is Worthy" "#8. Interested, not only in the production, but also in the conservation of the wealth of his country – provident, thrifty." *[If this statement is true and if Christians have no interest in producing or conserving wealth, then are we bad citizens?]*

"#10. A good person – obedient, honest, trustworthy, kind, sympathetic, loyal – a good American." *[Hmmm. Can we be an obedient, honest, trustworthy, kind, sympathetic, and loyal Christians, with no regard to earthly citizenship?]*

"Conclusion of the list: Remember that the American people have the greatest privileges and the most opportunities of any people in the world. But in order to enjoy these privileges and opportunities, it is our first duty to make ourselves worthy of them." [*Based on the overall context of this biased book, it is obvious the privileges and opportunities are economically based. I also find the comment on making ourselves worthy of enjoying American privileges and opportunities interesting, especially since God loves us when we are not worthy of his love.*]

"A Good Citizen Eats Meat – Plenty of Meat" [*Surely this sentence was not influenced by the meat industry! There were drawings of a cow, a sheep, a calf, and a hog on the page.*]

"Employee's Health – Everybody benefits by sanitary working conditions." [*What about those without jobs?*]

"The Employee – Because he is in good health, contented and happy." [*Excuse me. What country is this? In my experiences in manufacturing, healthcare, and government jobs, it was the rare individual who was truly happy with their job.*]

"The Boss – Because his employees are in good health and turn out more and better work." [*More and better work equals more money for the boss and the owner of the company!*]

"Society – Because prosperous and happy employees and employers are good citizens." [*So, now being a good citizen is linked directly to being prosperous? Conversely, does this mean if people are poor they are not good citizens?*]

"The Country – Because co-operation between employer and employees makes the Country rich and powerful." [*Hmmm. Sound familiar? Greed and ego-power again. What happened to benevolence, humility, and unconditional love toward all humanity?*]

"Fundamentals – Code of the Junior Rifleman #10. I will do my part to make America, once again, 'A Nation of Riflemen.'" [*Keep in mind the title of the book, The Good Citizen's Handbook – A Guide to Proper Behavior. If Christians are not "riflemen" then are we neither good nor behaving properly? Why can't we become a nation of believing Christians instead of riflemen?*]

The author lists three, small-font pages of credits, many from school books, posters, Boy Scout and Girl Scout handbooks, federal government pamphlets and books, the National Rifle

Association, the American Heritage Foundation and others, with dates ranging from the 1920s to 2000.

It frightens me to think that those who buy this offensive book might not read it as a compilation of old, biased publications but will instead read it as a valid and current guide for good behavior. This is a good example of how government propaganda, disguised as helpful publications and posters, has influenced our thinking into the narrow-minded ego-power and greed mindset.

Even with this biased ego-power, average citizens have no power. Individual citizens have no power to influence Congress when lobbyists with unlimited bank accounts rule the day. Our politicians love to glorify democracy but hate to make any real improvements. As mentioned before, when viewing C-SPAN's coverage of Congress, remarks made on the floor remind me of children who whine when they do not get their way. It is as though our theoretical representatives believe we belong to them instead of the other way around. How is it possible for our representatives to know our wishes when they have poorly paid and overworked staffers infrequently replying to our inquiries and recommendations? How can they claim to know what is best for us when their replies indicate they are pursuing their personal agenda with no consideration of our needs? "It means that the leaders...do not own the people and have no right to steer the people blindly towards their salvation."[101]

Those in Congress and other political positions are not leaders. They are figureheads with ego-power linked to their title of office. Those who do not follow God and do nothing to glorify him and honor his power and love through faith-based actions are spinning their ego-wheels and going nowhere.

> The oppressors do not perceive their monopoly on *having more* as a privilege which dehumanizes others and themselves. They cannot see that, in the egoist pursuit of *having* a possessing class, they suffocate in their own possessions and no longer *are*; they merely *have*.[102]

Most Americans have many possessions – too many. Some are in boxes in closets that have not been opened for years. Why are they there? Short-sightedness and the need to boost our egos by opening the top of the box and visually (and artificially) confirming our identities. For me, statistically, and in reality, richer than most others in the world, my label is *middle-class*. As a Christian, class must not matter and possessions have no true spiritual value. Some of our possessions are conveniences in the area of food, clothing, and shelter. Some have no intrinsic value other than being artistic, so those are ego-possessions. Having lots of books used to be a source of pride for me. Why? Because I thought having lots of books (and yes, all were read, several times) made me look smart to those who saw my library. How childish. After sorting through dozens of books, those not used on a regular basis were donated to the closest small library. It may not be much, but it is a start in the move away from loving things and moving to loving others.

In the New Testament, the rich man walked away, because he only had possessions and no longer was able to deal with the spiritual. Our society almost succeeded in convincing me that to have many things was more important than doing many things to serve others. Daily life was an automatic habit. Eric Fromm stated: "It is not enough that men are not slaves; if social conditions further the existence of automatons, the result will not be the love of life, but the love of death." Automatons can be equated with those who do the same thing over and over, all while expecting something new and innovative to happen, like Congress. They are lobbyist-driven with no real concern for the non-rich voter. Their efforts focus on creating laws that benefit the rich and their big companies with no concern about the fact that many laws currently enacted are not being enforced. Once again, we must be reminded that human governments usually fail over time. God's kingdom can never fail.

Some might have a difficult time linking automatons to the love of death. It seems interesting that the only time Americans come together emotionally is when a disaster happens. We are conditioned to automatically respond in pre-programmed ways. The focus then becomes how fast can we design and erect a memorial to the dead! Jesus tells us to let the dead bury the dead and get on with carrying out our role as Christians – teaching others the path to eternal salvation. As a veteran of the Vietnam War, I have been to the Vietnam memorial wall several times. It is always emotional for me, because of my friends who died. But I do not stand there for weeks on end feeling sorry for myself. The visits I have made are usually over within a few minutes, and then I get on with the day. I have not researched how many monuments have been constructed in America since World War I, but believe I am safe in stating ninety-nine percent of them memorialize someone or some group that is dead. When was the last time you personally saw a monument celebrating someone who was still alive? The closest are pink ribbons celebrating those who have survived breast cancer. Why is there not a giant pink monument on the mall in Washington D.C. for those brave people? Why are we obsessed with death when Jesus tells us to focus on eternal life? Could it be that we are automatons?

Some will argue that all those yellow ribbons plastered on houses and vehicles celebrate life and the hope of a safe return of friends and family from war or other duty in *foreign* countries. American society as a whole has ignorantly chosen to place yellow-ribbon stickers and magnets as symbols of their support. Ignorantly because the original lyrics of the song dealt with a *prisoner* coming home after serving time for his crime not a soldier returning from war! Could this be a money-making ploy feeding on the automatic knee-jerk emotions of the country? Could this be a complete misinterpretation of an old metaphor? If this symbolic support is sincere and truly felt in the hearts and minds of those displaying yellow ribbons, would not Americans permanently paint the ribbons on their vehicles? Is it a subconscious sign that most ribbons are magnetic, and as a result, easily removable? Is this not temporary patriotism? What part of community psychology describes the model of superficial visual support for a futile government cause? In comparison, living for God is neither superficial, temporary, nor futile.

A few excerpts of the lyrics show using yellow ribbons simply does not fit what the original song tried to say: "I have done my time" -- we currently have an all-volunteer military. To state "I have done my time" could mean one's enlistment is complete or one will be returning from foreign duty, but the original song meant someone is being released from prison. "I'd soon be free" -- same thing with these words – one will be free from prison. Prisoners do not have freedom like those in the military. If one volunteers for active duty how can they be "free" just by returning to America? Are they not already free as Americans? "Put the blame on me." In the song, the one returning from prison stated that if the relationship between he and his woman failed, he was to blame. It is doubtful any American wishes for returning soldiers to feel they are to blame for failed political policies, useless wars, and futile deaths and injuries. "I'm really still in prison." Soldiers are not in prison, prisoners are! It appears someone with no understanding of the song or the military found a way to make money by creating and misusing magnetic yellow ribbons to signify America's support for the troops. Here is a novel idea, why not support them by providing the equipment they need? Why not support them by not starting a personal and political war in the first place? Why not support them by only using the National Guard on a temporary basis for state emergencies? How unwise can we be?

When traveling by air or ground vehicle, I wear comfortable clown clothes. The banner on the back of my clown coat says, "*War Is Costly. Peace Is Priceless.*" I have yet to be approached by someone in an airport terminal disagreeing with my public

　　　　　JOSEPH ALAN REDMAN

statement. Early in 2005 at the Dallas-Fort Worth airport, I was approached by four gentlemen wearing their corporate-logo, business-casual shirts, commonly known as *cotton handcuffs*. (You know – when you have so many articles of clothing with a corporate logo that you cannot afford to change jobs because you would have to replace most of your clothing!) They commented that they all heartily agreed with my banner. During the conversation I discovered they were all veterans of active combat during the Vietnam War. As one who completed nineteen months in Vietnam and later served as a Pershing missile-unit platoon commander during the Cold War, I feel I am qualified to comment on the ineffectiveness and futility of war.

> The Dalai Lama told 36,000 people at Rutgers Stadium that the concept of war was outdated and young people have a responsibility to make this century one of peace. 'This whole planet is just us,' the 70-year-old exiled monk said Sunday. 'Therefore, destruction of another area essentially is destruction of yourself.'[103]

Profound words from one who is not a Christian!

Jesus reminded us there will be wars and rumors of war during the last days, but he also commands us to turn the other cheek instead of going to war, going to court, or acting out in some other physically violent manner when we face those who threaten us. What part of "love your neighbor" do we not understand? I believe part of the reason we do not love our neighbor is because we fall short of fulfilling the second part of that command which is "as you love yourself." Many people do not love themselves, and therefore are incapable of loving others, especially those labeled *enemy*. When one hates himself, it is difficult to love others.

The banner on my clown coat is a superficial symbol of my belief in love and compassion over a belief in war. Why does the president wear an American flag lapel pin? Is it not understood he supports the troops sent to the war he declared? Is he not surrounded by military honor guards, marine door guards, and flown in military aircraft? Is it not understood he is an American? The greater question is, *What value is there in a superficial symbol?* The answer, of course, is none, unless the symbol is backed up by, or representative of, loving, faith-based action.

Jesus comments on the Pharisees and their symbols worn as part of their daily attire:

> Everything they do is done for men to see: They make their phylacteries wide and the tassels on their garments long; they love the place of honor at banquets and the most important seats in the synagogues;
>
> Matthew 23:5-6

And Jesus also comments on what may be the origin of the term *lip service* by stating:

> These people honor me with their lips, but their hearts are far from me.
>
> Matthew 15:8

If people *honor* the American military by placing a temporary-magnetic yellow ribbon on their car but do nothing else to demonstrate sincerity of support, where then are their hearts? What kind of honor is this?

The New Testament tells us true religion is caring for widows and orphans. In Matthew, Jesus discusses giving support to the needy:

> So when you give to the needy, do not announce it with trumpets, as the hypocrites do in the synagogues and on the streets, to be honored by men. I tell you the truth, they have received their reward in full. But when you give to the needy, do not let your left hand know what your right hand is doing,

so that your giving may be in secret. Then your Father, who sees what is done in secret, will reward you.

Matthew 6:2-4

There is little benefit to public display of symbols, ribbons, flags, and public giving to the needy, based on what the New Testament tells us. God's priority seems to be on what is done, those actions that actively demonstrate our faith in Him versus what is visually portrayed on the side of a car, a lapel, or a flagpole, including fish symbols and crosses. Being a Christian means active, one-on-one interaction with other humans. It is important to remember that Jesus did not only say he loved us. He showed us His love by action.

Chapter Four Thought Questions

1. Do you believe in pledging allegiance to a country? Why? Why not?

2. Do you spend more time each month balancing your checkbook and checking on your investments than you do reading the Bible?

3. Are you proud of America? Of being an American? Why? Why not?

4. If you claim to be patriotic, have you voluntarily served your country? How? Why? If not, why not?

5. Do you know the words to the national anthem of America? Do you sing them out loud? Why? Why not?

My Challenge Tasks

1. List all the reasons you can stating why you are patriotic.

2. List all the reasons you can stating why you are a Christian. Which list is more valid and important to you? Why?

3. Explain why you vote or do not vote in every election. What does being unequally yoked with unbelievers mean to you?

4. List ways that being a Christian conflicts with the model of being an American patriot.

5. If you display flags and ribbons on your vehicle, explain how this actively demonstrates your Faith. How does this glorify God?

WHAT MATTERS?

The world is my country, all mankind are my brethren, and to do good is my religion.

Thomas Paine

In this chapter, I address a wide variety of topics that, at first glance, do not seem related to each other. Simple observations combined with facts and references will show how mixed up we can be when it comes to identifying those things that are truly important to us. In this discussion, I define the rich as those who fall into the leisure class as described by Thorsten Veblen in his remarkable book titled, *The Theory of the Leisure Class.* Written in the 1800s, Veblen's description of America is clearly based on solid examination of our culture in that it still fits America in the twenty-first century. My thoughts are not judgmental in nature, but they are critical of those thoughts and actions that detract from the work God expects us to do as Christians.

What matters to the rich during their short visit here on earth? Food? Clothing? Shelter? Jobs? Power? Status? Titles? Possessions? Houses full of stuff? Phones? Beepers? Computers? Cars? Appearances? Perhaps.

What matters to the poor? "In the gutter, people are forced to forget what they are as they run for their lives."[104]

Hmmm – does she have a newer (write something you really desire here) than I? Fill in the blank with any *thing*, (purse, watch, beeper, phone, laptop, electronic music storage device, etc.) and you have what is a quite common view of life on earth by rich Americans. Most advertising is designed to make one feel inferior unless the product or service being sold is immediately purchased. It is amazing that each item we supposedly must have in order to be a complete human costs only $19.95 and can be purchased through a phone number or Internet web site shown on the television. How do they manage to make everything we need and sell it for the same price? Amazing! But wait! If you call now we will double your order! It just does not get any sadder than this! Especially when we consider the most wonderful gift possible, God's Son!

Evidently, buying lots of stuff is what matters to many Americans. Those who buy lots of stuff probably think they are doing better than their parents because of all they can buy and *own*. Is this what really matters?

> Among all these and other contenders for the American purpose of life, one seemed to win out…the American dream, the ideal that each generation of whites, whether immigrant or native-born, was to become more successful and prosperous than the parent generation.[105]

My parents spent their childhood years on farms in Oklahoma. After a career in the army, my father retired in 1968. My mom left the earth in 2008, but, prior to her spiritual relocation, she and my father kept both the small freezer in the refrigerator and a full-size freezer stocked full of food. As of this writing, my father is in his 80s, eats very small meals, and has enough money in the bank to take care of his daily needs. He has access to a military commissary so is able to buy groceries for a little less than those who shop in regular stores. And yet, because both my parents had very little in the way of possessions as children, as retired adults they always had a full freezer and refrigerator. Their words indicated that none of that matters, but actions speak much louder than words. To them, the appearance of a full freezer and refrigerator seemed to indicate success. Several days without power from a severe storm would immediately change that perception. "The idea is that a presentable image *(cars, church buildings, accoutrements)* makes substance immaterial. All that glitters 'is' gold."[106]

For several years, the worship services my wife and I attended were held in what most would call a fancy shed. Unfinished wood planks lined the floor. The roof was metal as were the hinged sides. During the warmer months, three of the sides could be raised so everyone could view the pasture and pond. It was not uncommon for horses or cattle to wander through the area during the worship service. Children were not isolated in a nursery away from the service. They routinely wandered through the crowd, casually walking around the preacher during the service. We even had an occasional visit by the local dog looking for a treat. We had plain light bulbs for light – no fancy chandeliers. The chairs were salvaged from yard sales and were either folding metal or fiberglass. Propane barn heaters provided heat during the cold of winter. There were six ceiling fans to move the air, but with the sides open, the breeze was quite adequate to keep us cool. The success of this little worship group was not based on how fancy a building we had but on the actions we took to show we love God and our neighbors. The Christians who attended were not rich but had hearts of gold. If someone had a need, either as the result of a fire or illness, everything that could possibly be done by this small group was done out of compassionate love with absolutely no concern over who got the credit. The local community knew of this generosity and was amazed the congregation gave money away to those in need instead of building a fancier building.

After the new building was built, complete with a full kitchen and indoor plumbing and restrooms, real fluorescent lights and a propane heater, combined with the departure of one of the "favorite" preachers, attendance plummeted. I believe it was a combination of what I call preacher worship and the loss of the rustic, community feel to the worship service. The group still meets, but the number in attendance continues to drop. Why? There are four or five men who do the preaching, and there are five different views of the New Testament Church and how it should function. The congregation is confused at the different views they hear each Sunday morning, and without strong leadership, the group will fade away. It has moved to where it cannot be identified as anything other than another denomination. We now worship in a congregation spiritually closer to how the church was set up in the New Testament.

To many in America, our little worship group does not matter. It does not matter that most of our members do their best to balance their home budgets, spending what is needed and always sharing what they have with others, whether money or food. It does not matter that we work at being good stewards of the monetary blessing God has given us. Instead, what seems to matter to many Americans is, how much you spend, and how much you own. "In our time there is no necessity for misers – they have all been converted into consumers. Both are caught by the attempt to take the whole world into their home and possess it."[107]

The same thing applies to so-called *religious* structures – buildings costing millions of dollars. A denominational group in Dallas, Texas, has decided to raise funds to build a $130 million dollar facility for their worship activities, including a three thousand seat auditorium. Apparently they have forgotten that this world will end along with every thing we think we own. And, all those multi-million dollar buildings will vanish. Will God walk around during the final judgment saying, "Wow! Nice building! How many hungry people starved because of what you spent on all your nice furniture, choir robes, and musical instruments?" From attending worship in big buildings and in small sheds, I have noticed Christians seem to be happier and more active when expressing their collective faith in the sheds. I can't help but wonder if the leaders of the group in Dallas believe their

JOSEPH ALAN REDMAN

expensive building will result in their members being happier than before? It looks as if a little love of money has crept into the fold in Dallas.

> But within the same society there is only a very weak relationship between finances and satisfaction with life; billionaires in America are only infinitesimally happier that those with average incomes.[108]

What? Are we saying money cannot buy happiness? Not us, but God. Happiness comes from loving and serving God through loving and serving others. Once again, possessions do not matter. People do! "…beyond the threshold of poverty, additional resources do not appreciably improve the chances of being happy."[109] It will be interesting to follow the progress of this denomination in the future to see how well they function in the community. There is no mention anywhere in the New Testament about money or possessions being required for happiness. In fact, one of the few references using the word happy, is in 2 Corinthians 7:9 where Paul is happy because the recipients of his letter repented. (No mention of money!)

During many years in the corporate learning and development field, I often facilitated workshops on what people can do to identify their personal values. What do you (the reader) value? Many people mention family, health, God, and friends, in that order. I never heard someone say, "Oh, and I have as a personal value the ability to get as much stuff as I can!" But, many of these same people demonstrated, by their actions outside the classroom, their love of the material. They showed little value in anything dealing with community unless it was coaching their own child's soccer team, often verbally abusing the child in the process. The needs of the community were to be handled by the city council or other elected officials. The mindset was, "Don't bother me with your problems. I have to get my kids to soccer practice, pianos lessons, and a dance recital." Or, "Sorry, cannot make it to Wednesday Bible study this week – too much work to do!"

There are several seminar companies offering workshops in time management. During my years as a workshop presenter, I never offered a time-management class. When people would ask, I told them to focus on doing their job instead of surfing the Internet, talking on the phone to friends and family, and delegating work to the lowest level possible, giving people accountability and authority to grow in their respective jobs. I met a retired air force colonel who said his time-management skills consisted of taking the contents of his inbox every Monday morning (a real inbox, not an e-mail inbox), walking up and down the hallway giving folders to his subordinates, and telling them, "Here's an opportunity for you to excel today!" He emphasized skills development over doing the job to get a check so one could go buy something.

As a high school student in the 60s, I recall one history teacher writing on the board, "The family is the basic unit of Chinese culture." During recent visits to China and Tibet in 2000 and 2003 and Vietnam in 2010, I frequently observed this concept still exists. The family and the community are critical to the survival of the people, no matter the country. Granted, China and Vietnam are communist/capitalist countries and both governments still hold a tight grip on the people. That being said, the Chinese and Vietnamese people continue to be a strong example of how families and communities can work together for good. In addition to the strong sense of family and community, the Chinese, Tibetan, and Vietnamese people demonstrated openness, friendliness, and willingness to play and laugh, and a strong sense of spirituality. The average Chinese and Vietnamese family is monetarily poor but seems to be much happier than most western families. On other humanitarian clown trips, some of the Venezuelans and Haitians we met had neither television nor radios – but they equally seemed to be happy and were not afraid to instantly play and accept our offering of silliness, love, and compassion.

On a sunny afternoon in the barrios of Caracas, Venezuela, my wife and I were street-clowning our way from the top of a hill down to where our bus was waiting. Several children were playing in the street, and as we approached, they motioned to us to come into their home. The building was two stories high, and when we entered, we were greeted by the mother and several children. We began singing and doing simple magic tricks, chasing and tickling, anything to help lighten the day. A young girl, maybe in her early teens, came around the corner of the living room, struggling on hands and knees to join the fun. We did not know what medical condition caused her difficulties, but she joined in the fun along with the rest of her brothers and sisters. The living room had a dirt floor, a couch that had almost no support, a small chair, and a single light bulb hanging from a wire in the middle of the ceiling. In other words, they had almost nothing in their home. Yet they invited us in and played and laughed while we were there.

I have a simple illusion I perform with a regular pencil, and when the children saw the pencil, they were so excited to try the trick. When we finally left, we gave the mother more pencils and of course, red foam clown noses, which everyone put on their noses, causing even more laughter. The mother hugged us over and over again, thanking us for visiting. By the time we made out way back into the street, we were all crying and laughing and hugging and waving. After we returned home, people asked, "Weren't you afraid that you would catch something from them while you were in their house?" My heart is sad that every person I meet in the US has not had the blessing of playing and laughing with children in a home with a dirt living-room floor. Their conversation always leads me to believe their focus is on money and the appearance that they have money. Here are several additional thoughts to ponder:

God's politics reminds us of the people our politics always neglects – the poor, the vulnerable, the left behind.[110]

Scripture has a tremendous amount to say about money or material possessions. Sixteen of the thirty-eight parables of Jesus deal with money. One out of every ten verses in the New Testament deal with this subject. Scripture has 500 verses on prayer, less than 500 verses on faith, but over 2,000 verses on the subject of money. [111]

More quietly, people are withdrawing their trust from the professions, the corporations, the educational system, the religious institutions, the medical industry.[112]

Think about this: Professions, corporations, the educational system, religion, the medical industry, jobs we usually associate with regular pay and in many cases, high salaries. If these statements are true, where is trust being placed? If we cannot trust in the government, what governing institution can we trust? If we cannot trust the professions (political, medical, law, etc.), where will we go for our political, legal, and medical needs? If we cannot trust our educational system, where can we learn? If we cannot trust religious institutions, where do we *get* our religion? For many it does not matter because, "As long as I have insurance and money in the bank, I don't care about those people who cannot keep a job. Besides, all those homeless people could find a place to work and live if they wanted to." Oh, really? Jesus didn't talk about the homeless and the sick and the poor. He jumped right into the middle of them and helped them by loving actions. Jesus is the perfect teacher and our perfect example of how we ought to be. Instead of following his example, many are satisfied bragging about how wonderful America is when compared to the rest of the world. The reply I hear most often when sharing stories of our clown travels is one of deep appreciation for living in America, that rich and free country.

How is it then that the American federal government provides a set of statistics (*facts*) for use during presidential press conferences that differ completely from statistics on the same topics provided by other non-governmental organizations (the *truth*)? In May of 2006, a report was issued by Save the Children stating, "In the analysis of global infant mortality, Japan had the lowest newborn death rate, 1.8 per 1,000 and four countries tied for second place with 2 per 1,000 -- the Czech Republic, Finland, Iceland and Norway."[113] This item made the evening news for a few days then disappeared from the horizon as the big news companies found more murders and political news to cover. People talk about the future of the country without realizing infant mortality rates are a key factor in the future of any country. I suppose infant mortality rates are not a topic of discussion among most Americans who live under the illusion we are a great country.

Office visits in the hospital and nursing homes are part of my weekly rounds as a clown, and I am amazed at how many times I am asked if I saw such–and-such a story on the evening news. When I politely tell them I do not watch the evening news, I am met with looks of confusion, as if I had three eyes. The conversation then moves to where we discuss how one can be aware of what is going on without watching local news each night. When I tell them most of the local news deals with local crimes, fires, car accidents, and drug busts, with maybe two or three minutes of the broadcast covering global stories, I ask in return, "What would happen if you did not watch the local news for a week?" I remind them that when they go on vacation and return, the news is still the same, only the date is different. More crimes, fires, drug busts, accidents, oh, and the weather. One would think Americans do not care about infant mortality rates or any other vital news statistic and only care, instead, about the *dramatic* crimes that fill the evening news. Why would one have this perception?

A second reason that premature deaths are not the primary topic of our professional discussion is that viewpoints of poor people will inevitably be suppressed or neglected as long as elites control most means of communication.[114]

Any dictator would admire the uniformity and obedience of the (US) media.

Noam Chomsky

One day of watching any news program on television proves Americans receive almost no real news during that particular day. Entire broadcast days are filled with ego-driven *reporters* standing in hurricane rain hoping for something traumatic to happen or obnoxious lawyers *reporting* on only those trials or crimes fitting the melodramatic model. Weather *reporters* insult our intelligence by reading words on maps and pointing at arrows that we, the non-meteorologist, supposedly cannot possibly understand. Hmmm. If a cold front is approaching, will the temperature drop? I sure am glad to have a professional meteorologist available! Heaven forbid we go outside and look at the sky to figure out what is going on. All major news television shows have several women *reporters* whose sole purpose appears to be the attraction of male viewers interested in short skirts, not the *news*. Is it a mere coincidence the female news *broadcasters* sit with their knees at camera level during their shows? What? If you do not believe me, flip channels during the cable/satellite news broadcasts and focus on how much skin is being shown! It is obvious that legitimate reporting of true news does not matter. But, the ratings do! Apparently the truth in news is not important. But, news about pet food is!

Yes, we are off on another tangent again! The purpose of all this seemingly random jumping from topic to topic is to emphasize as many times possible, Christians are losing their focus on the importance of the Gospel, its message, and Jesus Christ. Even pet food can be a distraction!

In March and April of 2007, a recall was initiated by several manufacturers of pet food distributed in America. While the total recall affected only one percent of all the pet food sold in the country, one major network news organization's crawler at the bottom of the screen consisted of only the items of pet food recalled – no other news – for days on end! Two rescued cats living in our home allow us to be their staff, and I understand the need to properly care for pets and other animals. However, during the same time there was no news about the ongoing challenge of children dying from malaria or malnutrition. No mention was made about the trafficking of women and children into the U.S. for use as slave labor or other physical abuse. How did we come to the point as a society where pet food dominates the news instead of human issues? My point is that as Christians we cannot fall into the trap of being lured away from spiritual matters by short-term physical concerns. While not directly related to the topic of news, the lengthy list does show just how we allow our egos to be fooled into thinking physical things are valuable to our pets. Realistically, when it comes down to pet food from a global view, most pets eat table scraps. Reading the list of recalled food (shown below) seems like the menu of a fancy restaurant!

Pouch Kitten Chicken/Tomato

Pouch Senior Whitefish/Crab

Flaked Tuna

Sliced Chicken/Heart/Liver

Sliced Turkey/Gravy

Sliced Beef/Gravy

Flaked Chicken/Tuna

Sliced Salmon/Chicken

Sliced Chicken/Gravy

Sliced Oceanfish/Sauce

Sliced Senior Chicken/Gravy

London Grill Cuts

Pouch With Stew

Chicken Cuts/Gravy

Puppy with Chicken in Gravy

Adult with Beef in Gravy

Adult with Beef, Potatoes and Carrots in Gravy

Adult with Chicken in Gravy

Adult with Turkey in Gravy

Adult with Lamb and Wild Rice in Gravy

Weight Control with Chicken in Gravy

Active Maturity with Beef in Gravy

Variety Pack with Beef, Chicken, Lamb & Rice

Variety Pack with Beef and Chicken

Small Dogs with Chicken in Gravy

Small Dogs with Beef & Vegetables in Gravy

Variety Pack for Small Dogs with Beef & Vegetables and Chicken in Gravy

Beef & Vegetables in Gravy

Chicken in Gravy

Active Maturity with Beef in Gravy

Weight Control with Beef in Gravy

Puppy with Beef & Chicken in Gravy

Pouch Cape Cod Picnic

Pouch CO Cookout

Pouch Greek Banquet

Pouch Outback BBQ

Pouch Tuscan Grille

Yummy! Cape Cod Picnic. Outback BBQ. Weight Control. Active Maturity. London Grill Cuts. Tuscan Grille. The menus at the nursing homes I visit are not as diverse and exotic as these pet foods. Is it possible, since animals cannot read and probably have no idea what a Greek Banquet is, that pet food companies are hoping the ego of the pet owner will make them think their pet is getting the best of the best, which also allows for a higher price? There are two issues here: First, the shallowness of this entire concept of *gourmet* pet food, and second, the over-exaggerated emphasis placed on this *crisis* by the mainstream media. Pets do not have souls and there is neither a logical nor a spiritual reason anyone should be obsessing on the pet death rate when our child mortality rate in the U.S. is not very good compared to the rest of the world. Why focus on an imaginary pet food crisis when we have millions of people in the country that struggle to feed themselves each day? During the recent recession and dramatic struggles of the American economy, frequent calls for help in stocking local food banks went out over television and radio. The local food banks were running out of food.

Hunger in the US

• The Second Harvest Food Bank Network reported that emergency food providers served more than 33 million people in 2002. Nearly 38% were age 17 or younger.

• The USDA reported 21.8 million adults and 13.1 million children, a total of 34.9 million Americans were hungry or at risk of hunger in 2002.

• In spite of employment, many people still needed emergency food. In 2001, 39% of the households served by Second Harvest had one or more adults working full-time.

Food security status of U.S. households, 2009

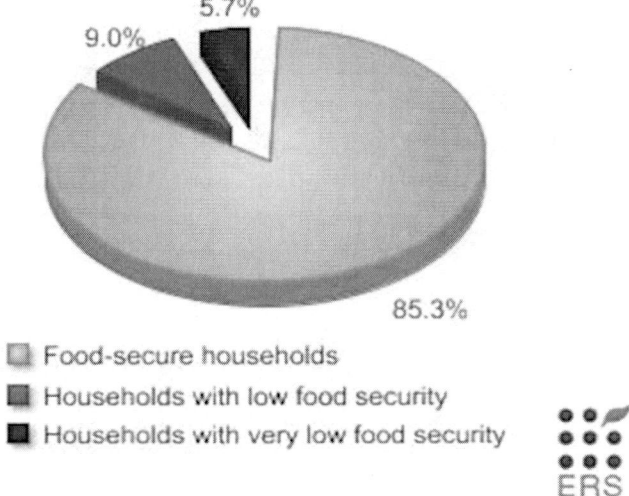

5.7%

9.0%

85.3%

- Food-secure households
- Households with low food security
- Households with very low food security

ERS

Note: Food-insecure households include those with low food security and very low food security.

Source: Calculated by ERS using data from the December 2009 Current Population Survey Food Security Supplement.

115

The "Food Insecurity" chart above shows an increasing rate of people not knowing if they will have food for their next meal. It is confusing to me as to why so much media time is spent on recalled pet food while seldom showing the facts about people who do not have enough food to eat every day.

With the rich elite, powerful corporations, and the government in control of mainline media (providing controlled content such as highly edited-for-the-negative television news and, supposedly leaked "classified" government information), Americans will end up in two camps. One will be those who are too lost to think for themselves, those who believe everything they see and hear on television and radio, and others who do the right thing and turn the media off. On more than one occasion, after returning from an extended vacation without television or newspapers, I find I have missed little that truly impacts my daily life. Same story, different day, body count higher. So, if the news does not matter, now can I go back to playing with my possessions? "Possession overload is the kind of problem where you have so many things you find your life is being taken up by maintaining and caring for things instead of people."[116] Working people devote much of their lives to paying bills, sending kids to college, buying cars and clothes, putting a little in the bank then trying to retire, so they can enjoy all their possessions that by then are worn out.

Many people with whom I have worked would drag themselves in to work on Monday mornings, exhausted from taking care of all their stuff on the weekend. The story is told of a person who says, "I can hardly wait for the weekend!" Then, when asked how the weekend was, they reply, "Had to work! Took stuff home. Made some calls. Now I can hardly wait for vacation!" After vacation, when asked how it went, the reply is often, "Had to work, took stuff with me. Made some calls. Checked my e-mail every day. Also kept my cellular phone with me on the beach in case somebody needed me for something important. I can hardly wait until I retire!" Then, after they retire and after sitting in the mall for a few months watching people walk by, they die. The obvious question is, why wait? Why not use your vacation days? (I am making the assumption the reader has vacation days available.)

When I worked in the health care field, many of the hospital staff did not use all their vacation. Several accumulated over 700 hours, almost three months of vacation time! They were also the ones who showed the most stress and complained about how they never had the time to do the job required. When asked why they never took vacation their frequent reply was, "Oh – but if I took vacation then I wouldn't be able to cash it in to buy Christmas gifts for my kids!" Or, "If I take vacation, everyone else will just mess things up while I'm gone." Translation: "I think I'm too important to leave the job for vacation." These were also the people who felt they were too valuable to miss more than a bathroom break during work. These were the people who had stacks of paper on their desks, shelves, and floor of their offices, and never had enough time in the day to do their work. These people have lost complete control of their lives in favor of a bigger bank account and more junk gifts for their kids. As a result, we are all struggling to find the time we want for those things other than our jobs, the commute, and our families.

One can only truly focus on one thing at a time. If the focus is on money (economic growth) then everything else suffers – time spent growing relationships, caring for families, caring for oneself. Does the greed ever end? Fortunately, there are an increasing number of organizations that have eliminated their policy of paying for unused vacation time and are, instead, mandating that vacation time be used. Even Jesus took time away from his work to rest, think, and pray. One of the most important personal actions a Christian can perform is taking time away from distracting activities and instead spending quiet time alone with God in prayer. We need to relearn that it is ok to carry on a running conversation with God, our Father who loves us. Without that constant connection with God, we easily become preoccupied with paying the bills.

Greed is also infiltrating into the lives of the young people of America.

> What may be the most discussed survey finding is a trend in students' value systems. Over the last 25 years, students have placed an increasing importance on "being very well-off financially" which is paralleled with the declin-

ing importance of "developing a meaningful philosophy of life." [117]

When was the last time you sat down with a piece of paper and a pen or pencil and wrote down your own personal philosophy of life? What about your personal vision? A personal mission? Personal values?

Where do children learn that greed is better than helping others? Surely not from their parents, the media, and their peers.

> Money is surprisingly bad at making us happy. Once we escape the trap of poverty, levels of wealth have an extremely modest impact on levels of happiness, especially in developed countries. Even worse, it appears that the richest nation in history – 21st century America – is slowly getting less pleased with life. [118]

When people become less pleased with their lives, this can develop into thoughts of taking one's own life. This is a serious problem for young adults under pressure.

> What good will it be for a man if he gains the whole world, yet forfeits his soul? Or what can a man give in exchange for his soul? For the Son of Man is going to come in his Father's glory with his angels, and then he will reward each person according to what he has done.
>
> Matthew 16:26, 27

It is clear the things that matter are not things at all. It is clear we are here on earth to do more than make money to buy things to use or throw away so we can go buy more things.
"We buy a wastebasket and take it home in a plastic bag. Then we take the wastebasket out of the bag, and put the bag in the wastebasket. Lily Tomlin, comedian." [119] If Christians are clear in their understanding that the souls of people matter, we will

find ways to prevent people from being labeled as disposable. Our mindset, in many instances, is to look at people who are not interested in the Bible or to look at those who once were part of our Christian family and have drifted away, and consider them as trash. They are no longer interesting or important to us, so we toss them back into the world and hope to never see them again. We forget the church is a hospital for those who are spiritually sick, and Jesus, acting through our faith-based and loving actions, makes us caregivers. By centering our lives on ourselves instead of serving others, we become just like the rest of the world.

Part of my reading schedule includes books either written by or written about Native Americans (a label incorrectly applied by white men). In these amazing books authored by wise men, I am always impressed with their complete grasp of how white Americans think.

> Perhaps these quotes, from an observation in the 1880s by Sioux Chief Sitting Bull, best describes why the Cherokee suffered the horror they did: 'The love of possession is a disease with them; they take tithes from the poor and weak to support the rich who rule. They claim this mother of ours, the Earth, for their own and fence their neighbors away.'[120]

What a profound observation! Sitting Bull may not have read the Bible, but I'm sure he would not have been surprised to learn it tells us the love of money is the source of many evils. Why do many feel they have to possess everything they see? Why do we allow ourselves to worry to the point of becoming sick when we find something we cannot possibly have? Do these things really matter? The most valuable gift we could ever receive, the love of God, is free! Jesus paid the price, and it is free, yet many ignore this wonderful gift. So what really matters here? I think you know by now.

The news regularly reports police arrests in China and other countries where fake name-brand items are being manufactured and sold as the *real* item. Select any famous designer and chances are his or her clothes, purses, shoes, etc., have been illegally manufactured for sale at greatly discounted prices. Why? So, we can walk around with our corporate-logo item out in public so others can see just how up-to-date and important we are. Many years ago, a nephew came to visit. As we drove through the countryside to worship on Sunday, the child pointed out the window and asked, "What is that?" The child knew the makes and models of most cars and had designer logos on his clothes, but failed to recognize *a cow*!

I do not know who coined the term cotton handcuffs, mentioned earlier, but the term is fitting for many corporate workers. For the reader working for a major corporation, do you feel tied to your job because if you left the company you would have to replace most of your wardrobe, so you wouldn't be walking around with your old company logo on the shirt? (Or pants, briefcase, phone holster, hat, shoes, pen, notebook, coffee cup, letter opener, etc.) In our home library, there is a special shelf filled with junk items emblazoned with corporate logos from companies for which we have worked in the past. Originally designed to provide recognition for work done or to improve company morale, they now proudly collect dust. To many, the corporate logo is a must-have item. These items are plainly little more than a waste of time and money. How much money could be invested in something other than temporary logo items? The failure of our materialistic culture continues with how much we waste every day. "Eighty percent of US products are used once and then thrown away."[121]

Have you ever been to a landfill? Guatemala City, the capitol of Guatemala, has the largest landfill in Central America. The site takes up forty acres and is over two-hundred feet deep. For a comparison, the Pentagon building in Washington, D.C. takes up about forty acres. Imagine that parcel of land covered with two-hundred feet of garbage. Workers in the dump recycle a million pounds of material each day, selling their found wares to anyone interested in buying plastic, metal, paper, or other recycled items that can be used again. The work is dangerous, and toxic fires from the methane build-up are a constant threat. There are several thousand people, aged fifteen and older, who work in the landfill. They are appreciative they have a job, in spite of the unsafe and difficult challenges they face. Until a few years ago, their families lived with them in the landfill, adding to the risk. After a massive fire in 2005, the government moved families out of the landfill and restricted who could work there.

On a humanitarian clown trip to the school located across from the landfill, our group played with some of the children whose parents worked in the landfill. They wore ragged clothes, shoes that did not match, and wolfed down the only food they would receive that day. The meals provided by the school, and everything associated with the school such as teachers and their supplies, are made possible by private donations. In the US, people who do not recycle waste at the curbside each week have no concern that their waste goes into a landfill and is covered with dirt, so it doesn't spoil the view of the neighborhood. Have we increased our lack of concern for what we waste to the point where we ignore what is taking place in the rest of the world?

A recent article about a gold mine in Australia stated nine hundred tons of excavated rock yielded one kilogram of gold. One kilogram is approximately thirty-five ounces. Therefore, about twenty-five tons of rock are excavated and processed for one ounce of gold. Some gold ends up in our cars and our computers. Most gold ends up in jewelry. Why do we want gold? So we can impress others with our gold cross on a gold chain thereby proving we are faithful Christians? So we can show off our wedding rings? So we can ignore the fact that in Africa, child miners who mine the gold earn about fifty cents each day? In addition to the greed need, I wonder what happens to all the rock left from the mining operation.

We are also obsessed with creating as many single-use products as possible such as: disposable razors, miniature packets of mustard and catsup, plastic syringes and disposable needles, paper and foam plates, bowls, and cups, plastic eating utensils, dozens of varieties of paper and plastic diapers filled with powders that collect and gel a baby's urine so it doesn't leak, dozens of plastic and metal pens and pencils, paper sticky notes of all sizes (with corporate logos), and on and on and on.

Years ago I started shaving with what was called a stainless steel safety razor. The handle unscrewed so the blade could be inserted, and with a little care, the blade was good for several shaves. There was nothing wrong with the old, single-blade safety razor. It performed well, and the stainless steel razor handle lasted forever. Now we need one with five blades, lubricant, an ergonomic handle in three colors, and a little battery-generated electric jolt to get our day started. Then, we throw it away. (Don't get me started on tooth-brushes!) We are conditioned to use something once then discard it. That wasteful mindset just might be part of the problem of dwindling membership in congregations across the country. "I got saved and enjoyed the pot-luck lunch, so now I can walk away and get back to my normal life." A mindset of "I can throw the church away too" is dangerous and can threaten the salvation of those who think that way.

Earlier I mentioned that I usually wear comfortable clown clothes. I make my own pants and have an old tuxedo coat for when it is cold. My socks are standard, striped clown socks, and my shirts are simple T-shirts with a variety of sayings printed on the front. I have never been in the company of other clowns where we discussed what designer we were wearing that day and have yet to hear, "Oh, today I'm wearing Patch Adams. Tomorrow I'll be wearing Emmett Kelly." Clown clothes are designed to be comfortable, silly, colorful, and functional. For clowns, we do not struggle with maintaining a full closet of this year's styles. But why do most people buy new clothes every few months? To be seen as up-to-date and fashionable? "...the expenditure incurred by all classes for apparel is incurred for the sake of a respectable appearance rather than for the protection of the person."[122] Please read that statement again. Clothing worn by people *unconcerned* with the latest style is, as a rule, designed to be functional – cool in the summer and warm in the winter. Many people want to dress in clothing that is clean and comfortable. Others want to have the latest fashion covered with the name of the designer. But, "No explanation at all satisfactory has hitherto been offered of the phenomenon of changing fashions."[123] Why do many feel a need for the latest fashion? Insecurity and misplaced pride.

Along with this observation, why do car and truck manufacturers insist on encouraging us to buy a new car every year? The 2000 Chevrolet Impala I drive looks exactly like the later models, has over 165,000 miles on the odometer, runs great, everything works, the paint is a little dinged up here and there, but it is still a safe and reliable car. Apparently I skipped the year in *How-to-Be-a-Guy* school where men were taught the need to have the newest model vehicle every year. I also missed the extra-credit assignment on why men feel the larger their truck and the louder the exhaust, the more masculine they are.

Chrysler and General Motors are in financial trouble and have declared bankruptcy. The federal government passed legislation *loaning* GM billions of dollars, so they won't fail and go out of business. Why do we need hundreds of variations of cars and trucks? Who do we think we're going to impress on judgment day by the size and color of our car or truck? Does "0 to 60 in 4.2 seconds" really matter? God does not care what kind of vehicle we drive, but is watching to see how we use it. If we use it for his glory – then what we drive doesn't matter. Others do not look to me as a role model based on the car I drive or the clothes I wear. Our hope must be to serve as a role model for others based on our

Christian actions only. If Jesus and the apostles could only have been effective if they wore only brand new clothes with designer labels, the church would not have survived.

People succumb to advertising by feeling inadequate if they do not have the newest and latest. This mindset filters down to our children who are also bombarded with targeted advertising. "...advertisements must be aimed not at getting them [*children*] but at getting their parents to buy things."[124] (Word in italics is mine.) If you have small children, how often do you go through the grocery checkout line without having your child express their desire to have you buy them something? Odds are they saw the product advertised on television. My daughter recently e-mailed relating the latest anecdote about our five-year old granddaughter. My son-in-law mentioned something about a commercial he was doing for his business and my granddaughter asked, "What's a commercial?" How refreshing to find a child who has no knowledge of television commercials!

Parents are shirking their duties by allowing their children to waste time and their minds in front of the television, with one result being the greedy desire to have the newest junk plastic toy, the most sugar-loaded cereal in the store, or the latest style of sport shoe. Exactly how many different shoes does one need? To drill down further, how many sports shoes does one need? Are we that far out of touch with what really matters? "The addiction to sports, therefore, in a peculiar degree marks an arrested development of the man's moral nature."[125] These comments were written in 1899, and the sentiment expressed so many years ago fits my sentiments today – exactly. While addiction to sports is spread wider than America, my thoughts will deal only with sports in America, something that seems to matter to many, especially men, many who claim to be Christians.

When we first moved to central Texas, my wife and I drove around Waco to find the grocery stores. On our way out of town, we drove by a large football stadium complex with a giant electronic sign, large advertising panels, and a massive parking lot. We discussed the enormity of the facility and commented that Baylor University had a nice stadium. It wasn't until a few days later one of my new co-workers corrected our first impression. We had driven by the high school stadium! High school sports in Texas, and in many states, are a powerful force impacting many families. The word *obsessive* comes to mind. It is both amazing and sad that so many young girls and boys live for participation in sports with the hope they will be good enough to get a scholarship to college and then, after graduating, be picked for a professional team so they can be rich and famous. Other than physical exercise, I argue that sports offer almost nothing genuinely beneficial to society. Under the ruse of *learning sportsmanlike conduct and teamwork* parents haul their children from event to event then behave like three-year olds on the sidelines during the event, yelling and chastising their children because they were not perfect during the game. These same parents then quietly escort their children into worship services on Sunday morning, leaving the impression they are so happy with their offspring.

One question – how much money is thrown away on uniforms, equipment, buildings, fields, transportation, coaching salaries, and advertising, at the high school, college, and professional level? Why is it that we, as a society, accept deplorable behavior of men and women sports *professionals* who are supposed to be parental examples for all children? Part of the answer is large egos fed by this *make-believe* tradition that provides public entertainment that is little different than gladiators of the Roman games. Why do so many parents value and encourage male-child slavery (football) dressed in helmets, pads, ready to *fight to win* and female-child exploitation (cheerleaders) waving pompons while wearing tiny tops and mini-skirts. Why do men fail to *grow up*? Perhaps it is easier to drink a few beers, watch the girls, yell at the boys, and wave a school banner than teach someone else about

JOSEPH ALAN REDMAN

God and then demonstrate that love and compassion by taking care of those in need.

God may have a reason for why we do not have a written record of Jesus's childhood. Other than beginning his studies as a young pre-teen, it does not matter what he did as a child. What matters is what he did as an adult that fulfilled prophecy and demonstrated how we must live our lives – in service to God and humanity. How many children are disappointed when they finally realize they are not going to become a millionaire from playing a game? How many parents teach their children that no matter how wonderful they are on the sports field, or how lousy they are on the same field, that God still loves them? But then how can a child understand God's love for them when their parents constantly criticize them for poor behavior?

Children also learn more than how not to behave from their ego-damaged parents. Some learn the fine *sport* of hunting. When we lived in New Jersey, hunters parked along the back roads as they prepared to hunt deer. It was quite amusing to see all the items they carried as they ventured into the *wild*.

> ...even very mild-mannered men who go out shooting are apt to carry an excess of arms and accoutrements in order to impress upon their own imagination the seriousness of their undertakings.[126]

The words written in 1899 describe hunters (men who go out shooting) today. My favorite phrase is "to impress upon their own imagination the seriousness of their undertakings." Shopping for food is hardly a serious undertaking in America. Why? Because we live in a rich country where food is plentiful and most do not suffer from hunger. (Many *do* suffer, but we have a tendency to ignore them.) Personally, I have no need for dozens of weapons, seasonal camouflage, deer stands, four-wheelers, duck calls, mounted heads and antlers, and memories of the hunt. I know there are others who do have that need. Contrary to man several thousand years ago, and contrary to people still living in jungle tribes along the Amazon river, modern man hunts to fill his empty ego, not to fill the freezer as he will tell you. Man wanted to feel important and needed, so the leisure class created this *sport* to fill their emptiness. We know from the New Testament that Jesus ate fish. We have no record that while he was walking on the water he stopped, grabbed a trophy-sized bass, and had it mounted for hanging on the wall, then went to the local bar to brag about the rod and reel he used.

The larger problem is man's desire for weapons designed to kill something or someone. How does one live a life of love and compassion for all living things while sitting in a tree stand waiting for a deer to walk by, knowing they already have a freezer full of food at home? Sport? These comments sound as if I am critical of these men and women who feel hunting is a necessary sport. My personal opinion is not important. However, as a Christian, I am concerned when these so-called sporting activities take priority over attending worship service, regular Bible study, and other activities of local congregations of the church. I base my comments on what I've experienced in my history, and know these activities can pull people away from what God expects us to do with our lives.

Let us return to another sport for a moment – football. "…the relation of football to physical culture is much the same as that of the bull-fight to agriculture."[127] Americans love their football. So do beer companies. So do advertising companies. So do car and truck companies. Professional football is the leisure class's legitimization of salaried slavery similar to gladiators in ancient Rome. There are team *owners*. Hundreds of thousands of fans spend millions of dollars to sit, drink beer, and watch either the players on the field or the cheerleaders on the big screens at the ends of the field. There are many who have filled their brains with sports statistics going back to the beginning of the game. How many of these same people know the books of the New Testament?

JOSEPH ALAN REDMAN

Football is not a metaphor for life. Football is a sport designed to make money for the team owner and the companies advertising their products during the game. Team owners definitely fall into the leisure class. "...the emergence of a leisure class coincides with the beginning of ownership."[128]

Poor people do not own much, especially not sports teams. The aftermath of hurricane Katrina showed that poor people in New Orleans did not have insurance, transportation, savings accounts, or any other needs that would have allowed them a way to escape the storm. One radio talk-show broadcast included a listener calling the radio station from his sport utility vehicle by cellular phone. He and his family were evacuating themselves from New Orleans. When asked by the program host where they were going, the man replied they were on their way to Disney World in Florida where they would stay for a couple of weeks. The man also stated that his insurance would take care of everything when they returned. I do not recall any phone interviews by the radio show's host with a poor person still stuck in New Orleans.

As a child, I was taught everything comes from God, and I should appreciate what I have. My view now is that which is good comes from God. Everything else is junk and comes from weakness caused by greed, which is, in turn, from the devil. Those who have money beyond what they spend for daily needs can afford to be leisurely. The poor must work multiple jobs and multiple shifts so that the leisure class can exist. Poor people don't own large organizations with dozens of employees. Poor people cannot buy more and larger facilities to manufacture the products they make. Poor people don't own a winter home, a summer home, a party home, and boats, cars, airplanes, and helicopters to support the wants of the rich. Those who have, as opposed to those who have not, have fallen into the empty well of self-satisfaction, knowing they have more than the poor. The leisure class believe they are most powerful, and they believe others will look at them and say they must be successful. "Gradually...accumulated property more and more replaces trophies of predatory exploit as the conventional exponent of prepotence *(having final authority)* and success."[129] Only God is all powerful. Only God can claim success in the physical world, because he created it. It belongs to him, and it is his to decide when it will all come to an end. Christians must always remember this.

Today, with the exception of rich hunters mounting exotic animal heads, skins, bodies, antlers, etc. in their homes, the average American demonstrates his prowess by the size of his house, the size of his property, the size of his vehicle, the size of his watch, the size of his bank account. He is proud of all that he has accomplished and boasts about those he has trampled and mounted as trophies during his climb to the top of the heap. And, chances are, he is unhappy and lonely, isolated from the rest of the world, only superficially friendly to those in the same class. How different would things be if those people shifted their focus to what really matters, God?

Chapter Five Thought Questions

1. Do you watch television shopping channels? Do you buy anything? Why? Why not?

2. Does your congregation have a monthly building payment? What percent of the monthly budget goes toward paying off the building loan? How does that compare to money spent on helping others?

3. What are your personal values? What is most important to you?

4. Who and what do you trust? Why?

JOSEPH ALAN REDMAN

5. What would happen if you did not watch, read, or listen to the news for a day? A week? A month?

My Challenge Tasks

1. If you work and earn vacation time – use it! Try volunteering to do humanitarian work during your vacation.

2. Identify the cotton handcuffs in your life. (List those that are separate from a required work uniform.) What can you do to replace them with spiritual links to God?

3. List what really matters then list how you are a Christian role model to others for what really matters.

4. Use a colored marker to highlight passages of your copy of the Bible when you study. Learn the books of the Bible so your study will be easier.

5. Make this year one of no gifts for your birthday and for other holidays. Encourage friends and family to donate money or time to their congregation or some local charitable organization instead.

INVESTING FOR THE
FUTURE

There is a higher form of patriotism than nationalism, and
that higher form is not limited by the boundaries of one's
country; but by a duty to mankind to safeguard the trust
of civilization.

Oscar S. Strauss

Investing for the future is one of many messages blasting through
television speakers each day. Call this company, and put your
money here to make millions by the time you retire! Buy gold!
Our society has wandered into a scorched desert of materialism
and worship of the almighty dollar, under the guise of investing for the future. My father was a career army man and, from
my birth through my high school years, we lived in Oklahoma,
Texas, South Carolina, Minnesota, Japan, and Germany. During
my childhood, very few stores were open on Sunday. We went
to worship then home to change clothes and eat lunch. The rest
of the day was usually spent with the family. We did not have a
lot of disposable income, so we almost always ate at home. Most
of my friends and their families went to worship also. The family was important. Today, all that has changed. What happened?
Why is the family no longer important to many in the country?
Why is worship attendance dropping at an increasing rate? Why
are there so many unwed mothers struggling to raise their family that isn't a complete family? One factor is the shift from the
family to the individual. Instead of thinking about *us*, we have

moved to the unstable edge of the *it's all about me* cliff. The local congregation and the family are being moved further down the priority list, replaced by our want of everything but that which we truly need: Family and God.

"Shopping centers have supplanted churches as symbols of cultural values. Indeed, 70% of Americans visit malls each week, more than attend houses of worship." [130] So that more money can be made by shoppers on weekends, when they are not at work, laws were changed and store owners driven by greed were able to open on Sunday. How convenient! Shopping centers, or malls, are large collections of stores selling few items we actually need. Prices are typically higher than in stores located away from the mall, and the center kiosks offer extraneous items with no true value or function. My wife and I have decided to leave the mall out of our shopping trips unless we need an item that we cannot get somewhere else. For the few things I need, they will be ordered through the Internet to save time for the activities I want to do such as my hospital clown visits and sermon and Wednesday night Bible study preparation.

When I do go to the mall, it seems everything is always on sale, especially mattresses. Why are people so gullible when it comes to sales and prices that always seem to end in either ninety-five or ninety-nine cents? On sale – only $299.95. Are we supposed to jump at the purchase because it doesn't cost three hundred? Wow – sure am glad we saved that nickel! Even so, if we want to buy more, we always have our credit cards! I have two cards and do everything possible to pay off the balance every month. One card has a low limit, and I take it with me when I travel out of the country. My other credit card company recently raised my credit limit to an obscenely high number because of my good credit rating. They must hope I will go buy a new car with my credit card. For those few purchases I do make in person, I am increasingly using cash instead of my credit card, so that the money is gone immediately, and I do not have to wait for a bill at the end of the month. In the past, there was a time when I had a high balance and paid only the minimum payment on the credit card. Unwise!

> Credit card use in the US is growing, with 14% of Americans holding more than 10 cards, a survey by one of the giant credit-reporting agencies has found. That's up from 2004, when 10% had more than 10 cards. [131]

Look in your wallet or purse and count your credit cards. More than two? Too many!

Beyond credit card debt, do you set aside any funds for emergencies so you don't have to use a credit card to replace a leaky faucet or pay the plumber for a costly repair? There are dozens of self-help books available that present information on setting up a stable, home budget. The common factor in all of these resources is creating an emergency fund, so credit cards don't become the automatic source for money in time of need. It takes a little time, but setting aside money each month is easily possible by cutting out the unnecessary wants from our shopping each week. If you drink two sodas each day, switch to water, and put that extra money into the emergency fund. Let's assume one dollar and fifty cents for the cost of a soda from a machine. In one month ninety dollars can be placed into the emergency fund. In one year, the total could be $1080, all from switching from sodas to water. You may even lose a few pounds in the process!

> "One-third of adults (33 percent), or about 75 million people, do not put any part of their annual household income toward retirement. This is up from 28 percent in 2008 and level with 33 percent in 2009. Though the proportion of adults who have *non-retirement* savings has increased over the years, three in ten (30 percent), or more than 68 million people, report that they have no savings and only 24 percent are now saving more than they did a year ago because of the current economic climate."[132]

This is not investing for the future. There is a big difference in being good stewards of our money and being greedy. God provides our needs, but he also expects us to use the money we have in a way that shows common sense. Some will say, "But I don't have any extra money to save. I'm using what I have to pay my bills, end even then I am falling behind!"

Why are so many struggling trapped with massive debt? First, low wage jobs. Sadly, some with lower-paying jobs fall into the second trap – being comfortable with high debt. Dumping all one's money into credit card debt is not investing for the future, materially or spiritually. Advertisers energetically try to convince adults and children to think otherwise.

> Children under 12 spent more than $24 billion of their own money in 1997, while directly influencing the spending of $188 billion more, McNeal reported in an April 1998 article in American Demographics. He estimates that by 2001, children's spending may reach $35 billion. [133]

One billion dollars annually equates to $1.9 million each and every minute, every day! What would happen if we cut spending on junk toys to a rate of $1.9 million dollars every other minute and instead provided better education and medical care for the poor? That would free up almost five hundred billion dollars to use more wisely. With a simple calculation we can easily see how five hundred billion could buy food for lots of hungry families. But targeted advertising frequently has a much more powerful affect on parents than using common sense. Time after time I hear a child whining in the grocery checkout line followed by the parent grabbing a piece of plastic junk, handing it to the child, then sighing as the child stays quiet for a few moments.

We love our children but often fail to give them the guidance they need. The examples they see every day by the actions of their parents often are not good examples. It seems that almost every year a cartoonist will draw a post-holiday cartoon of a small child playing with a cardboard box while the stack of new toys in the corner collects dust. When walking through the aisles of toy stores, I am amazed at the massive quantity of over-packaged toys and child-targeted merchandise available for purchase. Many of these toys have little to no learning or play value, they break easily, and are designed to encourage children to want even more. There is no telling how much oil could be saved if we simply stopped buying plastic toys with no play or learning value.

As a child, I remember being told, "Go outside and play." Most of my play involved other children and found objects – boxes, trees, bicycle parts, dirt, water, and beets. (Yes, I once discovered I could write my name on our brand new stone and concrete wall using a fresh beet. My parents did not appreciate my artistic display of creative thinking!) At the end of a day of playing outside, clean-up required simple soap and water, not backing up computer files, powering down electronic equipment, and recharging batteries. Why do parents not reduce the amount of junk toys and instead encourage children to play by using their own creative minds? One obvious answer is television and parents who are not at home because they have to work more than one job to pay off all their high bills.

"Children are a captive audience: The average American child watches an estimate between 25,000 to 40,000 television commercials per year. In the UK, it is about 10,000."[134] Using only the low number of twenty-five thousand, that equates to sixty-eight commercials every day. It is time Christian parents lead the way by shifting personal values from materialism to spiritual actions! Children viewing so many commercials every day learn the myth that having things brings happiness. Just look at the faces of all the people in the commercials. Buy this and be happy! "Money brings happiness only insofar as it lifts people out of poverty. Once that point is clearly passed, the link between monetary wealth and happiness is actually very small." [135] What this means for Christians is that allowing children to focus on getting instead of giving leads them down the false road in a wilderness filled with disappointment. Once again, when the focus is on *me*, all areas of our lives will suffer.

Friends seem to be more distant today than in years past. Friends are those people at the other end of some electronic piece of *communication* equipment. Personal skills are demonstrated not by what a person can do but by the number of framed credentials hanging on their office wall or number of initials after their names. Libraries are frequented by seniors looking for a cool place in the summer or a heated place in the winter. The wilderness can only be reached by purchasing the newest off-road sport utility vehicle. Afternoon naps are reserved for babies – sometimes. Is this investing for the future?

What happened to long, face-to-face conversations with close friends? What happened to letter writing in long-hand? (For those unfamiliar with the term *long-hand*, it means writing with a pen instead of a keyboard.) What happened to trading some home-canned vegetables and fruits for mowing a lawn or hand-washing a car? Why do so few people buy, read, and discuss books? (I recall reading a statement that only thirty percent of Americans buy and read books. I do not have a source document, but from talking to the many people I meet during my hospital visits, that percent does not surprise me at all.)

Why is wilderness now equated with *the new place to drill for oil?* America seems to be on the *let-us-explore-for-more-oil* bandwagon. After all, all the other rich countries are doing it. (You know – all those non-super power countries!) Every parent, at one time or another, probably told their child they were not allowed to go with friends to this or that event, saying something like, "If every body jumped off a cliff, would you jump too?" The message was, if everyone is doing wrong, why would you want to join in with them? "But fortunately, in reality, everybody does not do wrong. If everyone did, our civilization would have irretrievably collapsed."136 But in our current society where the rich and famous drive the moral compass of the people enamored with them, the results can be spiritually fatal. When those of the leisure class, especially celebrities, sports figures, and CEOs make the news with staggering salaries and bonuses far beyond what the average person makes in their entire working life, what is the message?

It is disturbing to see annual CEO salary surveys showing they are one of the largest groups who do the monkey-see-monkey-do things when it comes to ridiculous salary increases. In America, CEO salaries are now a hot news item, especially when comparing American CEO salaries to the rest of the world. The CEO salary arrangement is one of the clearest examples of *every-one-else-is-doing-it* greed in the world. This is materialistic investing at its best, and that type of investing can lead one off that spiritually fatal cliff.

> Kmart just replaced its CEO, Julian Day. During Day's reign, Kmart's sales dropped from 36 billion dollars in 2001 to 23 billion in 2003. Despite what seems like a dismal performance, Day will leave the job over 110 million dollars richer. He holds stock options currently worth 105 million dollars. He received one million dollars in salary for 2004 and will get an additional cash payment of two million dollars. He stands to receive another 1.5 million in long-term performance awards....What matters for Kmart executives is what always matters most for capitalists. Their aim is not to produce and sell things that people need or to provide jobs. Their goal is to find the quickest way to turn a profit.[137]

Kmart, like Walmart, is a store backed by powerful people whose primary job is to get as many products possible for the lowest cost possible with little or no concern for the effect on anyone else, especially the manufacturers of those products. They both sell many non-food items no one really needs. Plastic junk, which wastes oil, clothes with the appropriate designer label (manufactured by abused and underpaid employees), newly invented household items designed to save us time, etc., etc., etc. Most of these non-food items are not made in America. Slavery is alive and well in the world of *what else can I buy for as little money possible?* For some strange reason, customers do not seem to care that the stuff they buy was made by a child working more than ten hours a day for one or two dollars, if they are lucky. Most are completely unaware of the high level of child abuse that takes place so we can have our stuff. Many believe abuse of children only has something to do with sex. It encompasses so much more than that evil. The following information includes complaints by child workers.

> In Managua, Nicaragua, one of the countries that signed the Central America Free Trade Agreement currently being considered by the US Congress, workers also complained of exceedingly long work hours. Some workers alleged that doors were locked and they were not allowed to leave the garment factory until the Wal-Mart quota was filled. For this they made about 23 cents per hour.[138]

A recent television advertisement presented by Walmart shows what some call "people of color" bragging that they started as a cashier, and within a few months were promoted to a manager position. This all sounds well and good, but what is missing is the part about how now that they are a manager and are salaried instead of being paid by the hour, they can be told to work fifty, sixty, seventy hours a week with no overtime pay. Convenient! The sad thing about all of this is that, if the CEO really cared, he would make immediate changes. Greed blocks logical thinking and loving action. Greed pushes away compassionate thoughts. The love of money is not a Christian value, yet most CEOs state they are worshipping Christians. This is investing for the future?

Psychologists talk about how the super-rich aren't interested in more money but more power over others. An example of how this control over others works is shown by the following:

> However, by 1998, the poor and middle groups had lost some ground to the wealthy. The richest group controlled 49.2 percent of wealth, the middle group just 15 percent, and the poor just 3.6 percent. That same year the richest 5 percent of the population controlled 21.4 percent of wealth. The trend toward the greater concentration of wealth by the rich has accelerated throughout the 1990s. While the relative income of the poorest families in the United States declined by 11.6 percent since 1980, the income of the richest group increased by 17.7 percent. [139]

The only one with complete control and power over all is God, no one else. God does not have a problem with someone being educated and making money. God does have a problem with a society where access to education is based on how much money you have. I believe God does have a problem where people and corporations do everything possible to avoid paying taxes, especially when we are specifically commanded to pay taxes. God does have a problem with those who are too rich to be bothered with helping the poor. We cannot control the rich and their greed. We can only control our thoughts. But, we are reminded that God will judge us all.

"In 2000, the average CEO earned more in one day than the average worker earned all year. In 2000, 25% of workers earned less than poverty level wages."[140] CEOs do not really lead or manage their organizations. Hourly employees, first-line supervisors, and secretaries run the whole thing. In the 1980s, when I worked for a household products company, all the managers were brought to the corporate office for a three-day planning event. From the CEO down to all the various managers in the company, all met away from their respective manufacturing, research and development, and other company facilities. The only management representatives left in the manufacturing facilities were the first-line supervisors. With the CEO, vice-presidents, and managers, we spent three days working on defining our corporate vision, mission, and values. I do not know what happened in the other plants, but, in the one where I worked, the production and quality numbers for those three days were the best they had been in a long time, all without the presence of any higher-level manager!

"Between 1990 and 2000, average CEO pay rose 571%. Between 1990 and 2000, average worker pay rose 37%."[141] Will this glaring inequity result in a true physical rebellion in America? Or will disgruntled workers simply get a weapon, kill their boss and a few co-workers, then kill themselves as is reported in the news almost every week? As mentioned earlier, when people become so distressed with their physical situation, they cannot see that they have to work out their spiritual state of affairs first then let God take over. The result is a worker returning to where he was just fired, killing his boss, then turning the weapon on himself. Instead of this physical rebellion, we need a spiritual rebellion, rebelling against the evil influence of ego and greed.

In the past several years, after so many stories about high-level corruption in many corporations, protestors marched, shouted tired phrases from the 1960s into megaphones, a few arrests were made, and little happened as a result. In most instances, a company spokesman was sent to the lobby to deal with the leaders of the protests, loudly expressing the corporate values posted on the wall behind the security desk. Some CEOs are so isolated from the rest of the world they no longer understand the concept of strong personal values based on Biblical principles.

> How screwed up are the priorities of our business leaders? Well, Adelphia's John Rigas considered himself so moral that he refused to carry Playboy Channel on his cable sys-

tems – but thought nothing of "borrowing" $3.1 billion from his company's coffers.[142]

The defining word is *hypocrite*. Jesus was very plain in his criticism of hypocritical behavior.

CEOs are easy targets when it comes to misplaced values and poor personal behavior. But what about the average person who minds their own business every day and never makes the news? Since we are still discussing investing for the future, remember the long pet food list? The list can be expanded to include pet medicines. When we go to a doctor, we hope she will treat us with the most effective tools and medicines so that we can get back to our normal routine and live a long life. A strange phenomenon is happening across the country that directly impacts the lack of money available for savings accounts and emergency funds. We've moved beyond health care for our families to the other members of our families, our pets. In several recent Bible study classes, more than one person stated they knew their animals would be in heaven waiting for them when they died. These same people spend thousands of dollars to care for their animals, often at the expense of their own well being.

"Americans have begun to medicate their dogs, cats and sometimes other pets much as they medicate themselves. They routinely treat their pets for arthritis, cancer, heart disease, diabetes, allergies, dementia, and soon maybe even obesity. They pick from an expanding menu of mostly human pharmaceuticals like steroids for inflammation, antibiotics for infection, anti-clotting agents for heart ailments, Prozac or Valium for anxiety, even the impotence drug Viagra for a lung condition in dogs."[143]

"Keeping more than 130 million dogs and cats alone, Americans bought $2.9 billion worth of pet drugs in 2005. Though equal to only 1 percent of human drug sales, the market has grown by roughly half since the year 2000."[144]

One local veterinarian is honest when offering treatment advice for animal owners. He will explain all the medications, tests, and treatments available, but will sincerely and honestly tell the owner the better option might be to put the animal down instead of spending thousands of dollars to extend the life of a cat by a few months. On the other hand, another veterinarian in my community now offers ultrasonic teeth cleaning for pets with bad breath. Is this investing for the future? It is true that animals should not be abused or neglected, and they do serve a role as companions and comforters. But it is a sad observation that many people treat animals better than the poor. God gave us no command in the New Testament to treat animals better than the poor. God tells us to care for and feed the hungry. He tells us to give to the poor. He tells us to comfort all men.

We are forgetting what the church is and what our mission as members of the church must be. Previously I mentioned the silliness of luxurious *worship* buildings. First of all, people make up the true church, not buildings. Second, there is no command from God to build any building for worship and no command to load up the building with statues, candles, orchestras, robes, and on and on and on! Until the time of Constantine, the early church met in homes or borrowed spaces for larger groups. We have no Biblical or historical record of all the extra ornaments, clothes, procedures, and holidays that now fill what many denominations call worship services and church activities. A large number of these so-called religious factions resemble cults more than they resemble the early church that Jesus established.

> The consumption of ceremonial paraphernalia required by any cult, in the way of shrines, temples, churches, vestments, sacrifices, sacraments, holiday attire, etc., serves no immediate material end. All this material apparatus may... be broadly characterized as items of conspicuous waste.[145]

Christians claim Jesus as their one example of perfection. There is no evidence of Jesus wearing expensive robes, jewels, hats, collars, implementing formal policies and procedures, or wearing crosses hanging on gold chains around his neck. There is no evidence he raised money to build multi-million dollar buildings for worship. There is no evidence he had the latest model donkey for transportation with a fish bumper sticker on the back. There is no evidence he used any high-tech, audio-visual equipment when speaking to crowds of worshippers. He never used PowerPoint during a sermon. There is no evidence Jesus engaged in any kind of conspicuous waste activity – ever. There is no record of Jesus investing money or anything material during his short stay on earth. In other words, all his efforts were devoted to teaching God's plan with love and compassion.

I am not convinced those groups who claim to be religious demonstrate this to the world by the size and grandeur of their buildings, robes, orchestras, hats, jewels, collars, or multiple levels in the chain of command. Why do some denominational groups believe they need to create their own organizational by-laws? Is the Bible not good enough for them? Could it be their hope of establishing a false reputation for themselves? If Jesus is the true head of the church, why do some denominations feel they need a US headquarters complete with fancy buildings and highly paid staff? "The possession of goods…becomes a conventional basis of reputability."[146] I seem to recall members of the first church selling what they had and giving it all to the poor.

In America, one's reputation is often preceded by the fragrance of their money and things piled up in their houses. The children we played with in Tibet have nothing in comparison to American children. They have no toys. They do not seem to have soap or toothpaste. Their worn and faded school uniforms provided by the government appear to have never been washed with detergent and fabric softener in a machine. They do have unlimited joy and love and a sense of play. They also have devotion to *their* god. Now who is reputable – the rich American or the Tibetan child?

> With expensive mission trips, sprawling campuses and dozens of sports and eclectic ministries, megachurches have been accused by some of lapsing into a materialistic suburban faith -- wasting collections on frills and grand complexes rather than concentrating on preaching the unadorned message of Christ.[147]

How much money is spent by *cults* (another word for religious groups as defined by Thorstein Veblen) on buildings, utilities, vehicles, property, equipment, salaries, television programs, websites, advertising, etc., contrasted with how much is given to the poor? Earthlings invest in the future with money. Christians invest in the future by asking God to grow their faith, and then by actively demonstrating their faith through acts of compassionate love.

Chapter Six Thought Questions

1. Do you go shopping on Sunday? Why? Why not?

2. How many credit cards own you? How many are maxed out?

3. Do you have a written monetary plan and a written spiritual plan for your family?

4. What matters to you? Why?

5. Do you believe that when you die you cannot take it with you? Why do you still have so much stuff?

My Challenge Tasks

1. Become debt free.

2. Prepare and live by a monetary plan.

3. Prepare and live by a spiritual plan.

4. List those things you absolutely need to live as a Christian, and then get rid of the excess. Either donate to a charity or have a yard sale then donate the proceeds.

5. Perform every day based on intentions driven by heavenly values – those things that matter most to God with complete compassion and love for others.

THE TEMPORARY STATE
OF AMERICA

All nations have present, or past, or future reasons for thinking themselves incomparable.

Paul Valéry

Some citizens of America believe they live in a *blessed* country because of the statement "In God We Trust" printed or stamped on their money. Some believe they are blessed because America claims to be a *Christian nation*. Others believe the founding fathers wrote the constitution as a Christian-inspired document, and that the constitution will last forever as an example to the rest of the world. We are proud that God blesses us!

The following table contains excerpts from constitutions of many countries around the world. Many constitutions refer to the Universal Declaration of Human Rights. Several countries who do not have any reference to God in their constitution do, however, include the statement, "So help me God" in their various oaths of office. Some Middle-Eastern countries, with Islam as the official religion, use "God" instead of "Allah" in their constitutions. Keep in mind that the main document of the US constitution does not make any reference to God.

Sample of World Constitutions with a reference to God

1	Albania	… with faith in God
2	Antigua and Barbuda	… acknowledge the supremacy of God
3	Argentina	… invoking the protection of God
4	Australia	… humbly relying on the blessing of Almighty God
5	Bahamas	… respect for Christian values;…indivisible Unity and Creation under God
6	Bahrain	In the name of God, the Merciful and Compassionate
7	Brazil	… under the protection of God
8	Chili	… invoking the name of the Almighty God
9	Columbia	… invoking the protection of God
10	Denmark	… citizens shall be entitled to form congregations for the worship of God
11	East Timor	… faith in God
12	Ecuador	… invoking the protection of God
13	Egypt	… in the name of God
14	Equatorial Guinea	Conscious of our responsibility before God
15	Ethiopia	… ALMIGHTY GOD. THE SOURCE OF ALL BENEFITS
16	Fiji	SEEKING the blessing of God
17	Gambia	In the name of God Almighty
18	Grenada	… acknowledging the fatherhood and supremacy of God
19	Guatemala	Invoking the name of God
20	Honduras	… invoking the protection of God

21	Indonesia	By the grace of God Almighty;... belief in the One and Only God
22	Ireland	... under God
23	Kenya	ACKNOWLEDGING the supremacy of the Almighty God of all creation
24	Kiribati	...acknowledging God as the Almighty Father on whom we put our trust
25	Liberia	Acknowledging our devout gratitude to God
26	Liechtenstein	... by the grace of God
27	Madagascar	... affirming their belief in God the Creator
28	Marshall Islands	... trusting in God, the Giver of our life, liberty, identity, and our inherent rights
29	Nauru	... acknowledge God as the almighty and everlasting Lord and the giver of all good things
30	Nicaragua	... from faith in God
31	Nigeria	... nation under God
32	Palan	... divine guidance of Almighty God
33	Panama	... invoking the protection of God
34	Papua New Guinea	... under the guiding hand of God
35	Paraguay	... pleading to God
36	Peru	... invoking God Almighty
37	Philippines	... imploring the aid of Almighty God
38	Poland	... those who believe in God as the source of truth, justice, good and beauty
39	Puerto Rico	... placing our trust in Almighty God
40	Rwanda	Trusting God Almighty

41	Western Samoa	IN THE HOLY NAME OF GOD, THE ALMIGHTY, THE EVER LOVING – WHEREAS sovereignty over the Universe belongs to the omnipresent God alone, and the authority to be exercised by the people of Western Samoa within the limits prescribed by His commandments is a sacred heritage
42	Solomon Islands	… under the guiding hand of God
43	South Africa	May God protect our people
44	Saint Kitts and Nevis	… the nation is established on the belief in Almighty God
45	Saint Vincent and Grenadines	… the Nation is founded on the belief in the supremacy of God
46	Sudan	In the name of God, the creator of man and people, the grantor of life and freedom, and the guiding legislator of all society
47	Switzerland	In the name of God Almighty! (Switzerland is the only country who uses an exclamation point when referencing God.)
48	Tonga	Since it appears to be the will of God that man should be free as He has made all men of one blood
49	Trinidad and Tobago	… acknowledge the supremacy of God
50	Tunisia	In the name of God, the Compassionate and Merciful
51	Tuvalu	AND WHEREAS the people of Tuvalu, acknowledging God as the Almighty and Everlasting Lord

JOSEPH ALAN REDMAN

52	Ukraine	... aware of our responsibility before God
53	United Kingdom	Magna Carta... by the grace of God;...having regard to God; ...unto the honor of God
54	United States of America	(During the Civil War the Confederate States of America Constitution) ... invoking the favor and guidance of Almighty God
55	Vanuatu	... faith in God
56	Venzuela	... invoking the protection of God
57	Yugoslavia (1931)	... by the grace of God

149

God is impartial and does not hold one nation or one person above another. (See Acts 10:34) To claim we are a Christian nation simply because the word "God" was used in letters and some state documents written by the founding fathers, and later engraved on building façades and printed on our money, is faulty logic. If using the word "God" is so important, what about the countries listed in the table above? Are they left out of God's plan because they are not America? I know from conversations with friends and acquaintances that there are some who feel the Bible was written only for America, and that it is not a timeless library of books written for all people of all time no matter where they happen to live.

Any legitimate student of American history knows we are not and never will be a Christian nation. We are a denominational nation and are rapidly moving to being a pagan nation. When one considers recorded history, the high number of civilizations and governments that have preceded America, and the number of governments and countries that have come and gone in the past two-hundred years alone, it is obvious we are but one small part of global history as it stands today. If the past is any indication of the future, America will most likely go the way of all other governments recorded in the history books – into oblivion to be discussed by archaeologists hundreds or thousands of years from now. (I highly recommend the following books: *Unchristian America* by Michael Babcock; *The Search For Christian America* by Mark A. Noll, Nathan O. Hatch, and George M Marsden; and *The Myth Of A Christian Nation* by Gregory A. Boyd.)

Let us look at a brief comparison between American government and the church established by Jesus.

America	The Church
Follows a constitution written by a group of men, over a few months, inspired by anger against the British Empire.	Follows the Bible written by a group of men, over thousands of years, inspired by God.
The constitution has been amended twenty-seven times, so far.	The Bible is complete and has never been amended.
America is driven by greed and a desire for power, classic signs of capitalism.	Christians are driven by their love for God and the desire to help others.
Continuously creates and enacts laws to keep the country running.	The laws and commandments in the Bible were written once and have not been added to.
Elected officials holding office higher up the chain of command (president, vice-president, etc.) usually come from the wealthier white male class and are highly educated.	The Church was established by a carpenter with no money involved. He was not elected, did not campaign, and spent no money to become the Son of God.
Politicians seem to focus on being elected, then re-elected, and obtaining funds for projects in their home states, regardless of the true value to the state and the country. The focus is always short term.	The Church is focused on teaching the Word of God and following the example of Jesus. The focus is on the long term – infinity!

America had a starting point, and will have an ending point, either through collapse of the government, or on judgment day.	The Church had a starting point and will never end.
The state of America is temporary.	The state of the Church is permanent.
Many Americans act as if the country will be around forever.	Many Christians also act as if America will be around forever – at least those who are driven by the same values of greed and power. Other Christians live with the hope of eternal life, separate from any hope, thoughts, or feelings for America, because America doesn't matter! Sadly, they are in a minority.

Tourists are impressed, either favorably or unfavorably, when visiting Washington D.C. The buildings, inspired by ancient Roman architecture, are large, grandiose, massive, and reek with the stale air of human power. Visitors to Rome can view what are now ruins of similar buildings.

> Even the most beautiful and impressive bourgeois buildings and public works are disposable…closer in their social functions to tents and encampments than to Egyptian pyramids and Roman aqueducts, Gothic cathedrals.[150]

When we lived in New Jersey, we routinely drove over a small, two-lane concrete bridge built in the 1930s. There were never any repairs to the bridge, even though it was heavily used each day by thousands of vehicles. Throughout New Jersey, during the eight years we lived there, we witnessed many repair jobs performed on much newer bridges. Why? Built-in obsolescence. America even knows how to design disposable roads and bridges! In Tulsa, Oklahoma, in 1972, I stopped on the side of the road and stood in amazement and stared at a new on-ramp to a bridge that was about four feet lower than where it was supposed to be. Part of the ramp existed from the lower road surface, and part of the ramp jutted out from the upper roadway of the new bridge. Obviously they were supposed to join in the middle, but someone goofed. Both ramps were torn down, and the process began again. Yet the small bridge in New Jersey, built in the 1930s, was still there, and, from what we could determine visually, had never needed or been repaired.

The Michigan state department of transportation web site states, "A mile of freeway through an urban area costs approximately $39 million, while a mile of freeway through a rural area costs approximately $8 million." (www.michigan.gov) When, as a nation, we spend so much money on new construction, why do we have to go back and repair it within only a few years? Surely the short life of roads and bridges is not designed into the construction so the repair companies have job security. Let us see – if we build a road with rocks from the local quarry then drive overloaded gravel trucks over the road and damage the surface, we can repair the road with rocks from the local quarry, again and again. Somehow this does not seem to be good stewardship. It must also serve as a reminder that our home in heaven and the love of God are permanent. Everything physical will be destroyed at the end of time.

Events taking place along a rural road in central Texas are evidence of how local quarry operations are destroying what once was prime farm land. This particular company buys farms from families or individuals who have either died or moved away, then excavates the land for the sand that lies below the dark, fertile soil. They dig until they reach the water table then move on to another piece of property. The water table in this part of Texas is not very deep, perhaps twenty to forty feet at the most. The photograph below shows the result. What once was farm land is now an opening exposing the water table. This particular *lake* is about forty acres, and there are dozens of excavations along just this one highway that runs for about five miles. My question is, what impact will there be on the water table now that there is a dramatic increase in the area available for evaporation? I am neither a farmer nor a road construction engineer, but I do not see how permanently removing excellent farm land for the sake of road-construction sand has any long term benefit to anyone other than the quarry company owners. With complaints of not enough farm land available to feed the nations and much of the rest of the world, I often wonder why sand from the ocean or the desert cannot be used instead. There will be those who argue the cost of transporting sand from the coasts to construction sites in Kansas would be prohibitive, causing an increase in construction prices. Think about the options. Which has more spiritual value, feeding the poor or building cheaper buildings and roads?

Another excavation a few miles from the forty acre lake is 106 acres. The difference is this ruined farmland has magically been transformed into a "hunting paradise."

In addition to not taking care of the health of the land, our health care for humans also shows how human-designed systems are filled with defects. We do not know how, and do not have a viable plan, to care for the health needs of the people, no matter their age. Bridges are part of the material infrastructure and people are part of the social and spiritual infrastructure. Both are important. We are a rich country with miserable health care services. Once again I want to look at infant mortality and use facts to show how America is not the land of milk and honey so many denomination preachers proclaim each Sunday morning. Keep in mind infant mortality is only one factor in the grand picture of healthcare in the US. The problem is staggering and more complex that we can imagine. Here is a recent headline: "US has second worst newborn death rate in modern world, report says."[151] From the article we read,

American babies are three times more likely to die in their first month as children born in Japan, and newborn mortality is 2.5 times higher in the United States than in Finland, Iceland, or Norway, Save the Children researchers found. Only Latvia, with six deaths per 1,000 live births, has a higher death rate for newborns than the United States, which is tied near the bottom of industrialized nations with Hungary, Malta, Poland and Slovakia with five deaths per 1,000 births.

The report goes on to say there is a high correlation between infant mortality and lack of education of mothers. Will any rich legislator read this report and take action? No. Will *Christians* in the *blessed* nation take action? No. Why do I say this? Simply because there are thousands of reports with startling results and the primary reaction will be for opponents to waste time and money debunking the report so Americans will be duped into thinking the problem does not exist at all. Our culture has developed to the point where we have become experts at ignoring facts. One person makes a factual statement and a hundred claim the fact is either misleading or completely false. News organizations spend large amounts of time and money challenging each other's stories hoping to prove their point so more viewers will watch. Once in a great while advertisers will realize the insanity taking place and will pull their advertising from programs that simply do not make any sense.

Those (especially Christians) who deny true, validated facts, and instead live in a fog of self-interest, are not aware of what is taking place in the world. This ignorance can be masked by the illusion of comfort, stability, and sameness from day to day, all while systems designed by humans are failing. Some have said America is collapsing while others deny the collapse altogether. All societies collapse – read your world history books!

> In the long run, rich people do not secure their own inter-
> ests and those of their children if they rule over a col-
> lapsing society and merely buy themselves the privilege of
> being the last to starve or die.[152]

America is temporary. Heaven is permanent. People who spend their entire lives investing/hoarding money so they can retire and be rich just do not get it. Several years ago as the year 2000 approached, a friend of mine mentioned the end of time was coming, and they were stockpiling food and gold so they would be ready. My son, at that time a teenager, asked, "If the end of the world is coming, why do they need food and gold?" My friend's confusion was caused by a book claiming the world would end in 2000. As I write, I have a pamphlet warning me the end of the world will be in 2011. Another states everything will be burned up in 2012. My Bible tells me only God knows the hour and the day.

There is a reason God tells us to put our treasure in heaven and not on the earth! But many don't care. Our culture has lost any semblance of being a Christian nation (not that we ever had any in the first place!) and without a foundation of faith-driven actions there can be no stability in any culture or country.

> A culture is unsalvageable if stabilizing forces themselves
> become ruined and irrelevant... The collapse of one sus-
> taining cultural institution enfeebles others, makes it more
> likely that others will give way...until finally the whole
> enfeebled, intractable contraption collapses.[153]

What are the stabilizing forces? Could it have anything to do with a culture based on love and compassion? Could it have something to do with strong families and a strong sense of community? Statistics indicate a growing number of single-parent households in America. Some are divorced, but a growing number have never been married. Sadly, the family is not the primary unit of our cul-

JOSEPH ALAN REDMAN

ture. I think it might be the television set. Because of the failure of community and the family, and the failure of many fathers to take responsibility for their actions, children are growing up with poor social skills, poor study habits, little respect for others, and no traditional household to call home. Growing numbers of young people take to the streets instead of attending school, resulting in actions encouraged by loneliness and low self-esteem. For some, the action includes joining a gang for the support missing from the family at home. For others, it means committing crime as a means to get the attention missing from the home. One result?

> My intuition tells me they (*families*) will probably be coercive. This is already true of the most swiftly multiplying and rapidly expanding type of American households at the turn of the millennium – prisons.[154]

How sad that the fastest growing household in America is our prisons. Parents who are not present as their children grow, who show a complete lack of sincere concern for their children, and lack of concern for God in the family, can only result in the catastrophic failure of America. Putting more and more people in prison is not an answer to any problem. Continuing with the practice of executing death-row prisoners will not solve any societal problems. Texas almost seems proud to lead the nation in prisoner executions, and yet the crime rate in my county is much higher than it should be. With an increasing number of studies showing a low correlation between the death penalty and reducing violent crimes, isn't it time to use common sense and move away from being one of only a few countries leading the world in prisoner execution? As of this writing, there are only sixteen states in this so-called Christian nation who've outlawed the death penalty. Think about this number. There are still thirty-four states who allow convicted prisoners to be executed as punishment for their crimes. The command, "Put away your sword" comes to mind.

Distribution of world's prisoners

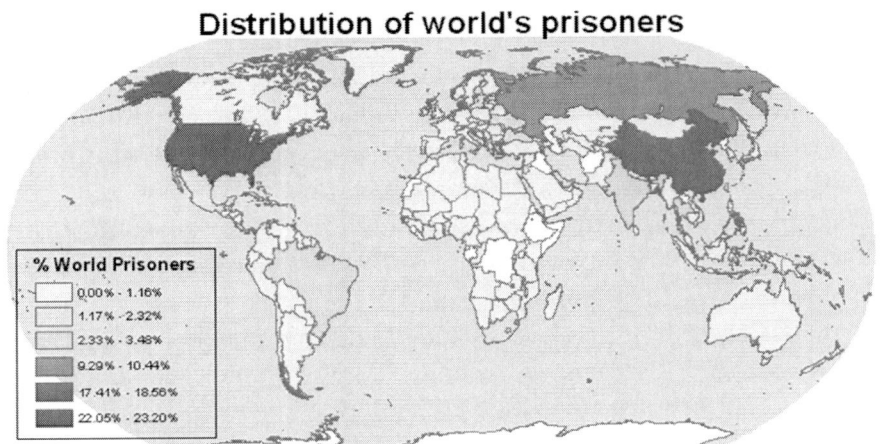

% World Prisoners
- 0.00% - 1.16%
- 1.17% - 2.32%
- 2.33% - 3.48%
- 9.29% - 10.44%
- 17.41% - 18.56%
- 22.05% - 23.20%

Data: World Prison Population List, 5th Ed.   Map: Prison Policy Initiative

The prison industry wants and need prisoners in order to make money. More and more private prison companies are taking the place of what used to be managed by the government. With more people in prison that any other country on the planet, why would we want to change the system when so much money is there to be made at the expense of people who made bad decisions by committing crimes? If we reduce the number of inmates, we will lose jobs and unemployment will rise. Right? So who benefits from putting people in prison? "Almost every government act… benefits one group more than another, and usually at the expense of everyone else."[155]

I accept the New Testament fact that governments are established by God and are designed to bring law and order to the land. I accept that without order, a society will fail. I do not accept human laws whereby convicted murders are killed for their crimes. I frequently wear a small button that reads, "Why do we kill people who kill people to show that killing people is wrong?" Think about it. With one in every one-hundred people in a prison, and the percentage is increasing each year, what will we do when the number in prison exceed those who are still free?

Realistically we will not hit that number, but the question still remains, why do we have more people in prison than any other country? Is this a sign we are blessed by God? Isn't this, instead, a sign of schemes to satisfy a small but powerful special interest group who has money and power to influence lawmakers?

Pick a topic from any senator's list shown on their websites, and you can be sure they will work hard for the special interest group either supporting or opposing the topic in question. The American government spends more money for the military than any other category, including social aid programs, social security, Medicare and Medicaid, and paying down the national debt. At whose expense? Yours, mine, and the civilians living in countries we invade. Now, with the Supreme Court's decision on eminent domain, there is no longer any private property. For Christians, that should not be a problem, right? If our home is not here on earth, does it matter whether or not the government takes land or property we *own*? It does when the motivation for taking the land is capitalistic greed under the guise of planning for the future, a temporary future on earth.

My point is, those we have elected to represent us are not doing their jobs very well. Few of the laws passed each year in Congress actually add anything beneficial to America. Many go un-enforced, and many never receive the funds required to implement them in a timely manner. If the American Congress continues to create laws which benefit only those at the top of the capitalistic food chain (many of which are somehow amazingly present in Congress!), does this process qualify as one God would bless?

Washington, D.C., has many historical national monuments. Some include the Washington Monument, The Lincoln Monument, The Korean War Monument, and The Vietnam Wall.[156] Thousands of people from all over the world come to visit the various monuments and memorials. To some, they consider these to be on *sacred* ground. How can anything man-made and temporary be sacred? A recent documentary was televised on the design and preparations for building a memorial to the passengers and crew of the plane that crashed in Pennsylvania on September 11, 2001. The architectural representatives talked about how this *holy* ground and this *sacred* ground would be here forever. So much for the entire creation being destroyed by fire on judgment day! When I visit Washington D.C. and watch people as they make their way past monuments and memorials, I am struck by how some approach as if they are approaching something to which they must be in awe. At the Vietnam Wall some leave mementoes as a way of showing respect to a friend or relative listed. Have we progressed to an emotional point in our lives where these temporary monuments are similar to idols? One definition of an idol is *an object of extreme devotion.* Take for example, the television show, "American Idol!" Based on this definition, one question is, have Americans built monuments and memorials that can be perceived as objects of extreme devotion to the point viewers sit fixated on their television screens? If so, are there Americans who admire intensely and blindly either a person or object, even after death? (Elvis and Marilyn Monroe come to mind!) By the way, both monuments and television shows are temporary.

As mentioned before, I have visited the Vietnam Wall several times. The names of five friends are etched into the black granite. Earlier in my life when my being an American came before my being a Christian, I must admit that my devotion to the wall was probably more important than my devotion to God. Based on the previous definitions of idols and idolaters it is likely I would have fit the definition. Fortunately, that has changed. Remembering my friends who died in Vietnam is something that is part of my life. Words cannot describe how close we were during our short time together in combat. The wall is their memorial, but it is neither holy nor sacred. It is a heartbreaking gash in the earth

JOSEPH ALAN REDMAN

that reminds us of the futility and complete waste of war. The Apostle Paul writes:

> For although they knew God, they neither glorified him as God nor gave thanks to him, but their thinking became futile and their foolish hearts were darkened. Although they claimed to be wise, they became fools and exchanged the glory of the immortal God for images made to look like mortal man and birds and animals and reptiles.
>
> Romans 1:21-23

Granted, the wall is not in the shape of a mortal man, animal, or reptile. But, in the area of the wall are two statues, one of male soldiers and the other of female nurses and wounded men, which are like mortal man. But do Americans worship at these monuments?

> Worship can be defined as:
>
> 1: to honor or reverence as a divine being or supernatural power
>
> 2: to regard with great or extravagant respect, honor, or devotion

While there may only be a few who fit the first definition, there are many who fit the second definition, and that is troublesome.

> The rest of mankind that were not killed by these plagues still did not repent of the work of their hands; they did not stop worshiping demons, and idols of gold, silver, bronze, stone and wood—idols that cannot see or hear or walk.
>
> Revelation 9:20

> Dear children, keep yourselves from idols.
>
> 1 John 5:21

No one can serve two masters. Either he will hate the one and love the other, or he will be devoted to the one and despise the other. You cannot serve both God and Money.

Matthew 6:24

Christians are either servants of all that is manmade and temporary, or we are servants of God. We cannot be both. Christians and veterans may show respect for the Vietnam Wall, but they must not worship it. We must only worship God. For all Christians, it is a safer path to be devoted to that which is spiritually permanent, not the temporary physical state of America.

Chapter Seven Thought Questions

1. What things do you believe a non-Christian would list as permanent?

2. What things do you believe a non-Christian would list as temporary?

3. How would a Christian answer #1 and #2?

4. Can you list all the current amendments to the US constitution?

5. Can you list any of Jesus's commands?

My Challenge Tasks

1. Research verses in the Bible describing the temporary state of our physical bodies and how we should care for them.

2. Research the various steps governments experience from beginning to end.

3. List the steps from your point of view then contrast your list with how you view the church.

4. List the machines and equipment in your childhood home and compare that list to your current home. Any real improvements and time savers or simply gimmicks?

5. Identify the idols in your life and develop a plan to replace them with actions that glorify God. Then implement the plan!

THE PERMANENT STATE
OF GOD

There are things a man must not do even to save a nation.

Murray Kempton

Whoever believes in him shall not perish.

John 3:16

Praise be to the God and Father of our Lord Jesus Christ! In his great mercy he has given us new birth into a living hope through the resurrection of Jesus Christ from the dead, and into an inheritance that can never perish, spoil or fade – kept in heaven for you.

1 Peter 1:3-4

All things created by man are temporary. All things God created that are non-spiritual in nature, such as animals and the universe, are temporary. God, Jesus, the Holy Spirit, heaven, hell, and our souls are permanent. In other words, if we can see it, it will be destroyed on judgment day. Things we cannot see, like our own souls, are eternal, as stated in 2 Corinthians:

So we fix our eyes not on what is seen, but on what is unseen. For what is seen is temporary, but what is unseen is eternal.

2 Corinthians 4:18

Fixing one's eyes means to stare at something. In this verse, it is a metaphor for faith – focusing on God. It is a difficult concept for humans to accept they are temporary, their house is temporary, their possessions are temporary, their religious denomination is temporary, and their country is temporary. The one true church established by Jesus is permanent, because it is based on the love of God which is spiritual and eternal. Religious denominations are based on ego and discord and are therefore temporary institutions. Once again, let us turn to the Bible to identify the true nature of God.

> For since the creation of the world God's invisible qualities—his eternal power and divine nature—have been clearly seen, being understood from what has been made, so that men are without excuse.
>
> Romans 1:20

Paul's comments indicate God's invisible qualities, such as eternal power and his divine nature, are something we humans can only comprehend on a simple level, because of the creation around us every day. We have no excuse when it comes to accepting these qualities of God.

> Now to the King eternal, immortal, invisible, the only God, be honor and glory for ever and ever. Amen.
>
> 1 Timothy 1:17

Once again, we learn God is immortal and invisible, and we are to honor and glorify him forever, a spiritual act.

> God, the blessed and only Ruler, the King of kings and Lord of lords, who alone is immortal and who lives in unapproachable light, whom no one has seen or can see. To him be honor and might forever. Amen.
>
> 1 Timothy 6:15-16

Paul continues to emphasize the characteristics of God as being immortal and invisible, at least to humans here on earth. Throughout the Bible, there are many characteristics of God written for us to read and accept. Some of these include:

A spirit: God is spirit, and his worshipers must worship in spirit and in truth.

John 4:24

Now the Lord is the Spirit, and where the Spirit of the Lord is, there is freedom.

2 Corinthians 3:17

Light and Love: Many songs of worship describe God as being light and love.

This is the message we have heard from him and declare to you: God is light; in him there is no darkness at all.

1 John 1:5

Whoever does not love does not know God, because God is love.

1 John 4:8

Consistency: Unlike humans, God remains constant in his actions and methods. There must be a high level of comfort to know God is consistent and will be around forever.

Every good and perfect gift is from above, coming down from the Father of the heavenly lights, who does not change like shifting shadows.

James 1:17

While traveling in Vietnam, China, Japan, and Tibet, it was common to see homes with small statues of their gods often surrounded with photographs of deceased family members. These shrines are where the family worships their god in the home. Worship in the home is a wonderful concept, but we do not need, and are not commanded to use, miniature god images for our worship to be acceptable. God is in heaven, not locked in a small statue.

> However, the Most High does not live in houses made by men. As the prophet says: "Heaven is my throne, and the earth is my footstool."
>
> Acts 7:48-49

> Be perfect, therefore, as your heavenly Father is perfect.
>
> Matthew 5:48

How can a mere human be perfect? The word perfect in this verse means mature and holy. Are we perfect? If we are Christians and have asked God's forgiveness for sin and are accepting his love by doing those actions to grow our faith so that we can be mature and holy, then we are perfect. Do we make mistakes? Of course, but that is why God gives us the opportunity every day to continue developing the love relationship we have through prayer.

Another characteristic of God is that he is faithful to his followers. The icing on the cake of freedom from sin is that when Christians are tempted, God will protect by not allowing us to be thrown off course by something we cannot handle. Every challenge we face here on earth are those challenges faced by all humans. This characteristic of God, that he gives us a way out of the difficult situation, is a model many struggle to accept. We often hear people complain, "Why did God do this to me?" A more appropriate response would be, "Thank you, God, for this challenge to demonstrate my faith in you through prayer and positive action filled with love and compassion!" Remember, Satan tempts, God tests.

> No temptation has seized you except what is common to man. And God is faithful; he will not let you be tempted beyond what you can bear. But when you are tempted, he will also provide a way out so that you can stand up under it.
>
> 1 Corinthians 10:13

God is good!

> "Why do you ask me about what is good?" Jesus replied. "There is only One who is good."
>
> Matthew 19:17a

If one accepts the Bible as the holy Word of God, and if one accepts these characteristics as a true definition of God, (as far as the human mind can comprehend something so magnificent) then perhaps the following quote will help solidify the significance of God, Jesus, and the Holy Spirit in our lives.

> "After 9/11, what were we asked to do? Shop! I mean, what an extraordinary thing — that we're supposed to shop as a way to resist terrorism. Christians all over the country should have said, 'Hey, that sounds pretty silly to us.' There's this extraordinary claim that September 11, 2001 changed the world. False. Christians should be saying, "No, A.D. 33 changed the world." We need to narrate 9/11 in the light of A.D. 33 and not vice versa. Nothing is more important for Christians than to demand the truth from our ministers."[157]

Chapter Eight Thought Questions

1. What words do you use to describe God? Are those words mainly positive or negative? Where did you learn this?

2. Why do bad things happen to good people?

3. What was your biggest mistake?

4. What was your biggest success?

5. Where is your greater focus – mistakes or successes?

6. What words did you use when expressing your emotions in #3 and #4?

My Challenge Tasks

1. Make a list of words you feel describe God in your life. During your prayers to him, praise him by using this list of words.

2. Take a piece of paper, and draw a line down the middle of the page. On the left side, list all the bad things that have happened in your life. On the right side, list all the good things that have happened to you. Which list is larger? What will you do to increase the number of good things in your life?

3. God forgets when he forgives. To help forget a mistake, write your mistake on a three by five note card. Pray for forgiveness, then take the card and burn it, scattering the ashes to the wind. Walk away.

4. Dedicate space in a special place where you can place all your successes. This can be as simple as a Look What I Did With the Help of God! folder. When you receive a thank you note, put it in the folder. If you do something and nobody sees, make yourself a thank you note and put it in the folder. When you are having a bad day, open the folder to see all you have accomplished with the help of God.

5. Write a poem using the words from #4 above – your biggest success, through God. Memorize it!

SELF-SPIRITUAL GROWTH

Patriotism is a kind of religion; it is the egg from which wars are hatched.

> Guy De Maupassant

Do your best to present yourself to God as one approved, a workman who does not need to be ashamed and who correctly handles the word of truth.

> 2 Timothy 2:15

If temporary America doesn't matter, but our permanent souls do, and if God does not bless America as a nation but blesses our souls as individuals, it is our loving obligation to work at spiritual growth so we can be workers approved by God. We must push our egos away to a place where they no longer interfere with our spiritual relationships with our Father in heaven. "The ego's relation to objects is one of consumption. The relation of the heart to things is one of breathing in, gasping, inspiration."[158]

Our egos are driven by the desire for objects – the physical items that are temporary. How childish! The child living in our egos loves to play. But that inner child also loves the material world because of the false hope that having possessions will make us happy. And, as we have seen before, having lots of money and possessions do not equate to an increase in happiness. Many years ago, when I served as a medic in Vietnam, we were issued a ration card for purchases from the Post Exchange, or PX, something like a military Walmart. We were allowed to purchase a limited number of cameras, tape recorders, amplifiers, speakers, watches, alcohol, and cigarettes during the thirteen-month tour of duty. That old ration card is in my scrapbook as a reminder of all the items I did *not* buy. I bought a watch, left it under a towel, and it was stolen when I went swimming in the South China Sea off the coast of Nha Trang. The stereo amplifier with speakers wore out in the 1980s. The movie camera never worked, so I tossed it in the trash. My final purchase was a TEAC tape deck that quit working after fifteen years. The end result was that in comparison to my buddies, my ration card did not see much use, and the things I did buy wore out and are gone, other than the original ration card. Several offers came from buddies to let them use my card for alcohol and cigarettes, but I refused to contribute to their desire to lose their health.

For some of my friends during that time in the army, they wanted to be happy by buying as much as they could from the ration card and sending it home to be waiting for them after their tour of duty was complete. The PX system actually allowed you to buy a car, and it would be waiting when you returned. Buying things does not equal happiness. Buying things does not help our spiritual growth.

> The US isn't alone. "In China, between 1990 and 2004, per capita income went from 5 percent of the US level to 16 percent," says Richard Easterlin, an economist at the University of Southern California and one of the founders of the happiness school. But happiness over that period stagnated. "Life satisfaction, if anything, seems to be declining. India, Chile, Turkey, Ireland—all of them show little or no improvement in happiness or well-being despite rapid economic growth."[159]

On what must our hope be centered? What is the source of our happiness? God and his love and compassion for us, and our love and compassion for others. Without that hope, many fall prey to those material things that can cause addictions. Some

Christians will say they are not addicted to alcohol, tobacco, or drugs because they never use any, and their facial expression and body language demonstrate they are quite proud of making that declaration. But there are many other types of addictions other than those listed above. What about junk food eaten at the desk in five minutes every day instead of a longer, healthier lunch? What about every person in the family either watching their own television or roaming the Internet on their own computer instead of meeting together for family time? What about not using vacation days, choosing instead to work. "Addictions indicate a taking in of the materialistic world view, as if possessing the world would produce completeness of soul."[160]

Just what is our soul? Webster defines soul as "the immaterial essence, animating principle, or actuating cause of an individual life." The Greek word is ψυχή (psuche /psoo·khay/), and can be translated as soul, life, mind, heart, and breath of life. In other words, the soul is that unique piece of our being that separates us from the animals, in that our soul will live eternally after our death. While our soul is within us, it is different than the physical body. Like the physical body, the soul must be fed and maintained in a healthy state. How? By constant prayer and contact with God through study of the Bible, and interacting with other Christians. This idea of the soul being fed must be taught to our children if they are to maintain these soul-life-support activities when they are adults. Then, when they (and we as we grow spiritually) are adults living and working in the world, this soul-education must continue to be an ongoing part of our daily life.

> While some problems are caused by bad people not caring what is wrong, most problems probably arise from good people not knowing or fully understanding what is wrong, particularly when what is wrong is a traditional or sanctioned way of doing something.[161]

JOSEPH ALAN REDMAN

As one radio commentator states, we spend too much time on the difference between right and left and not enough time on the difference between right and wrong. We often fall into the trap of making judgments about the ideas and action of others. Our role as Christians is to show love and compassion to all, not to judge.

Do not judge, or you too will be judged.

Matthew 7:1

A better option is to devote our time to study of the Bible and prayer to God so that we can more effectively demonstrate our faith to others. Unfortunately, in America, the idea of constant self-improvement and learning, in any area, is rapidly losing ground, as evidenced by failing school systems, and unbelievable and constantly increasing tuition rates at colleges and universities. This crumbling of the learning infrastructure also crosses over into the arena of spiritual growth. We are losing our ability to care for other humans, even when they are our children. "In cultures so deteriorated that nurturing and educating are in short supply, most of the intellectual and other advantages become reserved for an elite."[162] A more detailed look at tuition costs will confirm, in many cases, attending a university is rapidly becoming a luxury for the elite and the rich in America.

> Over the decade from 2000-01 to 2010-11, published tuition and fees at public four-year colleges and universities increased at an average rate of 5.6% per year beyond the rate of general inflation. This growth rate led the price to increase from 22% of the average tuition and fees at private nonprofit four-year institutions to 28% over the decade."[163]

In America, the average 2010 annual income was $34,142.

Nurturing and educating the soul is free. All one needs is a Bible, a teacher, prayer, love, compassion, focus, God, and time. There are 86,400 seconds in each day. How much time is spent in temporary activities and how much is spent in eternal activities?

Chapter Nine Thought Questions

1. How do you study the Bible?

2. What study helps do you use?

3. How do you know the difference between right and wrong?

4. Do you believe that if you simply live a good life you will go to heaven? Why? Why not?

5. In what ways do you judge others? Why?

My Challenge Tasks

1. Identify someone you believe to be a good student of the Bible, and ask them to help you improve your own study model.

2. Buy a Bible dictionary, an Exhaustive Concordance, a Bible Timeline, and an Interlinear Greek-English New Testament for your personal study library.

3. Make a list of what you learned as a child about right and wrong. Study the Bible to identify those actions that truly are wrong and those which are simply parental opinions about how a child should behave. Adjust your behavior accordingly – for the better!

4. If you do not know about the Biblical plan for salvation, find someone you trust to help guide you through the Bible for clarification.

5. Make a list of statements you use that may be perceived as being judgmental of others. Work on eliminating these sayings from your vocabulary and replace them with statements of love and compassion.

THE RESULTS OF LOVE

What difference does it make to the dead, the orphans, and the homeless, whether the mad destruction is wrought under the name of totalitarianism or the holy name of liberty or democracy?

Mohandas K. Gandhi (1948)

In the final analysis, love and compassion will rule over greed and ego. One of the most quoted passages from the New Testament is Matthew 5:3-12. We began our conversation discussing why America is not blessed by God and never will be. Therefore, who are the blessed and what are the results?

Blessed are the poor in spirit, for theirs is the kingdom of heaven. Blessed are those who mourn, for they will be comforted. Blessed are the meek, for they will inherit the earth. Blessed are those who hunger and thirst for righteousness, for they will be filled. Blessed are the merciful, for they will be shown mercy. Blessed are the pure in heart, for they will see God. Blessed are the peacemakers, for they will be called sons of God. Blessed are those who are persecuted because of righteousness, for theirs is the kingdom of heaven. Blessed are you when people insult you, persecute you and falsely say all kinds of evil against you because of me. Rejoice and be glad, because great is your reward in heaven, for in the same way they persecuted the prophets who were before you.

Matthew 5:3-12

JOSEPH ALAN REDMAN

Neither America, nor any other country or nation, can claim to fall under the coverage of this list of "Blessed are..." because this list deals only with individual people. Verse twelve is often excluded from the typical quote, but it is the most important verse from the passage. Countries do not have a reward in heaven – individual Christians do. The verse references the fact that people insult, persecute, and falsely say all kinds of evil against individuals, such as that against the prophets in the Old Testament. The reward is not in oil, cars, money, land, clothes, ego-power, title, or anything earthly. The reward is in heaven and heaven alone. Why? Because God loves and blesses individuals not nations.

God alone loves us unconditionally. To help us understand love, one of the greatest passages in the entire Bible is found in 1 Corinthians:

> Love is patient, love is kind. It does not envy, it does not boast, it is not proud. It is not rude, it is not self-seeking, it is not easily angered, it keeps no record of wrongs. Love does not delight in evil but rejoices with the truth. It always protects, always trusts, always hopes, always perseveres. Love never fails. But where there are prophecies, they will cease; where there are tongues, they will be stilled; where there is knowledge, it will pass away. For we know in part and we prophesy in part, but when perfection comes, the imperfect disappears. When I was a child, I talked like a child, I thought like a child, I reasoned like a child. When I became a man, I put childish ways behind me. Now we see but a poor reflection as in a mirror; then we shall see face to face. Now I know in part; then I shall know fully, even as I am fully known. And now these three remain: faith, hope and love. But the greatest of these is love.

> 1 Corinthians 13:4-13

A brief look at these verses on love will further prove the concept that eternal love comes from God and works through individual Christians, not nations.

Love is Patient. America is known historically for rushing to war. The false patience supposedly portrayed by waiting for UN sanctions to work only results in massive hardships for innocent citizens of the target country. Jesus teaches us to go the second mile, to turn the other cheek, and to give our cloak to the one in need. Jesus never once commanded any Christian to go to war to solve a problem. He would not approve of sanctions that damage the poor people of any country. His comment informing us that there will be wars and rumors of wars from the time of his resurrection until he returns for the final judgment is not a command for Christians to engage in or support war. What part of "put down your sword" do we refuse to understand?

Love is kind. America spends less than one percent (1%) of its annual federal budget on foreign aid. [164] "*Kind*" hardly defines this action. Switching the amount spent on the *defense* budget with the amount we spend on foreign aid to other countries would be kind.

Love does not envy. Other words for envy are jealousy, greed, desire, gluttony, self-indulgence, and many more. Enough said!

Love does not boast. People all over the world have a false pride in their countries. Americans are notorious for decorating everything they own including clothing with the American flag. They are, in effect, saying, "Look at us. We are better than you!" Is not boasting a form of idolatry?

Love is not proud. Many who were born in Texas actively demonstrate their pride by window and bumper stickers and license plate frames that seem to claim no other place on earth is better than Texas. When I travel internationally, it is common to end up in a situation where an arrogant and *proud* American is loudly proclaiming their status and frustration against some *foreigner* who is not treating them with respect.

Love is not rude. Operating a government without sincere concern for the poor and sick of the country may be the ultimate example of being rude. How frustrating it must have been for the elderly of America who were forced to struggle through the massive Medicare plan fiasco, many to the point where they were subject to being fined by not rushing to enroll in one of dozens of program options. As one who has the opportunity to visit nursing homes each week, it is obvious to me the designers of the program knew nothing about being elderly. *That* is rudeness. *That* is not love.

Love is not self-seeking. We are a selfish nation; otherwise we would not use more natural resources per capita than any other nation on the planet. We do not want to share anything we *rightly own.* (Tell that to *The People!*[165]) I laugh at our false pride at being Americans by birth when our forefathers illegally invaded in the first place! Americans are the pure definition of a self-seeking people.

Love is not easily angered. Gang violence. Domestic violence. School violence. Teen pregnancy. War. High prison population. Buildings of worship being burned. Former employees shooting former co-workers. Road Rage. Massive numbers of prescription medications for stress and anger management. Did I mention war? Not easily angered? Not in America!

Love keeps no record of wrongs. National Security Agency files. Federal Bureau of Investigation files. Central Intelligence Agency files. Politicians' egos. If we are a nation claiming to be "under God" and trusting in God, why have we not yet established a *Department of Good Behaviors and Activities?* Why are there no memorials for those who are still alive and doing God's work? Why is America a country that loves to live in the negative past? Lack of love and compassion and lack of faith in God stand out as one reason!

Love does not delight in evil. On the surface, at least to us, America may seem to not delight in evil. As far as the rest of the world, I am not so sure. By not delighting in God, we are delighting in evil.

> He who is not with me is against me, and he who does not gather with me scatters. And so I tell you, every sin and blasphemy will be forgiven men, but the blasphemy against the Spirit will not be forgiven. Anyone who speaks a word against the Son of Man will be forgiven, but anyone who speaks against the Holy Spirit will not be forgiven, either in this age or in the age to come.
>
> Matthew 12:30-32

By ignoring the Holy Spirit, one will not be forgiven – ever. By choosing to ignore God, his Son, his Word, and his love for his children, this country is delighting in evil. When the best-selling electronic games are those filled with graphic violence, this is delighting in evil.

Love rejoices in the truth. Polls indicate the word *truth* and *politician* do not compute! Frank Lloyd Wright once said, "The truth is more important than the facts." Here are a few samples of lies told to the American people.[166] [Bold in original text.]

> **The lie:** "The first atomic bomb was dropped on Hiroshima, a military base. That was because we wished in this first attack to avoid, in so far as possible, the killing of civilians."
> **The truth:** Though Hiroshima was the headquarters of a number of military units, it was mostly a civilian city. In fact, Hiroshima was rated a low military priority by the US Army; that's why it hadn't been bombed yet. 140,000 people, almost all civilians, died as a result of the bombing.
>
> **The lie:** "I have previously stated and I repeat now that the United States intends no military intervention in Cuba."
> **The truth:** Not only was the Bay of Pigs invasion organized and funded by the CIA, but Americans flew combat missions as well. One day after Kennedy made the above

statement, an American pilot was shot down on a bombing mission over Cuba. Castro recovered the pilot's body and kept it -- frozen -- for the next 18 years as proof. (He returned the body when he heard that the pilot's daughter was looking for her father who, she had been told, disappeared on a training flight.) Over 100 Cuban exiles, 14 Americans, and an unreported number of Cubans died in the invasion.

The lie: "As President and Commander in Chief it is my duty to the American people to report that renewed hostile actions against United States ships on the high seas in the Gulf of Tonkin have today required me to order the military forces of the United States to take action in reply."
The truth: There was no unprovoked Vietnamese attack on a US warship. President Johnson ran with the untrue story to gain support for American involvement in Vietnam.

The lie: "We did not -- repeat -- did not trade weapons or anything else for hostages -- nor will we."
The truth: Reagan approved the sale of over 2,000 anti-tank weapons to Iran in return for promises to release the American hostages there. Money from the sale of those weapons went to support the Contras' war in Nicaragua. (The White House needed this backdoor method to fund the Contras because Congress had banned military aid to them.)

The lie: Speaking after a White House presentation on child care, he told the nation, "I want you to listen to me. I'm going to say this again: I did not have sexual relations with that woman, Miss Lewinsky." (He also, of course, may have told the same lie under oath.)
The truth: Oh, he did it, alright.

This article does not include the lies told about why America went to war with Iraq, and the lies about weapons of mass destruction that have yet to be found there. America deals with distorting facts and hiding the truth for supposed security reasons, while God deals with the open and perfect truth, an importance difference! Lies are not a sign of love.

Love always protects. The Occupational Safety and Health Administration (OSHA) is tasked with enforcing laws and conducting inspections to ensure companies are maintaining safe working environments for their employees. There are thousands of laws and regulations on the books stating the same.

> And OSHA isn't even doing a very good job enforcing the standards it has on the books. American employers who are well aware that they are far less likely to be inspected by OSHA at work than they are to be pulled over for speeding on the way home from work. The AFL-CIO has found that it would take 117 years for OSHA to visit every worksite in those states covered by federal OSHA. Even if a workplace is inspected and violations are found, the fines levied by OSHA or MSHA are often absurdly small. Although the maximum penalty for a willful violation of an occupational safety and health standard is $70,000, most penalties are far smaller – even when a worker is killed. An exhaustive review of OSHA enforcement actions by Mike Casey of the Kansas City Star last year found that in 80 fatal and injury accidents, half of the fines Kansas City area employers paid were $3,000 or less. Even where fines are large, they are rarely high enough to present an effective deterrent. BP North America was fined $21.3 million for the 2005 Texas City refinery explosion that killed 15 workers and injured 170, but even that record penalty comes to only a few hours of profit for the giant corporation.[167]

JOSEPH ALAN REDMAN

This is protection? If managers in all business organizations used common sense and loved their employees as their neighbor, maintaining the workplace in a clean and safe manner, then we might not need an agency like OSHA.

Love always trusts. As mentioned many times before in this book, we are to trust God. Granted, there is a certain level of trust we demonstrate when we drive on the highway, get in an airplane, eat at a restaurant, etc. But, the news is full of stories about times when that trust fails. Highway accidents, plane crashes, and food poisoning are always there to remind us – In God We Trust! (Everything man-made we check!)

Love always hopes. If America is like the rest of the nations and empires of recorded history, we will not last forever. Therefore, eternal hope lies only with God, not a nation driven by ego and greed. I love my wife and my children, but I love God more. I have hopes of a long life with my wife and playing with grand-children, but I have an even higher hope of life with God in heaven.

> Anyone who loves his father or mother more than me is not worthy of me; anyone who loves his son or daughter more than me is not worthy of me;
>
> Matthew 10:37

America does not and cannot demonstrate hope based on love of God over love of all else. Greed and egos are in the way of that love and hope. But, individual Christians can demonstrate that hope through faith-based actions.

Love always perseveres. The word is "always," not "occasion-ally." While in the history of America, there have been times where we have persevered, there are also times where we did not. *A People's History of the United States 1492 – Present* by Howard Zinn is an amazing book – read it!

Love never fails. Because America is a human institution, it is not perfect, and can fail at times. God's love never fails – ever. God always does the right thing. America does not and cannot.

Galatians 5:22-23 lists the fruits of the Spirit as: love, joy, peace, patience, kindness, goodness, faithfulness, gentleness, and self-control. We each have a spirit, and when our spirit is tuned to the frequency of God's love, we will bear the fruit described in this passage. A nation, because of how it is structured, cannot physically do this. Any fruit perceived to come from a nation actually comes through the actions of individuals. Peter reminds us of exactly what we need to be fruitful Christians. 2 Peter 1:5-9 instructs Christians to add to their faith the following behaviors: goodness, knowledge, self-control, perseverance, godliness, brotherly kindness, and love. America is not a nation of goodness. There are pockets of goodness, but on the whole we cannot be labeled *good*. Based on high-school dropout rates and the difficulty of paying for higher education, our national level of knowledge is not increasing well. Many adults cannot read beyond a third grade level. I know many who cannot speak in complete, intelligible sentences, and others who can speak in complete sentences, but, can only do so by using massive amounts of profanity.

There is little self-control in the country. As a nation, we are impatient. We do not have any desire to persevere in anything we do. We can barely keep our attention focused on a task for more than a few minutes at a time. Peter Block said, "The most common rationalization for doing things we do not believe in is that what we really desire either takes too long or costs too much." Our self-proclaimed godliness is superficial, at best. Brotherly kindness and love only make the news as something unusual. If, as a nation, we could add brotherly kindness, there would be no poor. Nations cannot add these things because nations do not have faith. The result of the lack of individual love (because of ego and greed) is a nation of those who do not care about others, which will eventually lead to a complete breakdown of an already

JOSEPH ALAN REDMAN

failing sense of community. "If their (*poor and disabled*) plight worsens or their numbers increase, it is prudent for cushioned members of a culture to take notice."[168]

Sadly, the cushioned members of a given culture are not really concerned about the poor, unless they get in their way or fail to show up to mow their lawn. The cushioned members of society do everything possible to insulate themselves from the poor – gated communities and private islands are only two examples. The New Testament states the poor will always be with us.

> The poor you will always have with you, but you will not always have me.
>
> Matthew 26:11

In 2005, Hurricane Katrina brought the poor and disabled to the forefront of the world, but only for a few days. Several years later, the big item on the news is abuse of hurricane-relief funds, and the fact many are still without a permanent home and much of the damaged areas have yet to be cleaned up. The same thing applies to the earthquake in Haiti in 2010. After a few weeks in the news, Haiti disappeared into the distant memory of most Americans all while promised aid was being held up for political posturing by members of Congress.

Child labor, both in America and in other countries, and the children's attempts to protest for better working hours and conditions, when contrasted with the increasing gap between the poor children and the rich few at the top of the pile, may result in a true revolution against the government. Whether physical in nature, or one of peaceful protests and massive feedback to Congress, only time will tell.

In America we tend to classify the poor as those with low incomes, stereotypically living in inner city areas. There is, however, another rapidly growing class of the poor we often forget – those in prison. We have already looked at prisons earlier, but it is important to look at some additional information in this chapter on the results of love.

Our society is driven by the need to incarcerate as many people as we can, whether legally in state and federal prisons, or illegally as in Guantanamo and secret prisons in other countries around the world, funded by American tax dollars. We also seem to pride ourselves in executing more prisoners than any other developed country with no valid statistics indicating the use of capital punishment reduces violent crime. In God we trust? Or is it trust in the money generated by this system of loveless treatment of those who have broken the law (and some who have not)?

> Compared to the world's other most populous countries, the 2.2 million people currently incarcerated in the US is 153% higher than Russia, 505% higher than Brazil, 550% higher than India, and over 2,000% higher than Indonesia, Bangladesh, or Nigeria (ICPS, 2006). [169]

Your tax dollars at work! The cost per inmate is higher than the average annual income of the regular American worker. Some quote Romans 13:1 when justifying the use of prisons as a social tool for reducing crime.

> Everyone must submit himself to the governing authorities, for there is no authority except that which God has established. The authorities that exist have been established by God.
>
> Romans 13:1

This means that as Christians living in America, or as Christians living in another country, we are obligated to obey the law – submit to authorities. If we violate the law, we may be fined or go to prison as a result. If a law or governing authority commands us to do something that goes against the teaching of the Bible, we will disobey the civil law, so that we can follow the expectations of God. Unfortunately, many people deliberately ignore both civil law and the Word of God.

JOSEPH ALAN REDMAN

> The Bible is the Word of God. That is to say, as a result of God's direct inspiration the words of Scripture, though put to pen by people, are in fact the words of God Himself. Through propositions expressed in ordinary human language, the Creator of the universe has revealed Himself and intonation about His creatures. The Bible's words are true, clear, and powerful if only because they are *His* words, breathed from His mouth, as it were.[170]

Some choose to ignore the Word of God completely.

Because many ignore God, and because many do not love our fellow man, love being a verb or action word, many do not show actions verifying compassionate love. If God-loving families and communities became the foundation of our country, how many people would end up in prison? If God-loving families and communities became the foundation, how many children would end up in detention centers and juvenile prisons? By ignoring children, for whatever reason, we sentence them to early suffering and death.

It is so sad we allow children to be the main target of greed-induced suffering. When adults focus only on getting more money to buy more things at the expense of their families and children, the children suffer.

> Chances of living merely to the age of five are low among the world's poor compared with the wealthy. In many developing countries, child mortality rates can be twenty-five to thirty times higher than the rate in the developed world. In fact, of the 10.8 million children under five who die each year, 10 million are from low-income countries—more than twice the number of children born annually in the United States and Canada combined.[171]

There are those who will say, "See. I told you so. Aren't you glad we live in America where we are blessed by God?" I wonder how they would reply if they knew the mean age of the homeless in

Chicago is nine years old. This may be one factor influencing where we are as a country when it comes to poor children.

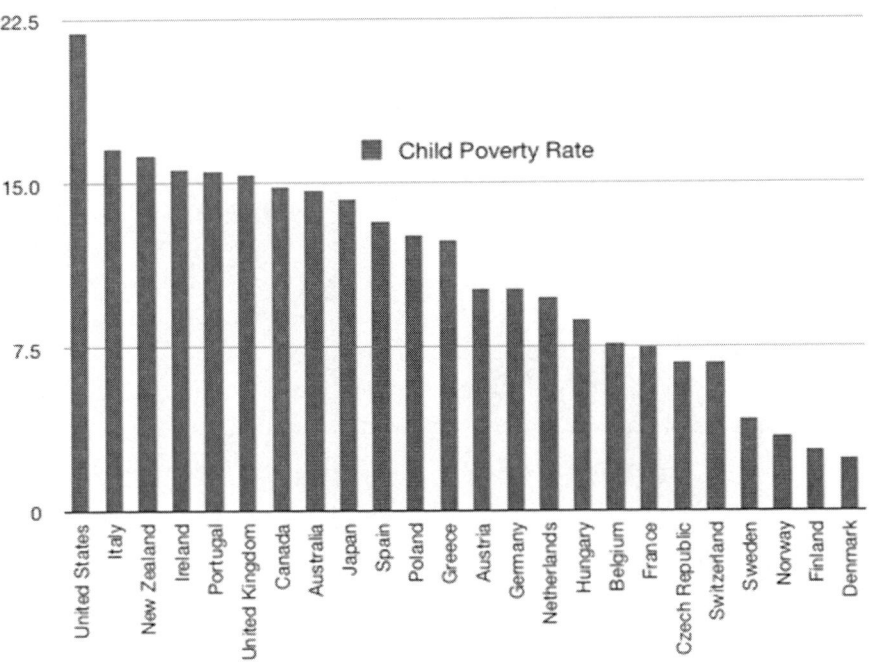

In 1968, while working at a field hospital in Vietnam, I was assigned to ride as a convoy guard. We were to drive from Nha Trang to Cam Rahn Bay to pick up medical supplies. On the trip, we saw dozens of children in ragged clothing with no shoes running beside the trucks begging for food. We tossed them all the fruit and candy we had with us at the time. In 2005, while clowning in a hospital in Russia, we observed families gathered in hospital wards pooling their resources so the children-patients would have something to eat. When I clown I usually carry high-protein bars in my bag for times when a meal is missed because of scheduling problems. Those bars were given to the families,

JOSEPH ALAN REDMAN

even though the quantity was small. How often have you seen someone standing on a street corner with a cardboard sign reading, "Will work for food?" How often do you buy them a meal or give them a handout or give them work to do for pay? How often have you thought, "They might be an angel?"

> Do not forget to entertain strangers, for by so doing some people have entertained angels without knowing it.
>
> Hebrews 13:2

During a humanitarian clown trip to Vietnam in 2010, while visiting a one-thousand-bed pediatric hospital, we noticed all the families who had a child in the hospital pooling their food and water, forming instant mini-communities where each child was taken care of by a group of parents and siblings, grandmothers and grandfathers. We have completely lost this concept of community in America. We are becoming a nation of thumb-texting, long-distance-communicating hermits.

Having enough food to feed the world is not the problem. Food surpluses are typically high on any given day. The unwillingness to distribute the food because of power, ego, corruption, and greed is the problem. Humans are the problem. "…poverty results from actions of other human beings."[172] If poverty results from the actions of others can it be said that poverty can also be solved by the actions of other humans? If humans are the problem, God is the solution.

Jesus told the rich man to sell his possessions, and give them to the poor. By doing this, money would be distributed equally and all would have enough to buy the necessities of life, instead of the rich buying many material possessions they will never use or need. The rich man walked away. We see the same thing in today's world where the rich provide only a token effort to help the poor. The mindset of the greedy seems to be one of, "If they (the poor) really wanted to help themselves they could." The end results of this attitude? The greed of those who have, results in the poor growing poorer. There is no compassion. "…compassion is basically unlawful."[173] In America, if one shows compassion, he is looked at as being either weak or sexually harassing another person. There have been many occasions when, in my office, I would be talking on the phone to another employee, a customer, or a supervisor, and because I always close my personal/family calls with, "I love you," I would forget and accidentally say, "I love you." *Without exception,* people will either say thank you, or will say, "I love you too." It is as if they know and understand from where the comment came. Some will call that harassment. Some will call it carelessness. Some who do the same thing will call it *accidental compassion*!

Jesus preached love and compassion. Jesus lived love and compassion. Jesus died showing love and compassion. Jesus was raised from the dead and lives at the right hand of God, waiting for the judgment, again with love and compassion. And that was no accident. So, for the record, I love you, and that is no accident!

Apparently, contrary to what we may think about ourselves, America is not a more civilized and industrially advanced community, because we insist on going to war at the drop of a hat. Where is the love in that? A quick look at our crime rates and increasing number of lawsuits shows we are not civilized. Don't believe me? Get your thesaurus and look at all the other synonyms for *civilized* and see if we fit the words. (Do polished, advanced, civil, cultured, educated, enlightened, humane, refined, and sophisticated fit the description of America today?) Earlier in our history we may have been advanced in industrial development, but now it is cheaper to move those development functions to other countries with cheap labor costs. "In the more civilized communities…the spirit of warlike aggression may be said to be obsolescent among the common people."[174]

On the other hand, perhaps the common people, those who work for a living and care about other humans, do not have a spirit of warlike aggression, one of the identifiers of the leisure class. Maybe those people have a spirit of love and compassion and service toward others. Maybe those are the people who laugh at army recruiters when asked if they want to join, and devote their lives to serving others instead. "To resolve a conflict without violence is an art, and a sign of wisdom."[175] As evidenced by American politicians and military *leaders*, these high-bred gentlemen (and gentlewomen) of the leisure class can find no other way to solve conflict than to use verbal, then physical, force against their *enemies*. Why are there no weapons of mass community? Why are there no weapons of mass love? In reality, there is. It is called the church.

Remember our previous comments on Jesus and the sword? Here are a couple of charts showing gun death information. I am not advocating any ban on weapon ownership. I do question why a Christian focused on love and compassion, or any sane person for that matter, would feel a need to collect dozens of weapons. Weapons and ammunition are expensive. Could the money spent for *target practice* be better used for food and clothing for the poor? Just a thought.

Gun killings in developed nations 1999-2000

	RATE (PER 100,000 POPULATION)
UNITED STATES	3.97
CANADA	0.59
GERMANY	0.13
ENGLAND & WALES	0.14
AUSTRALIA	0.34
SWITZERLAND	0.51
SWEDEN	0.37
AUSTRIA	0.34
JAPAN	0.02
NEW ZEALAND	0.15

SOURCE:
INTERNATIONAL ACTION NETWORK ON SMALL ARMS (IANSA)

While I would love to see the complete elimination of weapons from the face of the earth, I realize it is a nice idea but not realistic given the false ego-needs and deep insecurities of many. It is important, however, to notice the strong correlation between homicides and handgun sales. Love and compassion will survive in the end. Power, greed, and ego will not. I recommend reading through *The Penguin State of the World Atlas Eighth Edition* completely revised and updated by Dan Smith, copyright 2008 by Myriad Editions Limited. Part three of the book deals with war and peace, and the details will startle the reader. It is past time to renew our commitment to working toward the results of love during our short time on earth.

Chapter Ten Thought Questions

1. Which adjectives in Matthew 5:3-12 describe you?

2. Which adjectives in 1 Corinthians 13:4-8 describe your love for others?

3. Which "fruits" in Galatians 5:22-23 describe you?

4. Which Faith add-ons in 2 Peter 1:5-9 describe your Faith?

5. To whom do you say, "I love you?" Why? How often?

My Challenge Tasks

1. Make a list of the adjectives from #1 above. Identify one activity you will do to demonstrate how the adjectives describe you. Build it into your daily living.

JOSEPH ALAN REDMAN

2. Do the same for the adjectives from #2 above.

3. Do the same for the adjectives from #3 above.

4. Do the same for the faith add-ons in #4 above. (Wow – are you going to be busy doing all these great works of love and compassion!)

5. Visit a nursing home (over and over and over), and become accustomed to sharing hugs and saying, "I love you." They truly need your love and compassion!

CONCLUSIONS

We kill because we're afraid of our own shadow, afraid that
if we used a little common sense we'd have to admit that
our glorious principles were wrong.

Henry Miller

The reader may think it is the role of Christians to hate America.
We must not hate anything except sin and those things God
hates. There are those who claim hate is the opposite of love, and
if one does not love something, then he must hate it. Not true.
Apathy is the opposite of love. Genuine Christians must be apathetic toward America and enthusiastic about God. Christians
must love God. America just happens to be where some of us
live. We can love God anywhere on the planet. If we are to love
God more than we love our families, it stands to reason that any
love of country is pretty low on God's priority list. If we accept
Jesus as the perfect teacher, then we must look to him for guidance and example. For me, no matter how hard I look, I do not
see any evidence of extreme earthly national patriotism or any
involvement in politics in his life. He was devoted only to the
kingdom of God and the salvation of mankind.

Christians can vote, although the end result is rarely one that
will glorify God and His kingdom. We must pay taxes. We must
do our best to obey the law. If we disagree with where the country is going, we may write to our senators to share our thoughts
instead of engaging in violent protest. I voluntarily joined the
army in 1966 and served as an enlisted combat medic working
in a field hospital and flying in a medical evacuation helicop-

ter. Later, I voluntarily served as an officer in the army during the Cold War. I am proud of my service, but not to the point where it is my only reason for existing. Christians cannot live in their earthly past. I have a dear friend, David Roth, who is a folk singer. In one of his songs he writes, "It's ok to look at the past, as long as you don't stare." We cannot change our personal histories, but our hope and focus is in God, his Word, and his promises for our future spiritual lives. My view of life changes for the better every day. For years I lived in the past, doing everything I could to bring my war stories into any conversation. My medals and awards are now in a frame in the hall, away from view from the rest of the house. What changed?

Think about a piece of fabric made of all green thread. This was my military past. Even though the time involved accounted for a small part of my life, I allowed it to rule my daily living. I was stuck staring at the past. Over time, one small thread at a time, I have replaced the fabric of love for ego and "all that I did to win the war" with new threads of love, compassion, play, laughter, study, worship, trust, faith, and hope in God's promises. The fabric of my life still contains a few green threads, as it must, because I cannot change history. But, until I am dead, it is my responsibility as a Christian to continue weaving the fabric of my life with new threads provided by living for God while I am on earth. I do this by renewing my mind with Bible study, prayer, worship, and actively loving humanity. Considering the eternal nature of God, and considering we cannot begin to grasp the love, power, wisdom, and nature of God except from a limited human view, trusting in America does not matter. Trusting in God does.

APPENDICES

a) Blessing Word Summary

The following is a summary of the number of times the words bless, blessed, blessedness, blesses, blessing, and blessings found in the Bible.[176]

Bless	Old Testament = 89
	New Testament = 6
Blessed	Old Testament = 163
	New Testament =71
Blessedness	Old Testament = 0
	New Testament = 2
Blesses	Old Testament = 7
	New Testament = 1
Blessing	Old Testament = 54
	New Testament = 11
Blessings	Old Testament = 20
	New Testament =4

JOSEPH ALAN REDMAN

b) Universal Declaration of Human Rights

Adopted and proclaimed by General Assembly resolution 217 A (III) of 10 December 1948.[177]

On December 10, 1948 the General Assembly of the United Nations adopted and proclaimed the Universal Declaration of Human Rights the full text of which appears in the following pages. Following this historic act the Assembly called upon all Member countries to publicize the text of the Declaration and "to cause it to be disseminated, displayed, read and expounded principally in schools and other educational institutions, without distinction based on the political status of countries or territories."

PREAMBLE

Whereas recognition of the inherent dignity and of the equal and inalienable rights of all members of the human family is the foundation of freedom, justice and peace in the world,

Whereas disregard and contempt for human rights have resulted in barbarous acts which have outraged the conscience of mankind, and the advent of a world in which human beings shall enjoy freedom of speech and belief and freedom from fear and want has been proclaimed as the highest aspiration of the common people,

Whereas it is essential, if man is not to be compelled to have recourse, as a last resort, to rebellion against tyranny and oppression, that human rights should be protected by the rule of law,

Whereas it is essential to promote the development of friendly relations between nations,

Whereas the peoples of the United Nations have in the Charter reaffirmed their faith in fundamental human rights, in the dignity and worth of the human person and in the equal rights of men and women and have determined to promote social progress and better standards of life in larger freedom,

Whereas Member States have pledged themselves to achieve, in co-operation with the United Nations, the promotion of universal respect for and observance of human rights and fundamental freedoms,

Whereas a common understanding of these rights and freedoms is of the greatest importance for the full realization of this pledge,

Now, Therefore THE GENERAL ASSEMBLY proclaims THIS UNIVERSAL DECLARATION OF HUMAN RIGHTS as a common standard of achievement for all peoples and all nations, to the end that every individual and every organ of society, keeping this Declaration constantly in mind, shall strive by teaching and education to promote respect for these rights and freedoms and by progressive measures, national and international, to secure their universal and effective recognition and observance, both among the peoples of Member States themselves and among the peoples of territories under their jurisdiction.

Article 1.

All human beings are born free and equal in dignity and rights. They are endowed with reason and conscience and should act towards one another in a spirit of brotherhood.

Article 2.

Everyone is entitled to all the rights and freedoms set forth in this Declaration, without distinction of any kind, such as race, colour, sex, language, religion, political or other opinion, national or social origin, property, birth or other status. Furthermore, no distinction shall be made on the basis of the political, jurisdictional or international status of the country or territory to which a person belongs, whether it be independent, trust, non-self-governing or under any other limitation of sovereignty.

Article 3.

Everyone has the right to life, liberty and security of person.

Article 4.

No one shall be held in slavery or servitude; slavery and the slave trade shall be prohibited in all their forms.

Article 5.

No one shall be subjected to torture or to cruel, inhuman or degrading treatment or punishment.

Article 6.

Everyone has the right to recognition everywhere as a person before the law.

Article 7.

All are equal before the law and are entitled without any discrimination to equal protection of the law. All are entitled to equal protection against any discrimination in violation of this Declaration and against any incitement to such discrimination.

Article 8.

Everyone has the right to an effective remedy by the competent national tribunals for acts violating the fundamental rights granted him by the constitution or by law.

Article 9.

No one shall be subjected to arbitrary arrest, detention or exile.

Article 10.

Everyone is entitled in full equality to a fair and public hearing by an independent and impartial tribunal, in the determination of his rights and obligations and of any criminal charge against him.

Article 11.

(1) Everyone charged with a penal offence has the right to be presumed innocent until proved guilty according to law in a public trial at which he has had all the guarantees necessary for his defence.

(2) No one shall be held guilty of any penal offence on account of any act or omission which did not constitute a penal offence, under national or international law, at the time when it was committed. Nor shall a heavier penalty be imposed than the one that was applicable at the time the penal offence was committed.

Article 12.

No one shall be subjected to arbitrary interference with his privacy, family, home or correspondence, nor to attacks upon his honour and reputation. Everyone has the right to the protection of the law against such interference or attacks.

Article 13.

(1) Everyone has the right to freedom of movement and residence within the borders of each state.

(2) Everyone has the right to leave any country, including his own, and to return to his country.

Article 14.

(1) Everyone has the right to seek and to enjoy in other countries asylum from persecution.

(2) This right may not be invoked in the case of prosecutions genuinely arising from non-political crimes or from acts contrary to the purposes and principles of the United Nations.

Article 15.

(1) Everyone has the right to a nationality.
(2) No one shall be arbitrarily deprived of his nationality nor denied the right to change his nationality.

Article 16.

(1) Men and women of full age, without any limitation due to race, nationality or religion, have the right to marry and to found a family. They are entitled to equal rights as to marriage, during marriage and at its dissolution.
(2) Marriage shall be entered into only with the free and full consent of the intending spouses.
(3) The family is the natural and fundamental group unit of society and is entitled to protection by society and the State.

Article 17.

(1) Everyone has the right to own property alone as well as in association with others.
(2) No one shall be arbitrarily deprived of his property.

Article 18.

Everyone has the right to freedom of thought, conscience and religion; this right includes freedom to change his religion or belief, and freedom, either alone or in community with others and in public or private, to manifest his religion or belief in teaching, practice, worship and observance.

Article 19.

Everyone has the right to freedom of opinion and expression; this right includes freedom to hold opinions without interference and to seek, receive and impart information and ideas through any media and regardless of frontiers.

Article 20.

(1) Everyone has the right to freedom of peaceful assembly and association.
(2) No one may be compelled to belong to an association.

Article 21.

(1) Everyone has the right to take part in the government of his country, directly or through freely chosen representatives.
(2) Everyone has the right of equal access to public service in his country.
(3) The will of the people shall be the basis of the authority of government; this shall be expressed in periodic and genuine elections which shall be by universal and equal suffrage and shall be held by secret vote or by equivalent free voting procedures.

Article 22.

Everyone, as a member of society, has the right to social security and is entitled to realization, through national effort and international cooperation and in accordance with the organization and resources of each State, of the economic, social and cultural rights indispensable for his dignity and the free development of his personality.

Article 23.

(1) Everyone has the right to work, to free choice of employment, to just and favourable conditions of work and to protection against unemployment.

(2) Everyone, without any discrimination, has the right to equal pay for equal work.

(3) Everyone who works has the right to just and favourable remuneration ensuring for himself and his family an existence worthy of human dignity, and supplemented, if necessary, by other means of social protection.

(4) Everyone has the right to form and to join trade unions for the protection of his interests.

Article 24.

Everyone has the right to rest and leisure, including reasonable limitation of working hours and periodic holidays with pay.

Article 25.

(1) Everyone has the right to a standard of living adequate for the health and well-being of himself and of his family, including food, clothing, housing and medical care and necessary social services, and the right to security in the event of unemployment, sickness, disability, widowhood, old age or other lack of livelihood in circumstances beyond his control.

(2) Motherhood and childhood are entitled to special care and assistance. All children, whether born in or out of wedlock, shall enjoy the same social protection.

Article 26.

(1) Everyone has the right to education. Education shall be free, at least in the elementary and fundamental stages. Elementary education shall be compulsory. Technical and professional education shall be made generally available and higher education shall be equally accessible to all on the basis of merit.

(2) Education shall be directed to the full development of the human personality and to the strengthening of respect for human rights and fundamental freedoms. It shall promote understand-

ing, tolerance and friendship among all nations, racial or religious groups, and shall further the activities of the United Nations for the maintenance of peace.

(3) Parents have a prior right to choose the kind of education that shall be given to their children.

Article 27.

(1) Everyone has the right freely to participate in the cultural life of the community, to enjoy the arts and to share in scientific advancement and its benefits.

(2) Everyone has the right to the protection of the moral and material interests resulting from any scientific, literary or artistic production of which he is the author.

Article 28.

Everyone is entitled to a social and international order in which the rights and freedoms set forth in this Declaration can be fully realized.

Article 29.

(1) Everyone has duties to the community in which alone the free and full development of his personality is possible.

(2) In the exercise of his rights and freedoms, everyone shall be subject only to such limitations as are determined by law solely for the purpose of securing due recognition and respect for the rights and freedoms of others and of meeting the just requirements of morality, public order and the general welfare in a democratic society.

(3) These rights and freedoms may in no case be exercised contrary to the purposes and principles of the United Nations.

　　　　JOSEPH ALAN REDMAN

Article 30.

Nothing in this Declaration may be interpreted as implying for any State, group or person any right to engage in any activity or to perform any act aimed at the destruction of any of the rights and freedoms set forth herein.

c) Various Quotes of the Founding Fathers of America

Thomas Paine was a pamphleteer whose manifestos encouraged the faltering spirits of the country and aided materially in winning the war of Independence: I do not believe in the creed professed by the Jewish church, by the Roman church, by the Greek church, by the Turkish church, by the Protestant church, nor by any church that I know of…Each of those churches accuse the other of unbelief; and for my own part, I disbelieve them all.

From: *The Age of Reason* by Thomas Paine, pp. 8,9 (Republished 1984, Prometheus Books, Buffalo, NY)

George Washington, the first president of the United States, never declared himself a Christian according to contemporary reports or in any of his voluminous correspondence. Washington championed the cause of freedom from religious intolerance and compulsion. When John Murray (a Universalist who denied the existence of hell) was invited to become an army chaplain, the other chaplains petitioned Washington for his dismissal. Instead, Washington gave him the appointment. On his deathbed, Washington uttered no words of a religious nature and did not call for a clergyman to be in attendance.

From: *George Washington and Religion* by Paul F. Boller Jr., pp. 16, 87, 88, 108, 113, 121, 127 (1963, Southern Methodist University Press, Dallas, TX)

John Adams, the country's second president, was drawn to the study of law but faced pressure from his father to become a clergyman. He wrote that he found among the lawyers 'noble and gallant achievements" but among the clergy, the "pretended sanctity of some absolute dunces". Late in life he wrote: "Twenty times in the course of my late reading, have I been upon the point of breaking out, "This would be the best of all possible worlds, if there were no religion in it!" It was during Adams' administration that the Senate ratified the Treaty of Peace and Friendship, which states in Article XI that "the government of the United States of America is not in any sense founded on the Christian Religion."

From: *The Character of John Adams* by Peter Shaw, pp. 17 (1976, North Carolina Press, Chapel Hill, NC) Quoting a letter by JA to Charles Cushing Oct 19, 1756, and John Adams, *A Biography in his Own Words*, edited by James Peabody, p. 403 (1973, Newsweek, New York NY) Quoting letter by JA to Jefferson April 19, 1817, and in reference to the treaty, *Thomas Jefferson, Passionate Pilgrim* by Alf Mapp Jr., pp. 311 (1991, Madison Books, Lanham, MD) quoting letter by TJ to Dr. Benjamin Waterhouse, June, 1814.

Thomas Jefferson, third president and author of the Declaration of Independence, said: "I trust that there is not a young man now living in the United States who will not die a Unitarian." He referred to the Revelation of St. John as "the ravings of a maniac" and wrote: "The Christian priesthood, finding the doctrines of Christ levelled [sic] to every understanding and too plain to need explanation, saw, in the mysticisms of Plato, materials with which they might build up an artificial system which might, from its indistinctness, admit everlasting controversy, give employment for their order, and introduce it to profit, power, and pre-eminence. The doctrines which flowed from the lips of Jesus himself are within the comprehension of a child; but thousands of volumes have not yet explained the Platonisms engrafted on them: and for this obvious reason that nonsense can never be explained."

From: *Thomas Jefferson, an Intimate History* by Fawn M. Brodie, p. 453 (1974, W.W) Norton and Co. Inc. New York, NY) Quoting a letter by TJ to Alexander Smyth Jan 17, 1825, and *Thomas Jefferson, Passionate Pilgrim* by Alf Mapp Jr., pp. 246 (1991, Madison Books, Lanham, MD) quoting letter by TJ to John Adams, July 5, 1814.

"The day will come when the mystical generation of Jesus, by the supreme being as his father in the womb of a virgin, will be classed with the fable of the generation of Minerva in the brain of Jupiter." -- Thomas Jefferson (letter to J. Adams April 11,1823)

James Madison, fourth president and father of the Constitution, was not religious in any conventional sense. "Religious bondage shackles and debilitates the mind and unfits it for every noble enterprise."

"During almost fifteen centuries has the legal establishment of Christianity been on trial. What have been its fruits? More or less in all places, pride and indolence in the Clergy, ignorance and ser-vility in the laity, in both, superstition, bigotry and persecution."

From: *The Madisons* by Virginia Moore, P. 43 (1979, McGraw-Hill Co. New York, NY) quoting a letter by JM to William Bradford April 1, 1774, and *James Madison, A Biography in his Own Words,* edited by Joseph Gardner, p. 93, (1974, Newsweek, New York, NY) Quoting Memorial and Remonstrance against Religious Assessments by JM, June 1785.

Ethan Allen, whose capture of Fort Ticonderoga while com-manding the Green Mountain Boys helped inspire Congress and the country to pursue the War of Independence, said, "That Jesus Christ was not God is evidence from his own words." In the same book, Allen noted that he was generally "denominated a Deist, the reality of which I never disputed, being conscious that I am no Christian." When Allen married Fanny Buchanan, he stopped his own wedding ceremony when the judge asked him if he promised "to live with Fanny Buchanan agreeable to the laws of God." Allen refused to answer until the judge agreed that the God referred to was the God of Nature, and the laws those "written in the great book of nature."

From: *Religion of the American Enlightenment* by G. Adolph Koch, p. 40 (1968, Thomas Crowell Co., New York, NY.) quoting preface and p. 352 of *Reason, the Only Oracle of Man* and *A Sense of History* compiled by American Heritage Press Inc., p. 103 (1985, American Heritage Press, Inc., New York, NY.)

Benjamin Franklin, delegate to the Continental Congress and the Constitutional Convention, said: As to Jesus of Nazareth, my Opinion of whom you particularly desire, I think the System of Morals and his Religion...has received various corrupting Changes, and I have, with most of the present dissenters in England, some doubts as to his Divinity; tho' it is a question I do not dogmatize upon, having never studied it, and think it needless to busy myself with it now, when I expect soon an opportunity of knowing the Truth with less trouble." He died a month later, and historians consider him, like so many great Americans of his time, to be a Deist, not a Christian.

From: *Benjamin Franklin, A Biography in his Own Words,* edited by Thomas Fleming, p. 404, (1972, Newsweek, New York, NY) quoting letter by BF to Ezra Stiles March 9, 1790.

Speaking of the independence of the first 13 States, H.G. Wells in his *Outline of History*, says: "It was a Western European civilization that had broken free from the last traces of Empire and Christendom; and it had not a vestige of monarchy left, and no State Religion.... The absence of any binding religious tie is especially noteworthy. It had a number of forms of Christianity, its spirit was indubitably Christian; but, as a State document of 1796 explicitly declared: 'The government of the United States is not in any sense founded on the Christian religion.'"

The words "In God We Trust" were not consistently on all US currency until 1956, during the McCarthy Hysteria.

The Treaty of Tripoli, passed by the US Senate in 1797, read in part: "The government of the United States is not in any sense founded on the Christian religion." The treaty was written during the Washington administration, and sent to the Senate during the Adams administration. It was read aloud to the Senate, and each Senator received a printed copy. This was the 339th time that a recorded vote was required by the Senate, but only the third time a vote was unanimous (the next time was to honor George Washington). There is no record of any debate or dissension on the treaty. It was reprinted in full in three newspapers - two in Philadelphia, one in New York City. There is no record of public outcry or complaint in subsequent editions of the papers.

d) Why All Nations, Including the United States of America, Come and Go

An Explanation of Acts 17:26-28

26 From one man he made every nation of men, that they should inhabit the whole earth; and he determined the times set for them and the exact places where they should live. 27 God did this so that men would seek him and perhaps reach out for him and find him, though he is not far from each one of us. 28 'For in him we live and move and have our being.' As some of your own poets have said, 'We are his offspring.'

Acts 17:26-28

Point 1: All nations on the earth, from the creation until today, came from one man, Adam.
Point 2: God created men and nations to live on the earth.
Point 3: God determines the beginning time and the end time of each nation.

Point 4: God determines the location and boundaries of each nation.

Point 5: The reason God does these things is so that humankind would seek him, reach out for him, grope (as if in darkness) for him, and then find him.

Point 6: God is not far from any one of us.

Point 7: We all belong to God and would not be here if it was not for him.

Question 1: If the previous points are true, how does this motivate a person to seek God?

By determining the beginning time and location of all nations, God gives the leaders of those nations, and the people living there, a choice to seek out and find him. While there are some leaders with good intentions, Satan easily finds his way into their hearts by enticing them with power and money. The result is a land of spiritual darkness filled with people having no interest in God. (Notice that in the Greek, the word *grope* means reaching out as if in the dark.) When leaders and people decide they are not interested in seeking God, they are in spiritual darkness, and the scripture implies God will allow that nation to fail.

Throughout history, nations come and go, and other nations replace them. This does not show that God is ineffective, but instead, shows God's patience with us. He wants every one to come to him. If one nation cannot provide conditions for the people living there to find God, he will allow another nation to replace it with hope the people will then be able to search for and find him. Christians must understand that there will come a time when God ends time as we know it, followed by the final judgment.

Through Bible study, and through hearing the Word of God preached, each person must recognize the weakness of earthly nations and be motivated to search for God as the only opportunity for eternal light and spiritual salvation. Even though nations are determined by God, there is no salvation in a nation.

JOSEPH ALAN REDMAN

Question 2: Does it matter where the nations are located and how long they last?

It shouldn't matter to true Christians. Our citizenship is in heaven.

> 20 But our citizenship is in heaven. And we eagerly await a Savior from there, the Lord Jesus Christ, 21 who, by the power that enables him to bring everything under his control, will transform our lowly bodies so that they will be like his glorious body.
>
> Philippians 3:20-21 (NIV)

Our concern must be for our souls and the souls of those around us. Neither our nationality, our ethnicity, nor our physical place on the earth makes any difference. What matters is finding God.

ENDNOTES

1   In 2006 the army raised its maximum age for enlistment from thirty-five to forty-two after falling short of recruitment goals. The army later removed restrictions preventing certain felons from enlisting.

2   Simon J. Kistemaker, *New Testament Commentary 1 Corinthians* (Baker Books, Grand Rapids, Michigan, 1993), 22.

3   Jeremy Scahill, BLACKWATER – THE RISE OF THE WORLD'S MOST POWERFUL MERCENARY ARMY (Nation Books, New York. 2007), 94.

4   In June, 2007, a new railway from China to Tibet was opened, along with a mountain pass from India to Tibet. These two events will be quite destructive to the Tibetan culture, a long term goal of the Chinese government.

5   www.stanford.edu/group/scspi/pdfs/pathways/winter_2008/Smeeding.pdf Accessed 28 February, 2011.

6   www.digitalmoneyworld.com/gold-passes-800-per-ounce-god-bless-america Accessed 28 February, 2011.

7   Elizabeth Gettleman. "NO SEX PLEASE, WE'RE ORGANIZING – A nation of pack rats tries to get it together," *Mother Jones* magazine (July/August 2007), 20.

8   Louise Richardson, *WHAT TERRORISTS WANT - UNDERSTANDING THE ENEMY, CONTAINING THE THREAT* (Random House, New York, 2006), 58-59.

9   www.gallup.com/poll/144506/november-christmas-spending-estimate-outpaces-2009.aspx Accessed 5 March 2011.

10 www.nrf.com/modules.php?name=News&op=viewlive&sp_
id=370 Accessed 28 February, 2011.

11 For more information I recommend the information located on the
Internet at en.wikipedia.org/wiki/Christmas

12 John DeGraaf, David Wann, Thomas H. Naylor. *Affluenza –
the all-consuming epidemic* (Berrett-Koehler Publications, Inc.
San Francisco 2002), 13.

13 Reader's Digest, June/July 2010, pg. 108.

14 www.quotationspage.com/quote/24926.html

15 Jane Jacobs, *Dark Age Ahead* (Random House, New York, NY 2004),
114.

16 Ibid., 184.

17 Ibid., 216.

18 www.nmha.org/go/information/get-info/workplace/mind-your-
stress-on-the-job Accessed 28 February, 2011.

19 http://missourifamilies.org/FEATURES/healtharticles/health32.
htm Accessed 28 February, 2011.

20 Robert Sardello, *Facing the world with soul – the reimagination of modern life* (Lindisfarne Press, Hudson, NY 1992), 87.

21 www.apps.who.int/medicinedocs/en/d/Jh1467e/9.2.html
Accessed 7 March 2011.

22 www.statice.is/lisalib/getfile.aspx?itemid=6194 Accessed 28
February, 2011.

23 Media.gallup.com/GPTB/religValue/soo20812_2.
gif$imgrefurl=http:gallup/com/poll/9016/Worlds-Apart-
Religion-Canada-Britain-US.aspk&h=314&w=440$sz=1
0&hl=en&start=60&tbnid=s2fCFSCLGhFKCM:&tbnh-
91&tbnw=127&prev=/images%3Fq%3Dus%2Bchurch%2B
attendance%26start%3D54%26gbv%3D2%26ndsp%3D18%
26hl%3Den%26sa%3DN Accessed 28 February, 2011.

24 www.gallup.com/poll/141044/americans-church-attendance-
inches-2010.aspx Accessed 28 February, 2011.

25 xpress.sfsu.edu/archives/news/007333.html Accessed 28
February, 2011.

26 Words: Traditional; Music: Traditional, arr. By A. H. Howard (w.1992)

27 "SONGS OF FAITH AND PRAISE" Alton H. Howard, Editor. Howard Publishing Co., Inc. West Monroe, Louisiana, 1994.

28 Louise Richardson, *WHAT TERRORISTS WANT - UNDERSTANDING THE ENEMY, CONTAINING THE THREAT* (Random House, New York, 2006), 216.

29 Richard E. Rubenstein, *REASONS TO KILL – WHY AMERICANS CHOOSE WAR* (Bloomsbury Press, New York, 2010), 86-87.

30 peterslarson.com/2010/12/14/why-inequality-is-bad-why-id-rather-live-in-michigan-than-mississippi/ Accessed 7 March 2011.

31 In 2008 president Bush welcomed the Catholic pope with a twenty-one gun salute combined with the official song of the Vatican played by the United States Marine Band.

32 "PARADE" April 10. 2005, page 4.

33 Ibid.

34 This partial list is from Eva Golinger's *THE CHAVEZ CODE – CRACKING US INTERVENTION IN VENEZUELA* (INSTITUTO CUBANO DEL LIBRO, Ciudad de La Habana, Cuba, 2005), 251-267.

35 www.nationmaster.com/graph/hea_hos_bed-health-hospital-beds Accessed 7 March 2011.

36 Paul Farmer, *Pathologies of power – health, human rights, and the new war on the poor* (University of California Press, Los Angeles 2005), 20.

37 www.cdc.gov/nchs/data/hus/hus07.pdf#listfigures Accessed 28 February, 2011.

38 Ibid.

39 www.cdc.gov/nchs/data/hus/hus07.pdf#listfigures Accessed 28 February, 2011.

40 Ibid.

41 National Center for Health Statistics Health, United States, 2007 With Chartbook on Trends in the Health of Americans Hyattsville, MD: 2007, 22.

42 www.flickr.com/photos/jason_diceman/833096553/ "I, Jasondiceman, the copyright holder of this work, has published or hereby publishes it under the following licenses: Permission is granted to copy, distribute and/or modify this document under the terms of the GNU Free Documentation License, Version 1.2 or any later version published by the Free Software Foundation; with no Invariant Sections, no Front-Cover Texts, and no Back-Cover Texts. A copy of the license is included in the section entitled 'GNU Free Documentation License'". Accessed 28 February, 2011.

43 These are not what Americans call "soup" kitchens. This is usually a kitchen in the largest home (apartment) where full meals are prepared for the small community.

44 Paul Farmer, *Pathologies of power – health, human rights, and the new war on the poor* (University of California Press, Los Angeles 2005), 100.

45 www.scu.edu/ethics/publications/iie/v3n3/system.html Accessed 7 March 2011.

46 money.cnn.com/2005/07/08/news/midcaps/orphan/index.htm Accessed 7 March 2011.

47 Paul Farmer, *Pathologies of power – health, human rights, and the new war on the poor* (University of California Press, Los Angeles 2005), 176.

48 www.berkeleydailyplanet.com/issue/2010-02-25/article/34733 Accessed 7 March 2011.

49 Paul Farmer, *Pathologies of power – health, human rights, and the new war on the poor* (University of California Press, Los Angeles 2005), 232.

50 Joel Bakan, *The Corporation – the pathological pursuit of profit and power* (Free Press, New York, NY 2004), 55.

51 Vincent Bugliosi, *THE PROSECUTION OF GEORGE W. BUSH FOR MURDER* (Vanguard Press, Cambridge, Massachusetts. 2008), 241.

52 Ibid., 79.

53 Nicola Tyrer, *SISTERS IN ARMS – BRITISH ARMY NURSES TELL THEIR STORY* (Weidenfeld and Nicolson, London. 2008), 196.

54 Ibid., pg. 197.

55 Joel Bakan, *The Corporation – the pathological pursuit of profit and power* (Free Press, New York, NY 2004), 108.

56 Philip K. Howard, *The death of common sense – how law is suffocating America* (Warner Books, New York, NY 1996), 83.

57 See Appendix C for interesting quotes seldom identified with some of the founding fathers of America.

58 Philip K. Howard, *The death of common sense – how law is suffocating America* (Warner Books, New York, NY 1996), 174.

59 www.ncbi.nlm.nih.gov/pmc/articles/PMC2771575/ Accessed 9 March 2011.

60 Thorstein Veblen, *The theory of the leisure class* (Dover Publications, Inc., Mineola, NY 1994; original in 1899), 1.

61 http://dissidentvoice.org/2010/04/2010-us-spending-priorities-58-to-military/ Accessed 28 February, 2011.

62 www.armscontrolcenter.org/policy/securityspending/articles/us_vs_world.gif Accessed 28 February, 2011.

63 Thorstein Veblen, *The theory of the leisure class* (Dover Publications, Inc., Mineola, NY 1994; original in 1899), 26.

64 Ibid., 49.

65 Ibid., 184.

66 December 2005, WHO GIVES A $%&T? Are Americans charitable? Or chintzy? Edited by Clara Jeffery. Page 16-17.

67 Jo Wilding. *DON'T SHOOT THE CLOWNS – taking a circus to the children of Iraq* (New Internationalist Publications Ltd. Oxford, United kingdom, 2006), 28.

68 Ibid., 29.

69 Jim Wallis. *GOD'S POLITICS – Why the Right Gets It Wrong and the Left Doesn't Get It* (Harper, San Francisco 2005), xviii.

70 If we have 100 senators, who came up with the idea to equally distribute an odd number of booklets (51,599) to an even number of senators?

71 /heavylifting.blogspot.com/2010/05/selective-service-compliance.html Accessed 28 February, 2011.

72 LTC Kenneth Keskel, USAF, *The Oath of Office – A Historical Guide to Moral Leadership*, http://www.airpower.au.af.mil/airchronicles/apj/apj02/win02/keskel.html Accessed 28 February, 2011.

73 http://blog.hiddenharmonies.org/2010/08/map-of-u-s-military-bases-around-the-world/ Accessed 28 February, 2011.

74 www.america.gov/st/washfile-english/2005/September/2 0050909140731ESnamfuaK0.2867395.html Accessed 7 March 2011.

75 Louise Richardson, *WHAT TERRORISTS WANT - UNDERSTANDING THE ENEMY, CONTAINING THE THREAT* (Random House, New York, 2006), 100.

76 Ibid., 147.

77 Marshall Berman, *All That Is Solid Melts Into Air – The Experience of Modernity* (Penguin Books, New York, NY 1988), 77.

78 Ibid., 124.

79 Ibid., 278.

80 Jared Diamond. *Collapse: how societies choose to fail or succeed* (VIKING, New York, NY 2005), 462.

81 www.worldtrademag.com/Articles/Industry_News/368a 01c268af7010VgnVCM100000f932a3c0____ Accessed 7 March 2011.

82 Jared Diamond. *Collapse: how societies choose to fail or succeed* (VIKING, New York, NY 2005), 122.

83 Robert Sardello, *Facing the world with soul – the reimagination of modern life* (Lindisfarne Press, Hudson, NY 1992), 94.

84 www.identitynetwork.net/apps/articles/default. asp?articleid=65166&columnid= Accessed 9 March 2011.

85 Jim Wallis. *GOD'S POLITICS – Why the Right Gets It Wrong and the Left Doesn't Get It* (Harper, San Francisco 2005), 37.

86 www.bpfna.org/public/moore_redemp.html Accessed 10 March 2011.

87 www.christianitytoday.com/ct/2009/augustweb-only/131-41.0.html?start=2 Accessed 10 March 2011.

88 pewforum.org/Politics-and-Elections/The-Torture-Debate-A-Closer-Look.aspx Accessed 10 March 2011.

89 Louise Richardson, *WHAT TERRORISTS WANT - UNDERSTANDING THE ENEMY, CONTAINING THE THREAT* (Random House, New York, 2006), 236.

90 Vincent Bugliosi, *THE PERSECUTION OF GEORGE W. BUSH FOR MURDER* (Vanguard Press, Cambridge, Massachusetts. 2008), 241-242.

91 http://english.aljazeera.net/News/aspx/print.htm Accessed 28 February, 2011.

92 http://clearpathinternational.org/cpiblog/archives/000874. php Accessed 28 February, 2011.

93 Gary C. Schroen, FIRST IN – An Insider's Account of How the CIA Spearheaded the War on Terror in Afghanistan (Ballantine Books, New York. 2005), 38.

94 Ibid.

95 Ibid.

96 Louise Richardson, *WHAT TERRORISTS WANT - UNDERSTANDING THE ENEMY, CONTAINING THE THREAT* (Random House, New York, 2006), 219.

97 www.worlddialogue.org/content.php?id=108 Accessed 9 March 2011.

98 Mazisi Kunene, *EMPEROR SHAKA THE GREAT – A Zulu Epic* (Heinemann Educational Books, LTD, London, England, 1984), 226-227.

99   Paulo Freire, *pedagogy of the oppressed* (Continuum, New York, NY 1970), 91.

100 The Good Citizen's Handbook – A Guide to Proper Behavior Jennifer McKnight-Trontz, Chronicle Books LLC San Francisco 2001.

101 Paulo Freire, *pedagogy of the oppressed* (Continuum, New York, NY 1970), 168.

102 Ibid., 59.

103 www.washingtonpost.com "Dalai Lama Tells US Crowd War Outdated" Rosa Ciranni, The Associated Press, Monday, September 26, 2005. Accessed 28 February, 2011.

104 Marshall Berman, *All That Is Solid Melts Into Air – The Experience of Modernity* (Penguin Books, New York, NY 1988), 158.

105 Jane Jacobs, *Dark Age Ahead* (Random House, New York, NY 2004), 57.

106 Ibid., 136.

107 Robert Sardello, *Facing the world with soul – the reimagination of modern life* (Lindisfarne Press, Hudson, NY 1992), 96.

108 Mihaly Czikszentmihalyi, *Finding Flow – The Psychology of Engagement with Everyday Life* (Basic Books, New York, NY 1997), 20.

109 Ibid., 20.

110 Jim Wallis. *GOD'S POLITICS – Why the Right Gets It Wrong and the Left Doesn't Get It* (Harper, San Francisco, 2005), xix.

111 bible.org/article/financial-faithfulness   Accessed   10 March 2011.

112 Wendell Berry, *Life is a miracle – An essay against modern superstition* (Counterpoint, Washington, D.C. 2000), 94.

113 www.savethechildren.org/news/releases/release_050905.asp?station   ub=i_hpln_050906&ArticleID=&NewsID= Accessed 28 February, 2011.

114 Paul Farmer, *Pathologies of power – health, human rights, and the new war on the poor* (University of California Press, Los Angeles 2005), 144.

115 www.ers.usda.gov/briefing/food_security_2009_ers.jpg. Accessed 28 February, 2011.

116 John DeGraaf, David Wann, Thomas H. Naylor. *Affluenza – the all-consuming epidemic* (Berrett-Koehler Publications, Inc. San Francisco 2002), 39.

117 www.allbusiness.com/north-america/united-states-pennsylvania/1167548-1.html Accessed 7 March 2011.

118 www.wired.com/wiredscience/2010/07/happiness-and-money-2/ Accessed 7 March 2011.

119 www.facingthefuture.org/Portals/0/Documents/Articles/NIE_9a.pdf Accessed 7 March 2011.

120 www.danielnpaul.com/Col/1995/TrailOfTears.html Accessed 7 March 2011.

121 www.isreview.org/issues/53/garbage.shtml Accessed 7 March 2011.

122 Thorstein Veblan, *The Theory of the Leisure Class* (Dover Publications, Inc. Mineola, NY 1994; original in 1899), 103.

123 Ibid., 106.

124 Joel Bakan, *The Corporation – the pathological pursuit of profit and power* (Free Press, New York, NY 2004), 119.

125 Thorstein Veblan, *The Theory of the Leisure Class* (Dover Publications, Inc. Mineola, NY 1994; original in 1899), 157.

126 Ibid., 157.

127 Ibid., 160.

128 Ibid., 15.

129 Ibid., 18.

130 www.ncbi.nlm.nih.gov/pmc/articles/PMC1276635/ Accessed 7 March 2011.

131 articles.moneycentral.msn.com/Banking/CreditCardSmar ts/1In7AmericansCarries10CreditCards.aspx Accessed 7 March 2011.

132 www.nfcc.org/newsroom/FinancialLiteracy/files2010/2 010ConsumerFinancialLiteracySurveyFinalReport.pdf Accessed 7 March 2011.

133 www.mediachannel.org/originals/kidsell.shtml Accessed 7 March 2011.

134 www.globalissues.org/article/237/children-as-consumers Accessed 8 March 2011.

135 www.yesmagazine.org/new-economy/what-is-real-wealth Accessed 8 March 2011.

136 Jane Jacobs. *Dark Age Ahead* (Random House, New York, NY 2004), 211.

137 the-spark.net/np737602.html Accessed 8 March 2011.

138 walmartwatch.com/wp-content/blogs.dir/2/files/pdf/Wal- mart_pay_gap-final.pdf Accessed 8 March 2011.

139 www.nationsencyclopedia.com/economies/Americas/ United-States-of-America-POVERTY-AND- WEALTH.html Accessed 8 March 2011.

140 Arianna Huffington, PIGS AT THE TROUGH – HOW CORPORATE GREED AND POLITICAL CORRUPTION ARE UNDERMINING AMERICA (Three Rivers Press, New York 2003), Ibid., 12-13.

141 Ibid., 14.

142 Ibid., 270.

143 www.msnbc.msn.com/id/17489668/ns/health-pet_health/ Accessed 8 March 2011.

144 Ibid. Accessed 8 March 2011.

145 Thorstein Veblen, *The Theory of the Leisure Class* (Dover Publications, Inc., Mineola, NY 1994; original in 1899), 187.

146 Ibid., 19.

147 www.bakersfield.com/news/local/x486710076/Where-does-church-money-go Accessed 8 March 2011.

148 http//confinder.richmond.edu Accessed 28 February, 2011.

149 Obviously, this is in an ideal world! Actual practice often seems far from the truth of this statement.

150 Marshall Berman. *All That Is Solid Melts Into Air – The Experience of Modernity* (Penguin Books, New York, NY 1988), 99.

151 www.CNN.com; Jeff Green, Wednesday, May 10, 2006.

152 Jared Diamond. *Collapse: how societies choose to fail or succeed* (VIKING, New York, NY 2005), 513.

153 prorev.com/abu.htm155. Accessed 7 March 2011.

154 Jane Jacobs. *Dark Age Ahead* (Random House, NY 2004), 53.

155 Philip K. Howard, *The death of common sense – how law is suffocating America* (Warner Books, New York, NY 1996), 116.

156 Most Style Manuals and spell-check functions spell it "Vietnam." When I was there in 1968-1969, and again in 2010, the Vietnamese spelled the name of their country, "Viet Nam," – two words.

157 www.homileticsonline.com/subscriber/interviews/hauer-was.asp Accessed 10 March 2011.

158 Robert Sardello. *Facing the world with soul – the reimagination of modern life* (Lindisfarne Press, Hudson, NY 1992), 127.

159 www.portfolio.com/views/columns/economics/2008/06/16/Personal-Wealth-Vs-Happiness/ Accessed 8 March 2011.

160 Robert Sardello. *Facing the world with soul – the reimagination of modern life* (Lindisfarne Press, Hudson, NY 1992), 142.

161 www.garlikov.com/philosophy/ethpoint.htm Accessed 7 March 2011.

162 Jane Jacobs. *Dark Age Ahead* (Random House, NY 2004), 159.

163 www.collegeboard.com/press/article/0,,48884,00.html Accessed 28 February, 2011.

164 http://wcco.com/goodquestion/afford.foreign. aid.2.723442.html Accessed 28 February, 2011.

165 "The People" refers to what "Indians" or "Native Americans" call themselves. See *Walking with Grandfather – THE WISDOM OF THE LAKOTA ELDERS* by Joseph M. Marshall III, Sounds True, Inc., Boulder, CO 2005.

166 http://www.motherjones.com/commentary/columns/1998/10/prezlies.html Accessed 28 February, 2011.

167 www.commondreams.org/views06/0429-27.htm Accessed 28 February, 2011.

168 Jane Jacobs. *Dark Age Ahead* (Random House, NY 2004), 30.

169 www.nccd-crc.org/nccd/pubs/2006nov_factsheet_incarceration.pdf Accessed 8 March 2011.

170 www.mtio.com/articles/bissar99.htm Accessed 9 March 2011.

171 www.georgetownlawjournal.org/issues/pdf/96-2/Gostin-Article.PDF Accessed 7 March 2011.

172 Paul Farmer, *Pathologies of power – health, human rights, and the new war on the poor* (University of California Press, Los Angeles 2005), 143.

173 Philip K. Howard, *The death of common sense – how law is suffocating America* (Warner Books, New York, NY 1996), 157.

174 Thorstein Veblen, *The theory of the leisure class* (Dover Publications, Inc., Mineola, NY 1994; original in 1899), 152.

175 www.innerself.com/Behavior_Modification/lee_walton_4184.htm Accessed 9 March 2011.

176 Zondervan NIV Exhaustive Concordance, Copyright © 1999, 1990 by Zondervan

177 Universal Declaration of Human Rights: www.un.org/Overview/rights.html Accessed 28 February, 2011.